GREEN, BLUE AND GREY

Cal McCarthy, from Cork, studied history and economics at University College Cork before going on to work as a civil servant. During a career break he completed his MPhil with a thesis on the 1918 election. He currently works with the Department of Arts, Sports and Tourism. *Cumann na mBan and the Irish Revolution* (2007) was his first book.

GREEN, BLUE AND GREY

—∞∞∞—

THE IRISH IN THE AMERICAN CIVIL WAR

CAL McCARTHY

The Collins Press

FIRST PUBLISHED IN 2009 BY
The Collins Press
West Link Park
Doughcloyne
Wilton
Cork

British Library Cataloguing in Publication Data

McCarthy, Cal
    Green, blue & grey : the Irish in the American Civil War
    1. Irish American soldiers 2. Irish - United States -
    History - 19th century 3. United States - History - Civil
    War, 1861-1865 - Participation, Irish
    I. Title
    973.7'4

ISBN-13: 9781905172986

Typesetting by The Collins Press
Typeset in Berkeley Book
Maps by Design Image
Printed in Great Britain by J F Print Ltd

Cover photographs: (top) flag of the 37th Regiment New York Volunteer
Infantry 'Irish Rifles', courtesy of New York State Militia Museum;
(bottom) officers of the 69th New York State Militia at Fort Corcoran,
Va, courtesy of the Library of Congress

CONTENTS

PHOTO CREDITS

FOREWORD

Most Irish people are aware that the US was at war with itself in the 1860s. We know that the Southern states attempted to leave the Union and that the Washington government under Abraham Lincoln would not permit them to do so, and we know that the war resulted in a Northern victory and the emancipation of African American slaves.

The average Irish person will also be aware that thousands of Irish people departed this island for the New World in the nineteenth century. We have all heard of long-lost relatives who went to America and were never seen or heard from again and have seen Irish characters in films such as *Gettysburg*, *Gods and Generals* and even *Gone with the Wind*. Thus, we are partially aware that the Irish must have played a significant part in the history of nineteenth-century America and its civil war. Yet our history seems to revolve around the evolution of our own state. Studies of the lives of the millions of people who left this island are left for historians working in the countries those Irish emigrants helped to construct. Consequently, all our knowledge of Irish participation in the American Civil War is gained as a result of the hard work of American and Irish-American historians.

This book is an attempt to place as much of that knowledge as possible into a flowing narrative of the war itself. It is aimed at the reader who knows as little about the American Civil War as I myself did when starting my research. The book may not make any contribution to our overall knowledge of the subject; however, it is the first time that Irish participation has been merged with an account of th war itself. This text may also have some function as an introductory guide to the topic. Because the range of the text is quite broad, it was necessary to move the narrative along rapidly without dwelling on intense detail. It simply tells the story of the war by placing Irish units and famous Irish characters at the heart of most of the war's major battles. Those readers who then feel interested enough to explore the topic in greater detail can consult the bibliography for the more detailed and academic texts from which this book is primarily compiled. Included in that bibliography is a list of the websites I consulted while researching this text. Some of those sites are better than others, but all are a credit to the American and Irish-American historians who give so much of their time to maintain these pages for the benefit of all. In addition, I have included small appendices which will allow the novice reader to acquaint themselves with the rudimentary principles of the warfare which characterised the period.

I hope that this text may cultivate a new interest for the reader. Some of us grow weary of exploring Irish history from within the traditional parameters and it is always pleasant to broaden one's own horizons. This text is a peek behind the curtain at a wealth of Irish-American history already written by dedicated historians on the other side of the Atlantic. As such, they have constructed a part of the history of their nation, as well as our own. It is not a part with which we Irish are familiar, yet it is quite likely a part in which many of our own families were involved.

When Irish emigrants left this island, they were frequently mourned, almost as if they had died. Over time, they were forgotten and their history became part of the histories of other nations. Sometimes, however, their continued interest in Ireland played a vital part in the shaping of this nation. I hope that their story will still be of some interest on the island of their birth.

Cal McCarthy
May 2009

ACKNOWLEDGEMENTS

Firstly I want to thank the very many American and Irish-American historians who had essentially told this story before I wrote it. Although I have never met most of them, it is only fair to acknowledge that without their many years of work on various websites and books, this text would not have been possible. I wish to thank Nuala and John Tuthill for providing me with a home from home when I have to undertake research in Dublin. My thanks to my parents, and to AnneMarie and John, who accompanied me on my tour of the battlefields, and helped to formulate my understanding of what had occurred there. In addition I should mention the courteous assistance of the staff of the National Parks Service. I wish to thank my friends and colleagues at Leeside Nurseries and DAST, especially Mary, Derry, Clare, Ena, Noreen, Angela, Tadhg, Orla, Eamonn, Vera, Kathleen and Peadar. Finally I wish to thank all those who lent me their books and their intellects, among them Tom Curtis, Billy and Linda Wiseman, and Katie Lyons, whose understanding of nineteenth-century American politics was invaluable.

CHAPTER 1

ORIGINS OF THE CONFLICT AND THE IRISH INVOLVEMENT

In discussing the origins of the American Civil War, it seems fitting that we should begin by looking at the issue that most people on both sides of the Atlantic still consider to be the primary cause of the conflict: slavery. Slavery did not in itself cause the American Civil War, but it was a major factor in contributing to societal differences that divided North and South.

In the years after the Industrial Revolution, the Northern and Southern economies developed in radically different ways. The Southern climate was particularly suitable to growing cotton, and with the invention of the cotton gin, which quickly and easily separated cotton fibres from the seedpods, there ensued a cotton boom that revolutionised both the economy and society of the South. The South soon became economically dominated by cotton production, which depended largely upon slave labour. As that labour propped up an industry that was responsible for approximately half of all American exports, few Americans would have openly expressed any moral misgivings about the concept of slavery.

1

Meanwhile, the North marched headlong into the industrial era. Manufacturing expanded rapidly, heralding the foundation of factories, corporations and ironworks. The huge coal mines of Pennsylvania fuelled this rapid industrial expansion. With the growth of the industrial sector came the expansion of the financial sector and increased urbanisation of the Northern states. The industrialisation of the North meant that Southern cotton production became increasingly dependent on the processing and export facilities of Northern cities. Northern financial institutions also bankrolled the Southern cotton industry. Thus, two radically different societies were developing within the United States. Each depended economically on the other, but each sought political control of the other.

One of the weapons used in this elaborate political power game was the issue of slavery. Slaves were not citizens of the United States. However, they did count for both taxation and representation in Congress. This naturally led to a serious conflict of interests between the Southern states, who wanted slaves counted for representational but not taxation purposes, and the Northern states, which saw the advantages of taxing the South but not of giving them an increased representation in Congress. The 1787 constitution had attempted a North/South compromise by decreeing that a slave should count as three-fifths of a free person for both taxation and representational purposes. However, in the fifty years prior to the Civil War, the issue of political representation for 'slave states' remained a divisive one. As the population of Northern states grew rapidly, Southern representation in Congress continued to decline. Even with the three-fifths rule in place, Southern states simply didn't have sufficient populations to maintain their proportion of the House of Representatives. As states had an equal number of senators, maintaining the balance of 'slave' and 'free' states in the Union now became the primary factor in the maintenance of Southern political power. However, this delicate balancing act continued to prove divisive.

The most prominent illustration of this division was the acquisition of Louisiana by the USA under the terms of the Louisiana Purchase, a treaty with the French in 1803 which involved the acquisition of states from the Canadian border to the Mississippi Delta. Louisiana was a slave territory and it was feared that its admission into the Union would increase Southern representation in Congress, which caused considerable unease in Northern states. Some of them even argued that the purchase was unconstitutional. However, President Jefferson was convinced that French (and by extension, Napoleonic) control of Louisiana was a security risk to the United States and thus declared the purchase constitutional, although he later admitted that he had 'stretched the constitution until it cracked'.

By 1819, the Louisiana Purchase had been divided into five parts and the state of Missouri applied for admission to the Union as a 'slave' state. At this time, there were eleven 'slave' states and eleven 'free' states in the Union, so the admission of another slave state would have had an enormous effect on the balance of power. Some Northerners sought to block the admission of any more slave states to the Union, while Southerners vigorously opposed any such measure. Eventually a compromise was arrived at whereby Missouri would enter the Union as a slave state, but the free state of Maine would also join. Slavery was then prohibited north of the line 36° 30', an arrangement known as the Missouri Compromise.

The War of 1812 between the USA and the British Empire had also played a significant part in weakening the

Union. The war was supported by Southerners who felt that Britain was unnecessarily interfering with American shipping and westwards expansion. A group of New Englanders met at the Hartford Convention where some declared that since the government was not acting in their best interests, secession from the Union was an option. More moderate delegates proposed the repeal of the three-fifths representation law and a restriction of the admission of new states to the Union. The Hartford Convention was a good example of how smaller groups tended to prioritise their own interests above those of the Union. The Treaty of Ghent subsequently ended the War of 1812 and thus prevented the New Englanders from driving their demands any further.

The end of the War of 1812, in 1815, brought its own difficulties. The war had been an expensive one and now tariffs were doubled in order to pay for it. The depression of 1812 led to further economic protectionist restrictions. The industrialised Northern states reaped all the advantages of this protectionism, while the South saw only the cost of manufactured goods rising. The South was also suffering from decreased soil fertility, westwards migration and the consequential declining land values. Thus demands for the nullification of tariff laws became increasingly audible in the South. It was during this phase that John C. Calhoun rose to the height of his prominence. Calhoun began to champion the sectional interests of Southern states above the interests of the Union. In 1832 he proposed a 'theory of nullification' for a new tariff law in South Carolina. The South Carolina state legislature elected a special convention to issue an 'order of nullification' for the law. The state even went as far as raising an army to resist any measures President Jackson might take to implement the collection of tariffs in the state. Of course, Jackson could not allow a single state to nullify an

Act of Congress and his determination to prevent such a measure became evident to Calhoun, who eventually yielded, thereby averting military conflict. Crucially, no other Southern state had supported South Carolina on the nullification of tariffs. Within South Carolina, planters were becoming increasingly convinced that secession was the only way in which they could preserve the Old South. However, they knew they would need the support of other Southern states for this secession.

Controversy again bubbled to the surface with the proposed annexation of Texas in 1844. Texas, which had won its independence from Mexico in 1837, was slave territory and thus the South supported the annexation, knowing that the three-fifths rule would provide them with more representation in Congress. The North opposed the annexation, fearing the dilution of their congressional power. Eventually, Texas was divided up into five states and then admitted to the Union, with a ban on slavery north of the 36° 30' line.

In 1846, a territorial dispute between Mexico and the US boiled over into a military conflict known as the Mexican War. By 1848, the US had defeated Mexico and in the process secured vast new territories for itself. The admission of these new territories to the Union once again highlighted the North/South divide. In 1849 California was the first part of these new territories to apply for statehood. This triggered the great debate as to whether it should be admitted as a 'slave' or a 'free' state. Eventually the 'Compromise of 1850' seemed to cool the slavery debate. It dictated that California should enter the Union as a 'free' state, while the rest of the territory won during the Mexican War would be divided up into the territories of New Mexico and Utah. When these territories became states, their citizens were to decide on their slave or free status. In addition, the slave trade (but not slavery) was abolished in Washington DC and strict measures for the return of runaway slaves to their Southern owners were enacted.

The Compromise of 1850 could prevent conflict only in the short term, however, and soon the relentless expansion of the US once again resulted in conflict over the slave or free status of new territories. In 1854, the Kansas–Nebraska Act created two new territories west of the Missouri. The Kansas and Nebraska territories were to decide their own position on slavery. The Kansas–Nebraska Act completely contradicted the previous Missouri Compromise, which had 'forever prohibited' slavery in this area. Kansas was the scene of armed conflict between pro- and anti-slavery settlers in 1856. The conflict ended with the tragedy of Bleeding Kansas and represented the first occasion on which Northerners and Southerners had met in armed conflict.

Both sides were now becoming more extreme. Those who called for the abolition of slavery (Abolitionists) suddenly found support among a Northern population that had not previously seemed overly perturbed about the existence of slavery in the South. Meanwhile, moderate Southerners who might previously have been conscious of the cruelty inherent in slavery began to see abolition as a dirty word. Harriet Beecher Stowe's poorly researched novel, *Uncle Tom's Cabin*, highlighted the most extreme horrors of slavery and stirred anti-Southern hostility in the North. In 1859, the famous abolitionist, John Brown, seized the federal arsenal at Harpers Ferry, Virginia, intending to start an anti-slavery uprising. The action was a futile one and Brown was captured, tried and hanged. One of the military units called into action during John Brown's raid was a group of Irishmen from Richmond, Virginia, known as the Montgomery Guards.

Many Northerners considered Brown a martyr, while many Southerners suspected that he had been involved in a government-organised movement to end slavery. People everywhere were now much more receptive to radicalism.

That radicalism was again in evidence during the famous Dred Scott case. Dred Scott was a slave who, having been taken into free territory, returned of his own accord to a slave state. The question was whether or not he was now a free man. The court ruled against Scott, and tensions between North and South again bubbled to the surface. The case seemed to be more about Northern versus Southern interests than the status of Dred Scott.

The presidential election of 1860 was predictably dominated by the North/South divide. The Democratic Party split along Northern and Southern lines, while the Republican Party worked only to promote Northern unity. Consequently, some Southern states decided that if the Republican candidate, Abraham Lincoln, was elected, they would secede from the Union. When Lincoln won the election, South Carolina was the first to secede and was quickly followed by North Carolina, Mississippi, Alabama, Georgia, Louisiana, Virginia, Florida, Tennessee, Arkansas and Texas. These states all seceded from the Union on the basis that the federal government was a league of sovereign states, and that any one of those states had the right to secede from the federation. In Georgia, one of the foremost advocates of secession was the Reverend Jeremiah O'Neill, a native of Lixnaw, County Kerry, who now declared himself 'a rapublican and a sacessionist and a satizen of Georgia', declaring that if seceding led to war, he would be the first to 'lade them into battle'.[1]

The American Civil War was the culmination of over fifty years of constitutional conflict between North and South.

From the very birth of the Union, two radically different societies began to emerge. One was industrialised and urban, the other agricultural and rural. Each society sought control of the political system and each saw slavery, and the three-fifths representation rule, as a means by which the South could exert greater or lesser control over Congress.

Continued expansion of the US meant further competition for political control between these radically different societies. American society was fragmenting on a geographical basis, and into this fragmenting society flooded millions of European immigrants. One of the larger immigrant groupings were the Irish, and in the twenty years prior to the Civil War, poverty and famine in their homeland had driven increasing numbers of them across the Atlantic to the New World.

CHAPTER 2

THE IRISH INFLUX

Tim Pat Coogan's seminal work on the Irish diaspora traces the origins of Irish emigration to the North American continent back several centuries before the beginning of the American Civil War. Indeed, people from the island of Ireland may well have been among the very first white people to set foot on the continent and may have done so as early as the sixth or seventh century. Ogham stones that may have been carved by early Irish Christians have been found all across the land mass that now comprises the modern United States. Coogan also presents evidence of an Irish-born soldier who seems to have resorted to the old Celtic tradition of headhunting when assisting the first British colonists in conquering the Native American population.[1]

However, it is generally accepted that mass migration from Ireland to America did not begin until the eighteenth century, when northern Presbyterians fleeing religious persecution in the form of 'penal laws' first sought refuge in the New World. These Presbyterians were descendants of the Scottish Presbyterians who had been planted in Ulster during the mid-seventeenth century. In the latter part of that century, they had supported the Protestant William (Billy) of Orange during the civil war he and James II fought for the kingship of Ireland and Britain. Thus, the term 'hillbilly' may have had its origins in describing these immigrants who went to the New World and settled in the Appalachian Mountains. Likewise, the term 'redneck' may well have been first used to describe the red scarves they wore to symbolise their support of the Scottish Presbyterians who had signed the 'Solemn Oath and Covenant' to resist pledging any allegiance to the Anglican Church as the official Church of Britain and Ireland.

Although also discriminated against by the penal laws, Irish Catholics did not generally have the means to settle in the New World in the seventeenth and eighteenth centuries. As such, their arrival in America in large numbers did not begin until the nineteenth century. Falling agricultural prices in the wake of the Napoleonic wars meant that over one million had already crossed the Atlantic before the Great Famine. America was then exporting huge quantities of timber to Britain and the empty ships returning westwards needed ballast for the voyage. Oftentimes, that ballast was provided by Irish emigrants. As many of them could not raise the money to pay for their crossing, ship captains allowed them to travel for free and then sold them as indentured labourers for periods of approximately five years. This system meant that Irish Catholic labourers were often treated worse than slaves. Slaves would still be the property of their owner after five years and thus he may have shown some concern for their long-term health. The same was not true of the indentured labourer.[2]

When they got to America, Irish immigrants took many different paths. Most remained in large east-coast cities like Philadelphia, New York and Boston, where they became an essential source of labour for the North's rapidly developing industrial economy. They worked on the docks and in the shipyards, on the railways and in the factories and foundries, helping to construct some of the most enduring architecture of North America. However, the presence of Irish immigrants was not unique to these population centres alone. Irish immigrants began to push westwards during the California gold rush of the 1840s and later into Nevada in pursuit of precious metal. The Irish generally settled wherever they could find work, and in an America that was by now developing two economies, that was not only in the industrialised North.

All through the South, these valueless (as opposed to slave) labourers constructed railways that still exist today. They quickly gained a reputation for being a tough and belligerent breed, so much so that one insurance company refused to cover risks related to Irish railway workers. They wrote to a Georgian lawyer (himself of Irish descent) as follows:

> Where two neighbours (citizens) have difficulties, our Company ordinarily feel no fear in taking a risk for either, but where the difficulty is with a citizen and one of the class of Irishmen such as you have about Staunton on the Rail Road, they always refuse the Risk when the fact of the existence of such a difficulty is made known, for in temper and disposition, that class of Irishmen are regarded as neither fish, flesh or fowl, and the fear always is that in order to vent their spleen or gratify their animosity they would, as is believed, injure the whole world to effect an enemy, in feeling or in property.[3]

In Georgia, the Irish toiled alongside the slaves to dig Augusta's industrial power canal. In a gesture of charity that

11

seemed to ignore the religious conflicts of the Old World, thirteen Protestants began the Hibernian Society of Savannah in 1812 to help Catholic immigrants fight poverty and yellow fever. Catholic Irish communities had a significant presence in Southern cities like Charleston, New Orleans, Memphis, Mobile and Richmond. In addition, Irish-American newspapers like the New York-based *Irish American* and the Boston-based *Pilot* had extolled the virtues of urban life in the South, which was probably a significant factor in the rise of the Irish population in Southern cities.[4]

David T. Gleeson has calculated that by 1860, Irish immigrants accounted for approximately 1.56 per cent of the South's total white population and up to 23 per cent of the white populations of some cities like Memphis and Savannah. Yet for all of the Irish influence in the South, there is no doubt that they were numerically stronger in the Northern states. Gleeson calculated that, by 1860, only 84,000 of America's 1.2 million Irish immigrants had settled in the eleven states that would make up the Confederacy.[5]

The Irish experience of the New World was not entirely positive. While the US offered them jobs, money and a future that would have been difficult to find at home, it also offered them the hatred and bigotry so often projected on immigrant groups. Foremost among the groups opposing further Irish immigration to America was a movement curiously known as the 'Know Nothings'.

The Know Nothing movement originated in New York in 1843 and was known as the American Republican Party. It soon began to spread to other states as the Native American Party and by 1855 had reorganised itself nationally as the American Party. The movement gained the 'Know Nothing' tag because of its semi-secret nature and its members' tendency to deny knowledge of the party's activities. The party sought political control where it could in order to stem the flow of Catholic immigrants into the US. They were convinced that Catholics could not be loyal to the United States, as their primary loyalties were to the Pope. The continued rhetoric of the Know Nothing faction led to spiralling violence against immigrant Catholic communities. The most infamous violent incident occurred when riots between Irish immigrants and Know Nothing supporters broke out in Philadelphia in 1844, though Irish families suffered at the hands of Know Nothings all over America. Soon, however, new issues were drawing the nation into a war with itself and Know Nothing politics became an unpleasant memory from the very recent past.

CHAPTER 3

THE LOSS OF INNOCENCE

As soon as the eleven Confederate states had seceded from the Union, the newly constituted authorities of those states began to seize all federal property as their own, including military installations. Since they were usually isolated, federal troops simply abandoned these installations under pressure, or even threat, from a hostile population. However, in Charleston Harbor, they insisted on maintaining occupancy of the now famous Fort Sumter. The government of South Carolina, and later the Confederate government, tried to negotiate the surrender of the fort without success. Meanwhile, South Carolina militiamen took possession of nearby Fort Moultrie in order to prevent Union attempts to resupply Sumter. Among these militia were the Irish Volunteers who had been raised in Charleston. The *Charleston Mercury* noted that the Irishmen were 'among the most efficient of our companies' taking part in the increasing militant activity in the city.[1] The Irish Volunteers were the first unit in South Carolina to volunteer for the war and would become Company K of the 1st South Carolina Battalion. Their flag was made for them by students at the Sisters of Mercy convent in Charleston.[2] In the end, the Irish

Volunteers were not involved in the shelling of Fort Sumter, which precipitated Lincoln's call for 75,000 volunteers to suppress the Southern rebellion. Up North, the Irish immigrants rallied to the Union banner and were soon flocking to the recruitment offices.

Michael Corcoran

The most famous Irish unit of the American Civil War was the Irish Brigade, although the formation of an Irish brigade was not authorised by the United States Secretary of War until September 1861. Meanwhile, the regiments which would eventually become the Irish Brigade began recruiting in the North. Those regiments were the 116th Pennsylvania Infantry, the 29th Massachusetts Infantry, the 63rd and 88th New York Infantry Regiments and the famous 'Fighting 69th', which would become the core regiment of the Irish Brigade. The 69th New York Volunteers was mostly comprised of the old 69th State Militia which had been formed by Irish immigrants in October 1851. In 1859, the Sligo-born Michael Corcoran was appointed Colonel of the 69th and brought the regiment to prominence when, in protest at the British government's ineffective response to the Irish famine, he refused to parade it for the visit of the Prince of Wales to New York in 1860. He was removed from command of the unit but was spared court martial by the desperate need for men created by the shelling of Fort Sumter. The remaining units that eventually formed the brigade were recruited in the twelve months following the shelling of Fort Sumter.

Of primary strategic importance to both the Federal and Confederate armies were their respective capitals in Washington and Richmond. The Union army placed 35,000 men under the command of General Irvin McDowell near Washington. Between McDowell and Richmond stood 22,000 Confederates under the command of General P.G.T. Beauregard. Meanwhile, a separate force of 18,000 Federal troops held the northern end of the Shenandoah Valley, which was a secondary route between the two cities. They were opposed by 12,000 Confederates under General Joseph E. Johnston.

Under considerable pressure from Northern politicians who sought an early victory over the Confederates, McDowell left Washington and moved south towards Beauregard's army, who were encamped near the town of Manassas. The plan was to engage the numerically weaker Confederates here, while Major General Robert Patterson was to prevent the Confederates in the Shenandoah Valley from reinforcing Beauregard by engaging them simultaneously. However, Johnston's Confederates slipped out of the Shenandoah to reinforce Beauregard at Manassas on the evening of 21 July 1861. Thus, McDowell was now engaged by a much larger Confederate force than he had initially anticipated. The First Battle of Manassas (also known as the First Battle of Bull Run) ended in a defeat which shocked the Northern army to its core.[3] It was here that General Thomas J. Jackson received the *nom de guerre* 'Stonewall' for standing fast against fierce Federal resistance before bayonet-charging

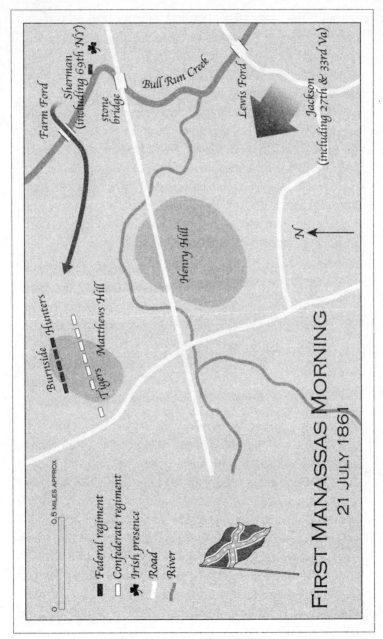

Farm Ford

Sherman (including 69th NY)

stone bridge

Bull Run Creek

Lewis Ford

Jackson (including 27th & 33rd Va)

N

Henry Hill

Burnside

Hunters

Matthews Hill

Tigers

0.5 MILES APPROX

Federal regiment
Confederate regiment
Irish presence
Road
River

FIRST MANASSAS MORNING

21 JULY 1861

them off the field. After Manassas, Lincoln realised that the war would not result in an early Northern victory and relieved McDowell of command, replacing him with Major General George B. McClellan. The North was shocked and the South was jubilant, but what of the Irish at Bull Run?

A number of primarily Irish units were engaged in the battle, where they received their baptisms of fire. On the Confederate side, the most famous Irish unit was the First Special Battalion Louisiana Volunteers. More commonly known as 'Wheat's Tigers', this battalion had already made its presence known within the Confederate army. Recruited largely from the Irish immigrant dock workers of New Orleans, the battalion forged a reputation for disorderly conduct. Another Confederate soldier described the unit thus:

> I got my first glimpse at Wheat's Battalion from New Orleans. They were all Irish and were dressed in Zouave dress, and were familiarly known as Louisiana Tigers, and tigers they were too in human form. I was actually afraid of them, afraid I would meet them somewhere in camp and that they would do to me like they did to Tom Lane of my company; knock me down and stamp me half to death.[4]

Their future brigade leader, Richard Taylor, later wrote that the Tigers' reputation was so 'villainous ... that every commander desired to be rid of it'.[5] By the time the Tigers arrived at Manassas Junction on 20 June 1861, men from the 18th Virginia Regiment noticed that some of them had been bucked and gagged for disorderly conduct. They fought their first engagement on 16 July, when, during a fire fight that their commanding officer, Major Robert Wheat (not of Irish ancestry), described as a 'nice little skirmish', James Burnes became the first of many wartime casualties, sustaining two broken legs. By 16 July, the Tigers had been designated part

Taken from atop Henry Hill, looking at Matthews Hill opposite. This gives an sense of the scale involved.

of Colonel Nathan Evans' brigade and were deployed on the extreme left of the Confederate line behind Bull Run Creek, near the famous 'stone bridge' on the Warrenton Pike.

On 18 July, McDowell's troops clashed with Confederates south of the stone bridge. The encounter was one that McDowell had sought to avoid, but his orders were countermanded by Brigadier General Daniel Tyler, who led Colonel Richardson's brigade in the brief clash. McDowell rebuked Tyler for disobeying his orders, and fearing that the Confederates would now reinforce this part of the line, decided to redirect his attention to the left, an action which made this Irish Tiger unit central to the First Battle of Manassas. Just before dawn on 21 July 1861, McDowell moved three Federal brigades towards the Tigers' position at the stone bridge, among them the 69th New York regiment (part of William Sherman's brigade), under the command of Corcoran.

Like the Tigers, the 69th had arrived at Manassas with a

The 69th Militia at Fort Corcoran.

record of some insubordination. A few weeks previously, some of the regiment's men had mutinied in protest at not having received any pay since joining the army. They had worked hard, constructing a fort (which they christened Fort Corcoran) overlooking Arlington and defending Washington's aqueduct bridge. Indeed, they had worked so hard on the project that within a week they succeeded in completing a job that Federal engineers had estimated would take a month or more. For poor immigrant labourers who had left whatever families they may have had to fend for themselves, the denial of pay, especially after such gargantuan effort, was a serious issue. On 5 July, two companies refused to report for duty unless they were paid. Corcoran promptly paraded the remaining companies and threatened to shoot the mutineers, whereupon the issue was resolved and the striking companies returned to duty. They were paid a week later and their chaplain left for New York to distribute the money among their dependants.

Stone bridge at Manassas.

By early morning on 21 July, these two ill-disciplined Irish units were in close proximity near the stone bridge on the Bull Run battlefield. However, they did not yet engage one another. The Tigers' first encounter came at about 3.30 a.m., when Confederate picket guards spotted the silhouettes of Federal troops moving through the woods to the east. Wheat awakened his men and readied them for action. Private Drury Gibson later remembered, 'We were anxious to meet the enemy, in fact our hearts jumped for joy when we saw their bayonets through the distant forest'. A skirmish developed, but in fact the Tigers were engaging only one of three Federal brigades, themselves engaged in a tactical feint, while two other divisions sought to outflank the Confederates on the left. It was at this point that Wheat's Tigers were immediately redirected, along with six companies under the command of Colonel Sloan, to engage the approaching Federals to the north. Amidst the confusion of battle, Wheat's Tigers were separated from the Sloan companies. The Tigers' first casualties at Manassas occurred when Hugh McDonald and James Wilson were mortally wounded by Sloan's men, who had mistaken them for Federals. Whether or not the Irishmen made the same error, they did return fire on Sloan's men and a skirmish between two Confederate units might have occurred but for Wheat's success in defusing the situation.

Although they would not have been aware of it at the time, this tiny group was now holding the left flank of the Confederate army against the approach of two entire Federal divisions. Upon reaching Matthews Hill, Wheat led one company, the Catahoula Guerrillas, up it in search of the approaching Federal troops, while leaving the remainder of the Irishmen under cover on the slopes of the hill. Reaching the summit of Matthews Hill, Wheat's company was soon engaged by an entire Federal regiment, leading to a quick retreat back down the hill and into cover on a small roadway.

The Federals immediately took the hill and a close-range artillery duel with Confederate cannon began. The cannon enveloped the hill and nearby cornfields in smoke and Wheat saw his chance to move the Irishmen up the hill under its cover. They moved beneath the smoke and through the corn up Matthews Hill until they emerged from its cover about fifty yards from the Federal guns. Firing their last musket rounds and brandishing bowie knives, the Tigers charged the Federal line and came within twenty yards of the Union troops. Then it was the turn of the 2nd Rhode Island to discharge their muskets at close range, stopping the Tigers' charge in its tracks, and the Irishmen immediately fled back down the hill.

The Tigers were scattered in the retreat, but eventually reconvened in the woods near the bottom of the hill. From here, Wheat attempted to order them back into the line, which was now being propped up by a brigade under the command of Brigadier General Barnard Bee. The Irishmen were reluctant to rejoin the fight, and while trying to coax them out of the woods, Wheat was mortally wounded by a Federal bullet. Without leadership, the Tigers were scattered to the winds during the frantic Confederate retreat from Matthews Hill to nearby Henry Hill.[6] Henry Hill was crowned by the house of the Widow Henry. Her deceased husband, Isaac, was the son of Irish immigrants. Mrs Henry was evacuated but begged to be returned to her house, just as it was becoming the centrepiece of the battle. She was killed when Federal cannon ripped her house apart in an attempt to dislodge Confederate sharpshooters.

As Wheat's Tigers retreated from Matthews Hill towards Henry Hill, two of them were asked to rejoin the fighting by Colonel Robert Withers when his 18th Virginia Infantry Regiment was ordered to reinforce the Confederate left. They refused to do so. 'From their brogue they were evidently Irish,' Withers commented before going on to praise the bravery of two other Irishmen who joined his regiment.[7]

Meanwhile, the Federal New York 69th, under the command of the aforementioned Corcoran, led Sherman's Brigade across Bull Run Creek and made their way onto the field just east of the now retreating Tigers. Moving west, they encountered their disorganised and retreating countrymen in a wooded meadow. The 69th engaged the Zouave Company of the Tiger Battalion and lost Colonel Haggerty, who was shot from his horse during the engagement. Anxious to continue his advance, Sherman ordered the 69th to cease their fire and the engagement broke off. Nonetheless, Colonel Ambrose Burnside expressed his gratitude to the 69th for their actions in his official report of the battle.

It was Sherman's brigade, with the Sixty-ninth New

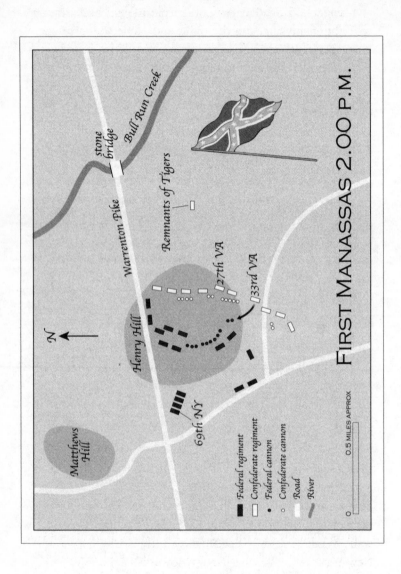

FIRST MANASSAS 2.00 P.M.

Bull Run Creek

stone bridge

Warrenton Pike

Remnants of Tigers

27th VA

33rd VA

Henry Hill

N

69th NY

Matthews Hill

0.5 MILES APPROX

Federal regiment
Confederate regiment
Federal cannon
Confederate cannon
Road
River

York Militia in advance, that arrived at about 12.30 o'clock, and by a most deadly fire assisted in breaking the enemy's lines, and soon after 1 o'clock the woods on our front, which had been so obstinately held, were cleared of the enemy.

Sherman's Brigade then formed up near Matthews Hill, with the Confederate army now deployed south of them on and around Henry Hill. Up on Henry Hill itself, Thomas Jackson had just arrived following a gruelling forced march out of the Shenandoah Valley and now readied the Confederate defences.

With Jackson was the most famous brigade he ever led, one that would earn a name which would echo through the pages of American history. With Jackson on that day stood the men of the Stonewall Brigade, with a considerable number of Irishmen in its ranks. Two of the brigade's regiments contained Irish companies. The colour company of the 27th Virginia was Company B, the Virginia Hibernians. This Irish company had been raised from among the Irish community settled in the mountainous terrain of Alleghany County. Meanwhile, among the ranks of the 33rd Virginia stood the men of the Emerald Guard, raised from among the Irish of Shenandoah County, many of whom were recently arrived immigrants seeking work on the Manassas Gap Railroad. Although no other specifically Irish units stood in the ranks of the Stonewall Brigade, their muster rolls reveal a healthy scattering of Scotch-Irish names.[8] It was behind Jackson and this brigade that Bee was alleged to have urged his men to form, pointing out that Jackson stood like a 'stone wall'. While Jackson placed his men, the Irish of the 69th New York were making their way towards Henry Hill.

The 69th, along with the rest of Sherman's brigade, was then attached to Brigadier General David Hunter's division, which was preparing to storm the hill. First up the hill was the 2nd Wisconsin Infantry Regiment. They charged the hill twice but could not breach Jackson's defences, leaving 112 casualties on the field. While the 69th watched, the next attempt was made by a Scottish-American regiment known as the Cameron Highlanders. The Highlanders also failed, leaving 198 casualties behind. When the Irishmen's turn came, they readied their arms and stormed Henry Hill shouting their regimental motto, *Faugh a Ballagh* (Clear the Way). They failed to clear Jackson from the hill and retreated in disorder. Corcoran was wounded in the charge, but continued to lead the regiment. Between 16 and 21 July, 192 men of the 69th fell in the Manassas area. The charge of the Irishmen of the 69th New York would appear to have hit the Confederate line between the Irish in the 27th and 33rd Virginia.

The stalemate on top of Henry Hill continued until about 2.30 p.m., when the 33rd Virginia, with the Emerald Guards among them, suddenly charged and overwhelmed Griffin's two-gun Federal battery on the southern side of the hill. Soon, however, Federal infantry was pushing the isolated Virginians back. It was at this moment that the Virginia Hibernians, along with the rest of their regiment and the men of the 4th Virginia, came to the assistance of their Irish comrades when Jackson ordered a furious bayonet charge that sent them crashing into the right of the Federal line. Soon the bayonet charge extended all across Henry Hill and the Federals were completely overwhelmed by its fury.

Now the whole Union army was in full retreat as Jackson bayonet-charged down the hill. The scene was disorderly, but it was Corcoran who brought some order to the retreat. His extreme exertions in bringing order to the chaos were mentioned by Sherman in his official report. But Corcoran himself was eventually captured by the Confederates when his wounds forced him and the few men who would not abandon him to remain in a house near Bull Run. Meanwhile, the remainder of the 69th, now led by Captain Kelly, formed the rearguard for the entire Federal Army of the Potomac as it retreated in disorder towards Washington.

Up on Henry Hill, the Tigers were at the rear of the Confederate line trying to reorganise after their morning exertions over on Matthews Hill. They had also been instrumental in delaying the Federal advance long enough for Jackson to deploy his men on Henry Hill. Some of them had joined up with Bee's command in the Confederate line on top of the hill, while the Zouave Company joined Sloan's men at the Lewis House. Overall, their commander was very impressed by the actions of Wheat's Tigers at Manassas. Of their attempt to defend and later retake Matthews Hill, Beauregard wrote:

> ... in the desperate, unequal conflict to which these brave gentlemen were for a time necessarily exposed, the behaviour of officers and men generally was worthy of the highest admiration, and assuredly hereafter all there present may proudly say, We were of that band who fought the first hour of the Battle of Manassas.

Two Irish units had arrived at Manassas with an aura of ill discipline hanging over them, yet both had distinguished themselves on the field of battle. For the 69th, Manassas was the story of a brave but futile charge at an enemy who commanded Henry Hill. The story was a similar one for the Tigers, except that their charge occurred earlier in the day at Matthews Hill. It seems that the two units encountered one another briefly during the Confederate retreat from Matthews Hill, but there is no evidence to suggest that they met again at Manassas. However, given the proximity of the 69th to the

Emerald Guards and the Virginia Hibernians while they charged Henry Hill, we can say that, at the very least, two small groups of Irish Confederates were aware of the presence of a large regiment of Irish Federals.

After Manassas, the Federals retreated back to Washington, knowing there would be no quick victory in the war, while the Confederates were buoyed up by the knowledge that they could defeat the military might of the Union on the field of battle. Each could still aspire towards ultimate victory, but neither knew how long that might take. The innocence of so many on both sides, who had predicted a quick and easy victory, died on the slopes of two unremarkable hills outside Manassas.

CHAPTER 4

THE WAR IN THE WEST

In the meantime, with the Confederates happy to defend their own territory, the focus of the war shifted to a western theatre, which had formed east of the Mississippi River and west of the Appalachian Mountains.

When the state of Kentucky declared its neutrality in the war, it presented both sides with a problem. Each needed the state in order to control the Mississippi, but neither wanted to be the invading aggressor. Confederate Major General Leonidas Polk made the first move by occupying the city of Columbus on 4 September 1861. It later became apparent that Federal General Ulysses S. Grant had planned to do so on the following day. Thus, the city would have been occupied either way, but the fact that the Confederates beat the Federals to the punch meant that Kentucky never formally joined the Confederacy.

General Albert Sydney Johnston commanded Confederate forces in the western theatre. His appeal for fresh troops to add to his paltry force of 20,000 met with the approval of the Confederate government in Richmond, Virginia, and soon Brigadier General Felix Zollicoffer was dispatched to reinforce Johnston's command. Moving in on the right wing of Johnston's command, Zollicoffer's inexperience immediately caused difficulty. He had set up his encampments north of the Cumberland River. The unfordable river had the effect of cutting off his path of retreat should the Federal army attack suddenly. Brigadier General Crittenden was dispatched to take command of Zollicoffer's forces and quickly realised the error of the latter. He knew that his only option was to launch his own attack against Federal forces, which were already moving towards his position. This attack resulted in a Confederate defeat at Mill Springs, Kentucky on 19 January 1862. The victory at Mill Springs was the first significant Federal victory of the war and was widely celebrated in the Northern press. The offensive ground to a halt, however, when a cold Tennessee winter and a consequentially barren countryside stalled the Federal advance towards Nashville. The right of the Confederate line had collapsed, but the Federals had failed to push the advantage home.

Next on the Federal agenda was the capture of Forts Donelson and Henry, located on the Cumberland and Tennessee rivers respectively. The forts had been constructed by Confederate engineers in an attempt to deny Federal gunboats access to two rivers that plunged deep into Confederate territory and served as vital arteries of supply. The railway bridges that crossed the rivers also made the potential for devastating the Southern supply chain tempting to Federal commanders. On 6 February 1862, Fort Henry fell to an attack by Federal armoured gun-boats, commonly known as ironclads, coupled with difficulties involving the fort's low elevation and rising flood waters. Most of the garrison were evacuated from the fort before its collapse, including the Irishmen of the 10th Tennessee Infantry Regiment.

The 10th Tennessee was raised in Nashville, Tennessee, between April and September 1861 and consisted almost entirely of Irishmen living in Nashville. However, companies were also raised in Pulaski, Clarkesville and McEwen. In 1850s' Nashville, the Irish had formed themselves into a group known as the St Patrick's Club in order to combat the rise of anti-Irish Know Nothing politics. To a large extent, this organisation served as the nucleus of the 10th Tennessee. While enlisted men were primarily Irish Catholics, the officers of the regiment were mostly Irish Protestants. As these officers were elected, there is no evidence that the division was in any way class or politically motivated. In all, it is thought that 80 to 90 per cent of the 10th Tennessee were Irish Catholics, with the remaining 10 to 20 per cent Irish Protestants. The regiment was one of only two out of 669 infantry regiments in Confederate service that was predominantly Roman Catholic, the other being the 6th Louisiana.[1] Its first commander was Randal W. McGavock, who enjoyed widespread popularity among all the Irish of Nashville.

The Irishmen's first task was helping to construct Forts Henry and Donelson. Many of the men spoke Gaelic, and in the early days of the war were known to engage in something else that America had begun to associate with the Irish – heavy drinking and the rowdiness that went with it.

At Fort Henry, they spent the day of 4 February 1862 marching along the banks of the Tennessee River attempting to ascertain Federal troop positions as enemy gunboats appeared in the river and exchanged fire with the fort that day. That night, they amused themselves by drinking, playing cards and fighting. However, for all of the difficulties controlling the 10th while in camp, their behaviour in combat seemed better. During the evacuation of Fort Henry, they provided the rearguard for Confederate forces moving to Fort Donelson and skirmished briefly with Federals in pursuit. Their behaviour during the defence and evacuation of Fort Henry was commended by the fort's commander in his official report. McGavock himself commended his men for never once breaking their lines during the evacuation to Fort Donelson.[2] The capture of Fort Henry was a huge success for Grant. Now, however, he was determined to add to it and open up the Tennessee River for Federal navigation. Next on his list was Fort Donelson, where the Irishmen of the 10th Tennessee were about to meet with defeat.

At Donelson, the disciplinary credentials of the Irishmen were once again called into question. During their brief stay at the fort, the Tennessee Irish were brought into direct contact with the Irishmen of the 2nd Kentucky, and it seems that the kinship of the old country was not a determining factor in their relationship. The 2nd Kentucky had a few Irishmen scattered through its ranks and on 9 February 1862 the two Irish groups brawled with each other. The Tennessee men's numbers assured them victory in this little scrap, although two Fitzgerald brothers among their number had to pay for their indiscipline with counselling from the regiment's Catholic priest. The next morning, an entire company of the 10th had to be regaled with stories of the heroism of Irish soldiers in the Mexican War before they would obey the orders of Brigadier General Gideon Pillow and man an artillery position at the fort. Their own commanding officer, McGavock, and a number of his subordinates were also partially responsible for pleading the hated Pillow's case before the independent-minded Irishmen. In the end they obeyed the order, but were returned to the service of their own regiment only a few hours later.[3]

Grant had surrounded Fort Donelson by 12 February.

His intention was to block off any overland escape route for a Confederate force that already had its back to the Cumberland River, which was controlled by the Federal navy. The Irishmen of the 10th Tennessee were among the forces now hemmed in by Grant's vastly superior numbers and were about to earn their sobriquet 'the bloody 10th'.

On 13 February, the Federals made a number of probing assaults along the Confederate line. The 10th Tennessee was formed near the centre of that line on a hill commanding a heavily wooded slope, which Federal attackers would have to climb. They dug some five feet into the hill and placed breastworks in front of their rifle pits. Coincidentally, at the base of the hill was a small stream known as Erin Hollow Creek and locals tended to refer to the area simply as Erin Hollow. McGavock believed their position was so strong that no Federal commander would risk an attack on that part of the line. He was wrong.

The Irishmen had come under some artillery fire on 12 February but had survived the attack without sustaining any casualties. Indeed, it appears that their biggest concern was the noise that interrupted their card games in the pits.[4] The morning of 13 February began with another heavy artillery duel until Federal infantry emerged from the treeline around 11.00 a.m. They made their way up the hill under ferocious artillery fire until they closed within range of the Irish muskets and were then met with devastating musket fire, which drove them back towards the trees. Nonetheless, the Federals were quick to re-form and attack a second and even a third time, all to no avail. Each time, they were repulsed by the Irishmen and their brigade colleagues on the higher ground. Confederate artillery fire from behind and around the Irishmen also raked the Federal ranks, and as the foe retreated for the third time, a particularly gruesome event occurred that must have shaken this regiment of Irishmen, who were, after all, still novices when it came to such heavy combat. As the Federals retreated, the galling artillery fire actually succeeded in setting fire to the dry leaves at their feet. As the Irishmen looked on, the overwhelmed Federals returned to the safety of the trees, leaving their wounded comrades to burn on the contested ground between the lines. Soon, both Confederate and Federal soldiers co-operated in a rescue effort and succeeded in removing some of the wounded from the burning ground. Some of the Irishmen participated in the rescue operation, while their Catholic chaplain, Fr Henry Browne, assisted Federal chaplains of all denominations. Grey- and blue-clad soldiers were temporarily united in a mission of mercy. Unfortunately, not all of the wounded could be saved and the Irish of the 10th Tennessee were forced to witness one of the war's most disgusting spectacles.[5]

That night, as snow covered the singed ground and charred bodies at their front, the Irishmen and their comrades tried to sleep in sub-zero temperatures without the aid of blankets. As daylight crept over the field, it brought the return of artillery and sniper fire, but no all-out Federal assault. They would wait another cold night before their own commanders finally decided that their only hope was to break out of the Federal encirclement. The attack was planned for 4.00 a.m. on 15 February 1862. However, the Irishmen would not be involved and were merely expected to hold their own position while their comrades sought to break through the Federal right. The attack was unsuccessful and the dejected Confederate troops had retreated to the safety of their rifle pits by nightfall. At about 2.00 a.m. on the morning of 16 February, the Irishmen were ordered to abandon their rifle pits and follow the movement of the troops to their left. As soon as they left, the white flag was flown and the Confederate position surrendered. It seems that the Irishmen were not happy to give in without a fight, however, and for a brief period contemplated their own escape without any authorisation. McGavock in particular felt let down and betrayed by his superior officers. In the end, though, they accepted the surrender and their very short war was over. In May, the *New York Herald* reported that the green flag of the Nashville Irish had been captured by an Illinois Irish unit and would be presented to the Irish of New York's 'Fighting 69th'. While the story is an interesting one, the 10th Tennessee's historian Ed Gleeson's research has proven that no such presentation took place and no such Illinois Irish unit engaged the 10th in the vicinity of Fort Donelson.

Soon, however, the Nashville Irish were to meet with a famous Illinois Irish unit when they were transferred to Northern prisoner-of-war camps. The commissioned officers were detained in Fort Warren in Boston, while the enlisted men journeyed to Camp Douglas in Chicago. One of the Federal officers who met the Nashville Irish at Camp Douglas was an Irish-American by the name of James Mulligan. Mulligan commanded the 23rd Illinois Infantry, a unit sometimes referred to as the Western Irish Brigade.[6]

James Mulligan was born in Utica, New York, of Irish parents. His father died when he was a child and his mother moved to Chicago, where she married an Irish-American named Michael Lantry. Mulligan's strict Catholic upbringing and his education at the Catholic College of North Chicago ensured that he was renowned as a devout Catholic. Mulligan read law at the office of a Chicago congressman and qualified as a lawyer in 1856. For a brief period in 1857, the young Mulligan worked in the Department of the Interior in Washington. His extra-curricular activities included editing a Catholic newspaper and attending to his duties as elected Captain of the Chicago Shields Guards. When the war began, Mulligan was instrumental in recruiting a regiment from among Chicago's Irish population, which would come to be known as the 23rd Illinois Infantry, or Mulligan's Irish Brigade. The Chicago men were joined by a company of Irish from nearby Detroit, Michigan, who had failed to find a placement in any of their own state's regiments.

The 23rd Illinois was mustered into Federal service on 15 June 1861 and moved South into the state of Missouri, where Confederate forces were battling for control of the state. Mulligan's Irish were dispatched to a town called Lexington, where they were encircled by Confederate forces. The encirclement did not prompt surrender from Mulligan, who sought to hold the town against a vastly superior besieging force. He was unsuccessful and Lexington's Irish garrison surrendered on 20 September, having been under attack since 13 September. The men were paroled by their Southern captors but Mulligan was held prisoner until November of that year. He was eventually exchanged for a Confederate general and returned to Chicago to rejoin and reorganise his old Irish regiment, as the 23rd had been officially mustered out in October 1861. However, upon his return, Mulligan successfully applied to have the unit reinstated and have their service counted from their original muster date. Mulligan and his old regiment were reorganised at Fort Douglas in order to guard prisoners. Soon these Irish immigrants found themselves guarding their countrymen of the 10th Tennessee.

There appears to have been some bond between the Irish guards and prisoners and cordial relationships between these countrymen may have led to a number of Confederates expressing an interest in joining the Federal forces as part of

Mulligan's Irish Brigade. It was during this period that Mulligan wrote to the Federal General Halleck, informing him that a considerable number of Irishmen from the 10th Tennessee had expressed an interest in joining the 23rd Illinois. However, recruitment of prisoners was not allowed at that time. Just a few months later, when prisoner recruitment was finally permitted, only five of the Nashville Irish still expressed the desire to join, and subsequently none of these five men did so. Thus, it appears that the Nashville Irish were fiercely loyal to the Confederacy and either Mulligan had exaggerated the extent to which they would flock to his ranks, or the Confederate Irishmen had merely been indulging in the cordial relations that existed between them and their captors by telling the latter what they wanted to hear.

In June 1862, the 23rd Illinois were transferred back into active Federal service and their Confederate countrymen at Camp Douglas were left at the mercy of a harsher regime led by Colonel Joseph H. Tucker. Tucker was a different proposition from Mulligan and the Nashville Irish grew to hate him. A brief extract from the journal of Jimmy Doyle, of the 10th Tennessee, gives an insight into prison life during the war:

> The guards call this the Southwest box. I do not know north from south, east from west ... Last count there were 131 of us in here ... not even enough room to walk from one end to the other ... has got to be over 100 degrees in here. This is hell and Tucker is Satan. We get mush once a day but nothing to cook it in ... Everyone sick. Carried four more to smallpox hospital today. Then off to the death-house ... Johnny Diggons of A Company died right in here last night. Never could get the lad to the hospital.[7]

While the men of the 10th Tennessee sweated it out in Camp Douglas, the war raged on to the south. After the fall of Forts Henry and Donelson, the western Confederacy was severely threatened. Confederate garrisons at Nashville and Columbus quickly became untenable and were abandoned to Federal forces. Grant continued his own advance, turning his attention towards Corinth, Mississippi. He planned to join his forces with General Don Carlos Buell's Army of the Ohio, which would mean a combined command of 78,000 men could move on Corinth. However, Johnston and Beauregard, commanding the Confederate Army of the Mississippi, could not wait for these armies to combine and outnumber them. Thus, they marched their force of approximately 44,000 men out of Corinth and north towards Grant, striking Grant's army on 6 April 1862 near a small Methodist meeting house called Shiloh Church. Perhaps the most significant Irish presence in this battle came in the form of a 33-year-old Cork man who would become the highest-ranking immigrant in the Confederacy. It was at Shiloh that Patrick Roynane Cleburne first led troops into a major battle.

Cleburne was born in a rural area called Ovens, approximately 10 miles west of Cork city. He was the son of a wealthy Protestant landowner and was himself baptised in the Church of Ireland at nearby Athnowen. In an Ireland undergoing rapid political and social transition, Cleburne's family was known to be among the more liberal of their social class and even voted for candidates who called for Catholic Emancipation. There is no evidence to suggest that the Cleburne family remained anything other than loyal subjects of the British Crown and supporters of the Union of Great Britain and Ireland. However, in his youth, Cleburne served as an apprentice physician in Mallow, County Cork. The apprenticeship is worth noting because during Cleburne's stay in Mallow the town was a hotbed of Irish nationalist activity, with Thomas Davis resident in the town and Daniel O'Connell holding political rallies there. If Cleburne's stay in Mallow sowed the seeds of his questioning of British rule in Ireland, the seeds did not instantly bear fruit. In 1846, Cleburne failed his second entrance exam for the Apothecaries Hall medical college in Dublin. He did not wish to return to Cork as a failure and instead enlisted in the British army.

Cleburne concealed his privileged background from his superiors and began his military career as a common soldier. He enjoyed the military lifestyle and it was during his early years in the British army that he formed a lifelong attachment to military drill, tidiness of uniform and the general discipline of military life. However, the Irish famine and the military duties related to it also left a profound mark on the young Cleburne. His regiment was moved around between various Irish barracks during those bleak years and death greeted them at every port of call. While standing guard over prisoners interned at Spike Island for stealing food, Cleburne was deemed guilty of the negligence that allowed some of the men to escape. It is possible that his negligence was the intentional result of his compassion for the poor and his growing frustration at a British system of government that had little pity for the poor of Ireland.[8]

Growing weary of the declining situation in his homeland, Cleburne bought his discharge from the army and emigrated to America in 1849. He settled in Helena, Arkansas, and for a few years worked as a pharmacist. Employed by two doctors who owned the drug store where he worked, Cleburne was soon moving in the highest circles of Helena's society. Later he studied law and qualified as a lawyer in 1856. In 1859 he became a founding partner in the Cleburne, Scaife & Mangum law firm. The young Irishman became a prominent opponent of Know Nothing politics in the South, perhaps transferring his family's views on Catholic Emancipation to the American political theatre. He was even involved in a shootout with Know Nothing candidates on the streets of Helena. During the gun battle, Cleburne and his friend were injured, while a Know Nothing supporter was killed.

As the war clouds rolled in over Arkansas in the early 1860s, Cleburne was as keen as most other Southerners to assert their right of independence. In 1860 he joined a militia company known locally as the Yell Rifles. This company had a significant number of Irish among its ranks.[9] Owing to his experience of soldiering in Ireland, Cleburne was quickly elected captain of the group. In April 1861, the Yell Rifles and several other Arkansas militia companies were sent to Mound City for training. In May, Arkansas seceded from the Union and joined the rebellion. The 1st Arkansas Infantry Regiment was raised from among the militia groups at Mound City and Cleburne was elected as its colonel. Upon moving to Fort Randolph, Tennessee, however, the young Irishman was replaced as commander of the 1st Arkansas. His replacement did not last long and when he abandoned the fort and fell back to Memphis, convinced that he was about to be attacked by Federals, he was arrested by Cleburne and several other officers of the 1st, who charged him with incompetence. For this act, Cleburne and his fellow officers were court-martialled for mutiny. They were exonerated of the charges and soon returned to Fort Cleburne, which had been built by the 1st Arkansas on the banks of the Mississippi and named in honour of their Irish commander.

Cleburne and the 1st Arkansas spent the remainder of

1861 marching around Missouri and Kentucky, taking part in manoeuvres that preceded theoretical Confederate offensives that never occurred. Along the way, Cleburne formed a strong bond with one of his superiors, Brigadier General William J. Hardee. It was Hardee who appointed Cleburne a brigade commander in October 1861. After the fall of Forts Henry and Donelson, Cleburne's brigade was among the Confederate forces that fell back to Nashville and by 20 March 1862 they were among the Confederate army gathering in Corinth. The young Irishman was about to undergo the first major test of his leadership in battle.

At 6.30 a.m. on 6 April 1862, Cleburne led his brigade from their camp and across the Shiloh branch. Scattered among its ranks were a number of Irishmen. Three companies of the 15th Arkansas, including the Yell Rifles, were mainly Irish in their composition. In addition to the Arkansas infantrymen, a number of Irish served in the Helena Battery. Cleburne had taken on more Irishmen on 5 April, when the mostly Irish 2nd Tennessee was transferred to his command. The 2nd had one full company of Irish, yet its ranks were so heavily dotted with Irishmen that it was often known as the 'Irish regiment'.[10] Moving through the early morning, they were soon within sight of the Federal camp of William T. Sherman. They fell upon the camp but were repulsed by heavy Federal fire and appalling losses. Cleburne was forced to order the retreat back across the Shiloh Branch.

Although the attack had been a failure, Cleburne had demonstrated his ability to react quickly as battle plans went awry. The young Irishman seemed to have an uncanny ability to be at the very place he should be when a crisis developed. His movement between the regiments he commanded was timed to perfection. By 2.00 p.m. he was ready for another attack and had managed to rally his deflated men. He also changed his tactics, rushing the Federal camp rather than approaching as if on parade. Again they were repulsed and again Cleburne rallied them for a third charge. By now two of Cleburne's regiments were devastated, yet on the third occasion, they managed to overrun the Federal camp.

In the evening he was once again instrumental in opportunistically exploiting a weakness in the Federal flank near Shiloh's sunken road, which provided the most obstinate Federal opposition to the sweeping Confederate advance. It took the Confederates eight bloody attempts to break through Federal resistance in the road. Among the men flung at the Federal strongpoint were the 13th Louisiana, which was about one-quarter Irish, the 2nd Arkansas with one Irish company, the 3rd Confederate Infantry including a company known as the Shamrock Guards, and the 20th Louisiana, including four companies of Irish from New Orleans. The key that finally unlocked the sunken road for the Confederates was a peach orchard just to the east of the position. When that was taken around 3.00 p.m. by a brigade including some scattered Missouri Irish, the Federal garrison in the sunken road was surrounded and surrendered.[11]

When the attack succeeded in dislodging Federal forces from the area, Cleburne was so determined to follow it up that he did not even allow his men to return to the rear to replenish their ammunition. Instead, he had the ammunition drawn from the rear to the men on the field. Again he moved his brigade forward, attempting to exploit another weakness in the Federal line. The orders of Beauregard and the approaching darkness, however, put an end to the relentless Irishman's pursuit of the Federals.

On 7 April, Cleburne demonstrated his ability to follow orders, even when they made little sense to him. Against his better judgement, the Irishman led his brigade in a charge that he considered suicidal. He made his commanding officer aware of the potential disaster but still moved forward without the support of artillery. His brigade was repulsed, but once again Cleburne showed his aptitude for leadership by rallying what few men he could to slow down the Federal advance.

The Battle of Shiloh had been a Confederate failure. On 6 April 1862 they had driven Federal forces before them and hemmed them in on the banks of the Tennessee. Reinforced that night, however, the Federals had turned the tables and gained back every inch of the ground lost on 7 April. As the grey-clad Confederates trudged back towards Corinth, Cleburne made sure the retreat was orderly and that any supplies that could not be carried were burned lest they fall into Federal hands. Already the young Irishman had proven himself a capable commander, qualities that would steer Cleburne further up the Confederate ladder and eventually earn him the *nom de guerre* 'Stonewall of the West'.

Patrick Cleburne

CHAPTER 5

THE PENINSULA CAMPAIGN

Back in the eastern theatre, after the defeat at Manassas, Major General George B. McClellan replaced McDowell as commander of the Federal army of the Potomac. McClellan quickly reorganised and trained the army, but his natural caution made him reluctant to lead it southwards. Indeed, it was to be March 1862 before McClellan finally took the offensive once again, an offensive that became known as the Peninsula Campaign.

The campaign began when McClellan moved troops towards Richmond via the Yorktown peninsula. McClellan was a very cautious man and when the Federal government refused to send 38,000 troops (McDowell's corps) to the peninsula and announced that there would be no more recruitment at that time, he abandoned his plan for an all-out attack and decided to lay siege to Yorktown instead. Facing overwhelming numerical superiority, Confederate General Joe Johnston decided that discretion was the better part of valour and withdrew from Yorktown on 3 May, leaving it to the Federals. On 5 May, Johnson's rearguard successfully engaged the advancing Federals at the Battle of Williamsburg.

With the successful capture of Yorktown, McDowell was

now ordered to advance towards Richmond from the Shenandoah Valley. The Confederate capital was threatened by two Federal forces and from two different directions. The answer was to have Stonewall Jackson pretend to threaten Washington from the Shenandoah Valley. When Jackson started attacking Federal troops there, Lincoln soon lost interest in Richmond and, perceiving his own capital to be threatened, ordered McDowell back into the Shenandoah Valley in order to try and close a trap around Jackson. Jackson escaped the trap, Richmond was spared and the Confederates' minds turned to counterattack. That counterattack came at the Battle of Seven Pines, where the Confederates attacked McClellan's army, which had advanced right up the peninsula and now threatened Richmond. Making its first appearance in a major battle was the newly organised Irish Brigade.

When the 69th New York retreated from Manassas, their ninety-day enlistment in the Federal army was already over. For many, this meant they could return to their homes, having done their duty. For others, however, continued service was either an economic necessity or a moral duty. The 69th had lost its leader, Corcoran, at Manassas, and now it had a new leader: Thomas Francis Meagher.

Meagher was born in Waterford in 1823, the son of well-established and wealthy Catholic parents. His father was a merchant trader between Newfoundland and Waterford and became Waterford's first Roman Catholic mayor in over 200 years. This privileged position afforded him the means to have Thomas educated in Clongowes Wood, County Kildare, and Stonyhurst College in Lancashire. When his education was finished, Meagher toured Europe before returning home and becoming a campaigner for the repeal of the Act of Union. In 1843, Meagher became a founding member of the

Young Ireland group, which favoured militant action in the cause of Irish independence. When he delivered a fiery speech advocating such an approach, he earned himself the title 'Meagher of the Sword'. After the Young Irelanders' rebellion in 1848, Meagher was initially sentenced to death, whereupon he famously addressed the court as follows:

> No; I do not despair of my poor old country – her peace, her liberty, her glory. For that country I can do no more than bid her hope. To lift this island up – make her a benefactor to humanity, instead of being as she is now, the meanest beggar in the world – to restore to her, her native powers and her ancient constitution – this has been my ambition and this ambition has been my crime. Judged by the law of England, I know this crime entails upon me the penalty of death; but the history of Ireland explains that crime and justifies it. Judged by that history, the treason of which I stand convicted loses all its guilt, has been sanctified as a duty, and will be ennobled as a sacrifice.

Meahger's sentence was subsequently commuted to transportation to Van Dieman's Land. The transportation did not prove to be as permanent as the authorities would have wished, and in 1852, he escaped and headed for America.

Arriving in New York, Meagher teamed up with another escaped Young Irelander, John Mitchel. Together they worked on a radically anti-British newspaper known as *The Citizen*. The two Irish rebels were eventually split by the issue of slavery, and while Mitchel went on to become a Southern propagandist, Meagher supported the Union. He joined the Federal army and led Company K of the 69th at Manassas.

Returning to New York after Manassas, Meagher proposed the idea of an Irish Brigade, of which the 69th

John Mitchel.

Thomas Francis Meagher, leader of
the Irish Brigade.

would be the core unit. In September 1861, the secretary of
war accepted his proposal and he was promoted to brigadier
general and given command of the new Irish Brigade.
Initially the Brigade consisted of the 69th New York, 63rd
New York and 88th New York Infantry regiments, which
were trained at Camp California in Virginia. Spirits were high
before the reality of combat sunk in. John F. McCormack
described the camp as follows:

> In early December 1861 the New York regiments took
> up pleasant winter quarters at Camp California, near
> Alexandria, Virginia, where they were assigned to
> General Sumner's division of the Army of the Potomac.
> Christmas was fondly remembered by those who
> survived the war. Little John Flaherty entertained on
> the violin while his father livened the festivities with
> Irish tunes played on the warpipes. The canteen, which
> hardly ever seemed to contain water, was eagerly passed
> around. Said Private Bill Dooley: 'It is as well to keep up
> our spirits by pouring spirits down, for sure, there's no

knowing where we'll be this night twelve months.'[1]

The Irish Brigade was to have been joined by the 28th Massachusetts before departing for the Yorktown peninsula, but as that regiment had not yet finished recruiting, instead the 29th Massachusetts (mostly of non-Irish Puritan descent) joined the three New York regiments in the midst of fighting on the peninsula.

On Saturday 31 May 1862, the brigade was enjoying some rest and recuperation in the form of a steeplechase and mule race organised by Meagher. Their chaplain, born in America of an Irish father, described the steeplechase as 'the invention of wild Irishmen, who did not know what fear is'. He was a little less perturbed by the mule race, which he considered 'laughable beyond expression'. The amusements were brought to an abrupt halt when the Irishmen heard Confederate cannon that had opened 'their brazen mouths and belched at our troops the missiles of death'.[2] The brigade was listening to the opening salvos of the Battle of Seven Pines echoing across the Chickahominy River. Taking advantage of the recent rains, Confederate General Joe Johnston had attacked Federal troops south of the river in an attempt to crush them before their Federal comrades could cross the swollen Chickahominy. Soon the Irishmen were on their way towards the foe and were moving towards another Irish unit, the 37th New York Infantry.

The 37th New York was mostly raised from among the remnants of the old 75th State Militia, a pre-war Irish unit. Companies from Allegany, Ellicottsville and Pulaski were added and the 37th New York Infantry, or 'Irish Rifles', were accepted into state service in May 1861.

By the time the Irish Brigade broke camp on the northern side of the river, the 37th New York were in the thick of the fight, having been engaged since morning in preventing a

Confederate flanking movement directed against their brigade that day. Divisional commander Kearney was specific in his explanation and praise of the Irish Rifles' role at Seven Pines.

> It was on this occasion that, seeing myself cut off, and relying on the high discipline and determined valor of the Thirty Seventh New York Volunteers, I faced them to the rear against the enemy, and held the ground, although so critically placed, and despite the masses that gathered on and had passed us, checked the enemy in his intent of cutting us off against the White Oak Swamp.[3]

Three officers from the 37th were later commended for their courage during the engagement. Their commanding officer, Colonel S.B. Hayman, made the commendations as follows:

> The Adjutant of my regiment Lieut. James Henry was particularly distinguished for his daring zeal and courage and I commend him as worthy of special notice. Lieut. W.C. Green, who was seriously wounded, and who, before the engagement, was unfit for duty, I also deem worthy of special notice. I also recommend as worthy of commendation Capt. James R. O'Beirne and Lieut. P.J. Smith for zeal, judgement and courage. Each company of my right wing had an officer disabled, and two of these companies were left entirely without officers, yet the enlisted men acted worthy of their native courage.[4]

O'Beirne, born in Ballagh, County Roscommon, subsequently received the Congressional Medal of Honor for gallantry in maintaining the line at Seven Pines. Later in the war, he rose to the rank of major and continued to serve the US with distinction after the war. He was the last provost martial of the District of Columbia and was involved in the pursuit and capture of Abraham Lincoln's assassin, John Wilkes Booth.[5]

Crossing the treacherous Grapevine Bridge, which the flooded river had weakened considerably, and sloshing their way through swampy marshes that adjoined the southern bank, it was late evening by the time the Irish Brigade arrived at the Federal front line. The scene of the bloodiest Civil War battle up till that point affected Meagher, who reported it as follows:

> It was between 9 and 10 p.m. when the head of our brigade entered on the scene of that day's terrible conflict, and we were apprised of the fact and it was impressed upon us startlingly by the appearance of numbers of surgeons and chaplains with lanterns in hand searching over the ground to the right and left of our advance in column for the dead and wounded, who they said were scattered in every direction around. The surgeon of my brigade, two of the chaplains, and the quartermaster of the Sixty-third New York Volunteers, First Lieut. P. O'Hanlon, were here requested to give their services in the humane search after and relief of the victims of the battle-field. In half an hour after the brigade, having carefully looked to and secured their arms, laid down on the open field, the first time to rest for that day.

The Brigade lay there through the night while Confederate troops occupied the woods in front their position. Then, as dawn broke over the Virginian battlefield, a hurried breakfast was interrupted by firing at their front. General Sumner, who commanded the corps in which the Brigade had been placed, rode up to remind them that they had been held back since entering service, but now was their time to shine.

With the 63rd New York detached to guard bridges at the rear and the 29th Massachusetts not yet arrived to join the Irishmen, the Brigade's remaining two regiments were immediately deployed through the woods to secure the railway at the other side. The 88th New York encountered some difficulty along the way when their orders were initially countermanded and then reissued by an officer from the corps staff. The 88th's commanding officer, Lieutenant Colonel Patrick Kelly, reported the dangerous battlefield confusion as follows:

> By order of General Richardson, conveyed to me by one of his aides, I took the regiment across a belt of wood for the purpose of re-enforcing the, I believe Eighty-first Pennsylvania Volunteers, who were reported nearly out of ammunition, and if not immediately relieved the result might be serious. On emerging from the wood I found I had only two companies, in consequence of the regiment having been halted while in the wood by a staff officer who did not convey the order to me, who was then marching at the head of my regiment. I with the two companies continued forward to the open space now occupied by Hazzard's battery, and advanced them in line of battle toward the railroad under a heavy fire. Shortly after the rest of the regiment came up; and here I would thank Captain McMahon, of General Meagher's staff, for the assistance he rendered them in conducting them to where I was then hotly engaged and where they were much needed.

The Irish Brigade succeeded in holding their position as ordered and acquitted themselves well on the field of battle. However, it was not the Brigade's combat at Seven Pines that caused controversy, but rather the subsequent reportage of that combat. Meagher's official report seemed somewhat exaggerated in its praise of his men's conduct during their first major battle and some other Federal commanders felt that Meagher's exaggerations reflected poorly on the performance of their commands. When a depiction of Meagher personally leading an Irish charge at Seven Pines appeared in *Harper's Weekly*, the hackles of these commanders were further raised. One of them subsequently claimed that Meagher was drunk on the night of 31 May and was nowhere to be seen during combat on 1 June. Allegations of Meagher's overindulgence in alcohol continued to follow the Irish Brigade's leader for the duration of his command. Another Federal officer claimed that the general had only appeared after the battle was over, and that the depiction in *Harper's Weekly* was inspired by his movements after, and not during, the battle.[6] Yet for all the controversy surrounding Meagher, nobody sought to deny that his brigade had done what was asked of it at Seven Pines.

The Irish Brigade and their Federal countrymen were not the only Irish on the field. The Confederate Irish units were generally much smaller than brigades and were seldom even regiments. Instead, they were the smallest of military units, known as companies. One of those companies engaged at Seven Pines was Company I of the 8th Alabama Infantry Regiment. Known as the Emerald Guard, the company was the colour company of the regiment, meaning that it frequently exposed itself to danger in carrying the regimental colours on the field of battle. The colours were generally carried at the centre of a regiment and were followed by those men who could not hear orders above the battle din.

Company I often served beside another immigrant unit of the 8th Alabama, Company H, the German Fusiliers. It is estimated that up to 104 of Company I's 109 personnel were Irish born. A look at their regimental roster reveals many names that may have been Scotch Irish, and many that were more typically Irish. The company's flag had an Irish harp surrounded by a shamrock on its reverse and also cited the Gaelic war cry so often associated with the Federal Irish brigade, '*Faugh a Ballagh*', along with the phrase '*Erin Go Bragh*'.[7] However, it was regimental and not company flags that were carried into battle.

As part of the 8th Alabama, the Emerald Guards were members of the first Alabama unit to enlist for the war. They saw action at Winn's Mill and Williamsburg and thus were not entirely without combat experience upon arriving at Seven Pines. On the field that day, they lost their commanding officer, Captain Patrick C. Loughry. In total, the 8th Alabama lost thirty-one killed, eighty wounded and thirty-two missing. The Emerald Guards would not have been aware of the presence of Irish Federals to the north of their position, though in the coming days they operated in close proximity to their countrymen on the Federal side.

Seven Pines was a bloody and indecisive battle. The Confederates failed to neutralise the threat to Richmond and lost General Johnston, who was wounded during the affair. The loss of Johnston turned into a blessing in disguise, as he was replaced by perhaps the most beloved general in American history, Robert E. Lee.

Lee immediately began to bolster the Confederate army outside their capital by bringing reinforcements from every quarter. Soon he had approximately 85,000 men facing about 105,000 Federals. McClellan's army was still split on the northern and southern banks of the Chickahominy River. From 12 to 15 June, J.E.B. Stuart rode his Confederate cavalry right around the Federal position to reconnoitre the

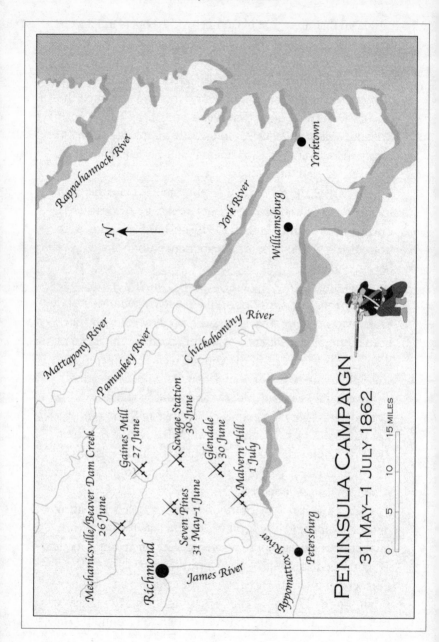

PENINSULA CAMPAIGN
31 MAY–1 JULY 1862

Yorktown

Williamsburg

Rappahannock River

York River

Mattapony River

Pamunkey River

Chickahominy River

Mechanicsville/Beaver Dam Creek
26 June

Gaines Mill
27 June

Savage Station
30 June

Glendale
30 June

Malvern Hill
1 July

Seven Pines
31 May–1 June

Richmond

James River

Petersburg

Appomattox River

N

0   5   10   15 MILES

Federal army. Stuart's raid also worked as a deception and McClellan became increasingly convinced that he was greatly outnumbered by the Confederates, thus his subsequent actions were cautious in the extreme. He began by slowly moving artillery towards Richmond, resulting in the first of the Seven Days Battles.

The Seven Days Battles were essentially a series of six battles fought over seven days from 25 June to 1 July 1862. The first of these was the Battle of Oak Grove on 25 June, which occurred when Federal troops attempting to move artillery closer to Richmond clashed with Confederate pickets. The result was indecisive, but it did not affect the Confederate counteroffensive that Lee had planned for the following day.

Lee knew he had to attack before the Federals had a chance to lay siege to Richmond, so he struck the Federal flank at Mechanicsville. The brunt of the attack was made by the forces of Major General Ambrose Powell Hill, who sustained about 1,500 casualties while the Federals suffered only 400. Nonetheless, McClellan was convinced that Lee's forces were numerically superior to his own and decided to withdraw to a more defensible position at Gaines Mill, where Lee attacked again.

As part of Major General James Longstreet's division, the 8th Alabama, with the Emerald Guards in their ranks, took part in a famous and bloody assault on the Federal position at Gaines Mill. They emerged from that victorious assault with the loss of half of the 350 men that had been engaged. Another Confederate unit present at Gaines Mill was the 1st Virginia Irish Battalion. This unit, smaller than a regiment, had been raised in the railroad and seaport centres of Richmond, Alexandria, Norfolk, Lynchburg and Covington, where clusters of Irish immigrants had worked. In common with so many other Irish units, they had gained a reputation for drunken rowdiness and in the spring of 1861 two of their number were imprisoned for mutiny. While in prison, the two Irishmen created more controversy by attacking their guards. The men were eventually brought to heel and sentenced to three months' hard labour. Although dogged by occasional disciplinary problems, the battalion had performed well in combat during Jackson's campaign in the Shenandoah Valley.[8] At Gaines Mill they came under fire during a charge: two of their men were wounded and one was killed. Their brigade commander complemented them on their 'coolness, bravery, and discretion'.[9]

Wheat's Tigers were also in action at Gaines Mill and sustained twenty-two casualties in a charge. Among the casualties was Major Wheat himself. The unit had continued to have disciplinary problems in the wake of First Battle of Manassas, and in December 1861, Michael O'Brien and Denis Corcoran became the first men of the Army of Northern Virginia to be executed for mutiny. Their bodies lay in unmarked graves south of Centreville until they were reinterred at St John's Episcopal Church in 1979.[10] After Wheat's death, the unit became increasingly disorderly and was eventually disbanded in August 1862.[11] Irish companies among the ranks of the 19th Virginia and 16th Mississippi also participated in the bloody Confederate assaults at Gaines Mill.[12]

On the Federal side, Irish units included the 9th Massachusetts Infantry, which delayed the Confederate crossing of Gaines Creek. These Boston Irish had moved out of camp early that morning, passing Gaines Mill on their way to New Cold Harbor. From there they were ordered back towards Old Cold Harbor, where they were then ordered to hold the crossing of Gaines Creek until Federal forces retreating from Beaver Dam Creek had taken advantage of it. The last of these forces passed through the ranks of the Boston Irish at noon. The Irishmen now attempted to delay the Confederate crossing long enough for their comrades to fortify a line behind them. The first piecemeal Confederate attacks spluttered out, having taken heavy enfilading fire from the Irish. But now, as the Irishmen looked towards the hill in front of them, an entire Confederate division was readying itself to carry the bridge and continue the Confederate advance. Among the forces that A.P. Hill was stacking up behind the hill was Maxcy Gregg's South Carolina Brigade, a brigade which contained the 1st South Carolina Irish Volunteers. Gregg's brigade clashed with the Boston Irish and after about two hours' fighting succeeded in carrying the bridge. According to Gregg's report, two non-Irish companies of the 1st South Carolina were primarily responsible for dislodging the Boston Irish. However, a post-war account written by the 9th's Daniel McNamara suggests that the 9th's holding action was defeated only when the full force of Gregg's brigade was brought to bear upon it.[13] If Confederate and Federal Irish did not actually clash at this crossing, they certainly came very close to doing so.

As the Irish 9th fell back from the crossing, they continued to delay Gregg's advance until he was forced to deploy large numbers to drive them back to what had now become the main Federal line. Hill now concentrated his efforts on breaking this line, and a desperate and confused fight rocked back and forth throughout the afternoon. Eventually, at approximately 7.00 p.m., the Confederates broke through near the left of the Federal line. Now, as Southern troops poured through the rapidly opening gaps, a full-scale rout was in progress. Only the impending darkness and the arrival of fresh troops from across the Chickahominy could save the troops on the northern bank. Enter the Irish Brigade.

The Irish Brigade had been sent by Sumner to assist Porter's command (the 9th Massachusetts among them), who were now falling back rapidly after the Confederate breakthrough. So commanding were the actions of the Irish 9th as they again covered the Federal retreat, this time with nine separate charges, that it was later claimed Longstreet confused their green flag as representing the Irish Brigade rather than a solitary regiment. Soon Longstreet's men were to encounter the real thing, as the Irish Brigade rushed to the assistance of their countrymen through the ranks of retreating Federal units. As they moved forward, they were loudly cheered by their retreating comrades, some of whom were rounded up by a company of the fighting 69th at bayonet-point. One French observer later wrote that 'they came in shirt sleeves yelling at the top of their voices'.[14] Upon their arrival, the commanding officer of Boston's 9th was alleged to have recognised his countrymen. 'Hello, General Meagher, is this the Irish Brigade?' he questioned through the evening gloom, and upon receiving a positive response from the Waterford man he supposedly replied, 'Thank God, we are saved.'[15] The Irish 9th then gratefully left their rearguard duties to their countrymen and slunk back across the river to count their terrible losses, the worst of any Federal unit that day.[16]

It seems that it was not only their fellow Irishmen that were grateful for the intervention of the Irish Brigade in covering the Federal retreat from Gaines Mill. During that organised retreat and related combat operations, at least one Federal general referred to the Irish Brigade's 'enthusiasm', which he stated had 'gained universal applause'.[17] Even the Confederate Major General D.H. Hill had reason to comment on the presence of the Irish Brigade as he pursued the retreating Federals at Gaines Mill:

> It was now fairly dark and hearing loud cheers from the Yankees in our immediate front, some two hundred yards distant, I ordered our whole advance to halt and wait an expected attack of the enemy ... The cheering, as we afterward learned, was caused by the appearance of the Irish Brigade to cover the retreat.[18]

Once again, Meagher's role at Gaines Mill proved controversial, with one historian later writing that he had led his men with 'the courage found in a bottle'.[19] It also appears that Meagher was arrested on 29 June, having failed to carry out a movement to the satisfaction of his superior.[20] Many within the Army of the Potomac were growing weary of the Irishman's continuous ill discipline.

Having retreated from Gaines Mill, the Federal army were engaged in a general withdrawal towards the James River, where they hoped to establish a new supply base. They were once again pursued by Lee's forces, with the latter's objective not only the defence of Richmond, but the complete destruction of McClellan's forces. The next Confederate attack came at Savage Station on 29 June, when Confederate attackers struck the Federal rearguard. Once again, the Irish Brigade was advanced through an evening twilight when it appeared that the Confederate attackers were making inroads. Once again, they successfully charged and routed the foe, succeeding in sabotaging a number of Confederate cannon that they could not draw away.

By now the Irish Brigade had been joined by the 29th Massachusetts. The 29th was about as non-Irish a unit as it was possible to find within the Army of the Potomac, but these sons of Boston's more privileged classes eventually came to admire the courage of their Irish comrades. One of the 29th's number mistook the 88th New York for the Fighting 69th, but nonetheless described their heroic intervention at Savage Station as follows:

> The musketry of the enemy swept their whole line from right to left; they staggered and huddled together ... and for an instant they nearly paused dreading to go on. Looking back they saw the Sixty ninth New York ... Passing their left flank, the Sixty-ninth New York, with fixed bayonets, ran straight toward the gorge and with an impetuosity so characteristic of them and such as few troops can withstand, rushed directly on the enemy's soldiers. The Vermont troops ... followed the brave example of the dauntless Irishmen, and in less than three minutes the railroad was ours.[21]

Once again, the Irish Brigade played a major part in holding the rear of the Federal retreat. But as the Federal troops continued their trek towards the James River, the Confederates kept on coming.

Only three days after their losses at Gaines Mill, on 30 June 1862, the 8th Alabama, as part of Longstreet's division (along with A.P. Hill's and Huger's divisions), converged on the retreating Federal army in the vicinity of Glendale or Frayser's Farm. The 8th Alabama and their Emerald Guards were part of Brigadier General Wilcox's Fourth Brigade, which was involved in the taking of two Federal artillery batteries that day, though the 8th were engaged by Federal infantry before they could get to the batteries. They held their ground and acquitted themselves well, sustaining heavy casualties.[22]

Meanwhile, the remainder of their brigade came into direct contact with a Federal Irish regiment, the 69th

Pennsylvania, which had been recruited from Irish militia units in Philadelphia. Curiously, it was initially designated the 2nd California, as it was raised to the credit of the western state. Later it became the 24th Pennsylvania and then 68th Pennsylvania. The unit then changed their designation to the 69th Pennsylvania in honour of their countrymen in the 69th New York after the governor of Pennsylvania, Andrew Gregg Curtin, had opposed the idea of their joining the New Yorkers as part of the Irish Brigade. At Glendale, the commander of the 69th's brigade was glowing in his praise of their gallant retaking of one of the artillery batteries initially taken by the 8th Alabama's brigade comrades:

> Another heavy attack broke McCall's centre and sent the fugitives shamefully through our ranks. Our line was advanced and Colonel Owen, Sixty-ninth Pennsylvania Volunteers, unsupported, pursued the victorious rebels back over the ground through which they were passing and crowned the crest of the hill where McCall had lost his artillery. Gallant Sixty-ninth! The line followed this noble example and McCall's position was held and the enemy discomfited.[23]

Brigadier General Joseph Hooker wrote of the 'almost reckless daring' with which the 69th had pursued the Confederates. It was also alleged that he personally congratulated the 69th on the field for having made 'the first successful bayonet charge of the war and saved the Army of the Potomac from probable disaster'.[24] Whether or not Hooker really made that statement, the 69th Pennsylvania was certainly instrumental in assisting the Federals in holding their ground and once again escaping Lee's grasp.

They did not outdo their countrymen of the Irish

Brigade, however, as the latter unit arrived yet again to shore up the centre of the line near Glendale in the nick of time on the evening of 30 June. As they made their familiar journey through the ranks of retreating comrades and passed their corps commander General Sumner, he was reported to have cried, 'Boys, you go in and save another day.' And once again, their comrades cheered the arrival of the green flag as the Irishmen charged forward with a rousing cheer and swept the field of the attacking foe.[25] That evening, McClellan's forces began to retreat to an easily defensible position on Malvern Hill. Lee would make one final futile assault, attempting to smash McClellan's army before it could reach the James River.

By the morning of 1 July, almost the entire Federal Army of the Potomac was camped on Malvern Hill. In order to win a decisive victory over the Army of the Potomac, Lee decided that his infantry should assault the hill directly after his artillery had bombarded it. Unfortunately for Lee, it was the Federal gunners who struck first, opening up one of the most intensive artillery bombardments of the war at about 1.00 p.m. By 2.30 p.m. their superior firepower had disabled most of the Confederate batteries, which had done their best to return what fire they could to the hill.

Up on the hill, the 69th Pennsylvania, fresh from their heroics the previous day, were being held in position behind one of the duelling artillery batteries. Eventually the Confederate fire was heavy enough that the Irishmen had to lie on the ground to escape injury. Perhaps in recognition of their contribution of the previous day, the 69th were moved out of the line of fire around noon. However, at approximately 3.00 p.m., their brigade was sent for and formed into a line of battle as Confederate infantry began attacking the hill. However, it was soon discovered that their summoning had been as a result of a staff officer mistaking the green flag of the 69th Pennsylvania for that of the Irish Brigade. When the error was corrected, the Pennsylvania Irish were once again returned to a safer position and Meagher's Irishmen were sent into the breach to rescue Federal units that had come under severe pressure from the Confederate infantry that were bravely storming the hill. Among the units that the Irish Brigade stormed forward to rescue was the 9th Massachusetts Infantry. As the brigade moved forward, the Irishmen of the 9th again recognised their countrymen and welcomed them with rapturous cheering. It was alleged that one Confederate officer on the hill was heard to remark, 'Here comes that damn green flag again'.

The fighting on the slopes of Malvern Hill was so heavy that the men of the Irish Brigade had to pick up the guns of their dead comrades when their own became too hot to fire. In the midst of this chaos, another group of Irishmen were thrown into combat – the men of the Confederate 10th Louisiana Infantry – and they now advanced towards their Federal countrymen.

The 10th Louisiana contained enormous numbers of Irish dockworkers from New Orleans. In all, some 26 per cent of their roster was made up of Irishmen. The contribution of those Irish to the fighting in which the 10th was involved can be deduced by looking at the dispropor-tionate number of casualties sustained by the Irish. Historian Phillip Thomas Tucker has pointed out that approximately 33 per cent of the regiment's casualties for the duration of the war were Irish, thus concluding that the Irish were often in the thick of the regiment's fighting.[26] The 10th Louisiana were described as 'New Orleans toughs and Mississippi river men, mainly Irish, and all skilled at alley fighting with hatchet and bowie knife'.[27] On Malvern Hill, in the late afternoon, these Irish 'toughs' slammed straight into another group of Irishmen who did not shy away from battle, and the result was a fight so ferocious that it shocked even battle-hardened Federal officers. Piles of abandoned and broken rifles were found on the spot where the Irishmen had clashed. Bayonets and bowie knifes cut through flesh and bone in a fierce hand-to-hand encounter, and when bayonets could not be fixed, muskets were reversed and used to club the enemy to death. In an accent distinctive to the American ear, one Federal Irishman explained, 'When the rebs went for our biys with bowie knives, biys went for the rebs in the way they wor used to'.[28]

As darkness fell on the Irish corpses that littered Malvern Hill, the 'rebs' retreated under the ferocity of the Irish Brigade's attack and the Federals had won the day, allowing the Army of the Potomac a safe retreat to Harrison's Landing. Of the casualties that the 10th Louisiana left on the field, almost half were Irish born.[29]

The Irish Brigade added to the growing reputation of their countrymen, coming to the rescue of other Federal units for the second day in a row. Lieutenant Colonel H.S. Campbell of the 83rd Pennsylvania Volunteers, having complained of the cowardice of one unknown Federal regiment, was particularly grateful to the Irish Brigade and wrote of his regiment's 'utter joy' when 'the gallant Irish Brigade dashed onto the field to save our utter destruction'.[30] However, the Irish Brigade's introduction to major combat operations and the reputation it had won for itself during the Peninsula Campaign came at a high cost. The brigade's chaplain, Fr William Corby, later recorded his memories of the Federal withdrawal towards the James River:

Our heroic brigade left 700 of its bravest officers and

men on the bloody fields behind; nearly every one of them Catholics, and we may almost say none without having shortly before received the sacraments. Let us hope that they met a favourable trial before the dread Judgement seat; and their hardships, thirst, hunger, and the blood flowing from their painful, mortal wounds, cried for pardon for past sins, and found a favourable echo in the Sacred Wounds of a benign Saviour, who had the last drop of His blood for the salvation of their precious souls. We leave them, as a tear drops to their memory, to meet, we hope, in the kingdom of peace.[31]

The Confederate assault on Malvern Hill was later referred to as 'murder' by D.H. Hill. The Confederates suffered some 5,500 casualties to about 3,500 for the Federals. McClellan completed his retreat to Harrison's Landing, thereby ending

The chaplains and men of the Irish Brigade, Harrison's Landing, July 1862.

the Peninsula Campaign, while Lee, having repelled the threat to his capital but having failed to break the Federal army, withdrew his forces to Richmond.

The Peninsula Campaign was over. Once again, a major Federal army had failed to take the Confederate capital and was forced to abandon its attempts. However, the Confederate defence of their capital came at a very high price in terms of casualties. For many of the Irishmen on both sides, the Peninsula Campaign had been their first taste of major combat operations. Their units acquitted themselves well and were frequently praised for their daring and valour. So impressed were Federal commanders with the Irish temperament on the battlefield that at Malvern Hill they specifically sought the green flag to reinforce their line of battle. Among Federals, the Irish had won a reputation for saving the day.

Yet for all of that, the misery of a soldier's life was the same for the Irish as it was for all others. Commanders reported heroism, valour, glory and horror in the line of battle, but when the battles were over, drudgery and discomfort were constant companions for all soldiers. For the 69th Pennsylvania, their heroic bayonet charge at Glendale meant little as they trudged through a rainy Virginian summer from Malvern Hill back towards Harrison's Landing on the James River. One of their veterans later wrote of their journey:

> The Sixty-ninth was given advance of the Corps, with instructions to march rapidly and push through any obstructions we would encounter. We arrived at the landing shortly after daylight, in the midst of a drenching rain. An encampment was formed in a ploughed field of the stickiest mud that could possibly be found: here we were allowed to rest. Our readers can

imagine the sweet repose enjoyed by troops marching almost constantly by night, and fighting by day, for four days and nights (some troops for seven days and nights). Thus ended the memorable 'seven days fighting' of the Army of the Potomac.

The government sometimes seemed a little ungrateful for all the services of the common soldier. Almost thirty years later, the above writer was still annoyed at one particular incident in the aftermath of the Peninsula Campaign that seemed to highlight that ingratitude:

> During our encampment here new clothing was issued, which was greatly needed as the men of the Sixty-ninth, just previous to going into the Battle of Savage Station were ordered to place their knapsacks in a pile in the woods until after the battle, which they did, but never recovered them, hence all their clothing was lost by order. The government in this case treated the men very meanly by charging them for the clothing they had drawn to replace that so lost.[32]

Conditions may have been even worse for the Confederate Irish, as the Confederate soldier was not as well equipped or well paid as his Northern counterpart.

Much Irish blood had already been spilled on the battlefields of America, yet the war was far from over. Indeed, its bloodiest chapters were yet to be written. For the Irish on both sides, far greater glory, fame, heartbreak and death awaited. The pages of Irish-American history would be forever dominated by the deeds these men were about to do in service of their adopted nation. Some of these sons of Erin would become icons of American history and some of their actions are still celebrated and commemorated today.

CHAPTER 6

BACK TO BULL RUN

On 3 August 1862, McClellan was ordered to withdraw all Federal troops from the peninsula. This effectively removed the dual threat posed to the Confederate capital from both the peninsula and the Shenandoah Valley and Lee was now able to concentrate exclusively on the Federal forces in the valley. The Federal forces had been increased by consolidating a number of commands into the Federal Army of Virginia and placing them under the stewardship of General John Pope. Pope had moved his command so far south that by 12 July he was already threatening Richmond's access to the valley. On 13 July Lee split his army in two, sending Jackson's two divisions to Gordonsville in order to oppose any southern movement by Pope, and keeping the remainder of his army in position in case McClellan turned back. The 1st Virginia Irish Battalion marched with Jackson to Gordonsville.

On 27 July 1862, Lee was feeling confident that the McClellan threat was receding and sent A.P. Hill's division to reinforce Jackson's wing of the army. This gave Jackson a force of about 24,000 men, large enough to attack the Federals if he decided it was opportune to do so. On 9 August, Jackson attacked Pope's forces when they moved south to capture the rail junction at Gordonsville, resulting in the Battle of Cedar Mountain. Although the Federals gained an early advantage in the battle, a counterattack by the Hill division eventually won the day for the Confederates.

The Irish battalion came into the Confederate line at Cedar Mountain at about 4.15 p.m. They were drawn up at the extreme left of their brigade in a densely wooded area with a small wheat field at their front. For approximately ninety minutes they stared at the wheat field and the woods on the other side in nervous anticipation of what might await them. Then, at about 5.45 p.m., the first of the blue uniforms began to emerge from the wood at the far side of the wheat. Soon, what looked to the Irish like an entire Federal brigade was moving at the double quick across the wheat in their direction. The limited range of their muskets meant that the Irish had to wait until the Federals were within 150 yards of their position before they could begin to defend it. The nerves of the Irish may have affected their aim and their first volley had little effect. They could only manage two further volleys before the Federal troops were upon them. The Irish fled the position in what their commanding officer admitted was a retreat that was undertaken 'rapidly and in great confusion'. The battalion officers attempted to hold the men in position and even to rally them after they had broken, but it was all to no avail. Arriving to reinforce the position, Brigadier General James H. Lane was disappointed at the 'disorderly manner' in which the troops he had come to support fell back. He found two lieutenants of the Irish battalion whose commands had deserted them and reassigned them to two companies in his own brigade.[1] Thus, the Irish battalion did not cover itself in glory at Cedar Mountain. Indeed, none of Jackson's division did. But greater glory was to follow.

By now, Lee knew that McClellan's force was being withdrawn and would be used to reinforce Pope, so he also knew that he needed to strike at Pope's army before it became too large for him to defeat. He now moved all his troops to join Jackson's group and attack Pope's eastern flank, cutting off his line of retreat to Washington and perhaps even crushing his entire army. Lee's operation was foiled, however, when a Confederate courier was captured with the plans and Pope rapidly withdrew and repositioned his army in a line at the Rappahannock River.

After some probing, Lee determined that the Federal lines were too strong for a frontal assault. Confederate cavalry raids around the Federal flanks also revealed that McClellan would reinforce Pope within days, presenting Lee with an overwhelming numerical disadvantage. What followed was one of Lee's most daring and debated tactical moves. Although his force of about 55,000 was already outnumbered by 75,000 Federals across the Rappahannock, Lee split his army in two.

On the morning of 25 August, the cavalry of Jackson and Stuart left the line of the Rappahannock under orders to round the Federal flank and break their communication lines. The Irish battalion marched with them. In a remarkably quick, efficient and gruelling movement, Jackson's forces reached Salem – twenty-four miles distant – by nightfall and one night later attacked the Federal supply depot at Manassas, a further 36 miles away.

By now, the penny had dropped with Pope and he realised that the Confederate army was split and could be destroyed one half at a time. He rushed his army back to Manassas to destroy Jackson's forces first, only to find that Jackson had mysteriously disappeared. Jackson's forces were eventually located at Sudley Mountain, near the very ground where the armies had clashed at the First Battle of Manassas twelve months previously. On 29 August, Pope attacked Jackson's half of the Confederate army, the Irish battalion among them.

The Irish had moved from Manassas towards Gainesville under cover of darkness on the night of 27 August. On the morning of 28 August, an intercepted dispatch alerted the commander of their brigade that superior numbers of Federal troops were moving in their direction from Gainesville. Immediately, the Irish battalion, under the command of Major John Seddon, was deployed on the Grovetown–Manassas road to guard against any potential Federal flanking movement. The remainder of their brigade engaged the Federals on a nearby hill and soon called for the Irish to reinforce the position. This was done and the hill was held until superior Federal numbers forced the brigade to withdraw towards Grovetown. That night, their brigade held the crossing of the Sudley Road over the old railroad before being ordered to rejoin Starke's division on the morning of 29 August. They were formed into a line parallel to and to the west of the Warrenton Pike along an unfinished railroad cutting that formed a magnificent defensive position for Jackson's entire line. It was over this railroad cutting, and Federal attempts to dislodge Jackson's men from it, that much of the Second Battle of Manassas was fought.

On the afternoon of 29 August, the Federals attacked to the left of the Irish battalion. They were attacking Starke's brigade who were located in an area known as the 'dump', which was a part of the railroad bed that was not yet filled in. The absence of an embankment made it perhaps the weakest point on Jackson's line. Among the defenders of Starke's brigade were two companies of Irishmen known as the Montgomery Guards and the Emmett Guards in the 1st

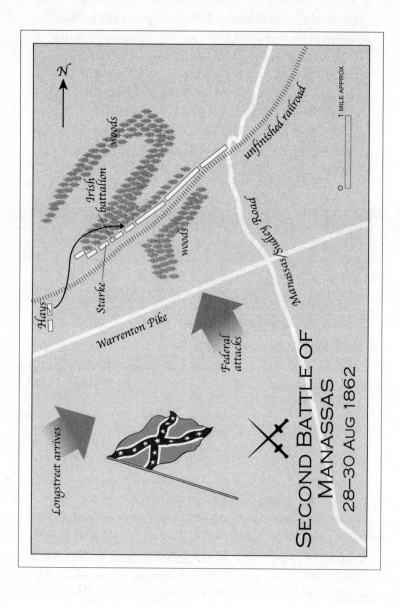

Louisiana under the command of Tipperary-born Lieutenant Colonel Michael Nolan. They were joined by a further two Irish companies within the 2nd Louisiana, known as the Orleans Light Guards and the Moore Guards, the Emerald Guards of the 9th Louisiana, five Irish companies in the 10th Louisiana and a 'significant number' of Irishmen scattered throughout the ranks of the 15th Louisiana.[2] Fr James Sheeran, a chaplain serving with the Louisiana brigade, later described the Irishmen's stand as follows:

> The 1st La. R.[egiment] was out of ammunition and in fact nearly out of strength as they had been fighting for several hours against ten times their number. Col. Nolan, who commanded the 1st, was expecting reinforcements every moment. To abandon his position on the bank of the R.R. [railroad] would have turned the tide of victory against us. The gallant boys of the 1st were not long in deciding what to do. Throwing down their empty guns they attacked and drove back the enemy with rocks which they found in abundance on the roadside. The other regiments as they got out of ammunition followed their example and soon it became a battle of rocks. It may appear strange, but it is nevertheless true that our men did as much execution with these new missiles of war as with their musket balls, for many of the Yankees were found on the field with broken skulls.[3]

As Federal troops attacked Starke's brigade, some of them emerged in front of the Irish battalion. It seems that they did not see the Irish or their entire brigade, as they were now lying down. The whole of the brigade charged the surprised Federal troops, driving them back into the woods in front of the railroad cutting and even out the other side. They were

joined in this endeavour by the stone-throwing Irish of
Starke's brigade. When Federal artillery tried to cover the
troops and assist in rallying them, the Irish battalion came
into their own, attacking the battery that fired and capturing
one of their treasured rifle pieces. The 15th Louisiana, with
its 'significant number' of Irishmen, also secured an artillery
piece for themselves and came up with an inventive method
for transporting it back to their lines. Fr Sheeran later
recalled:

> Now occurred one of the most laughable incidents of
> the war. The Yankees had placed a mountain Howitzer
> opposite the 15th Louisiana Regiment which very much
> annoyed the boys. Having repelled the attack of the
> New York Infantry, the gallant 15th boldly charged this
> battery which they captured with a large squad of
> Yankees. Desirous of securing their booty and the
> horses of the battery being killed, they harnessed the
> Yankees and compelled them to haul the artillery into
> our lines. The sight of some 50 Yankees hitched to a
> piece of artillery, with the 15th charging bayonets,
> coming across the battlefield at the double quick, drew
> forth a burst of laughter from our Confederate boys.[4]

The two brigades of Starke and Johnson drove Nagle's
attacking Federals right back through the Grovetown woods,
where a makeshift Federal line finally halted their advance
on the edge of the tree line. The great charge now over, the
Irish and their brigades returned to their original position
and held it through the night. As the Irish of Starke's and
Johnson's brigades returned through the Grovetown woods
to their positions in the 'deep cut' and the 'dump', they
probably were not aware that they were passing the front of
another group of Irishmen who held a portion of the railway

cutting in the woods to their right. They were the Irishmen of Harry T. Hays' brigade and an attack by Federal General Kearny was about to bring them into the action.

Hays' Louisiana brigade consisted of the 5th, 6th, 7th, 8th and 14th Louisiana Infantry Regiments, all of which had significant numbers of Irishmen among their personnel. At the beginning of the war, the 5th had had 94 Irish-born men among its ranks, while the 6th contained two distinctly Irish companies that were originally intended to form part of a Confederate Irish brigade. Also among the ranks of the 6th was a company known as the Calhoun Guards. The Calhouns took their name from John C. Calhoun, who was the son of an Irish immigrant, and were primarily composed of Irishmen. The 7th contained four Irish companies, among them the Irish Volunteers and Sarsfield Rangers. Another Confederate soldier noted that the 7th Louisiana 'was composed mostly of Irishmen'. The 8th included a primarily Irish company known as the Cheneyville Rifles. Company E of the 9th Louisiana was known as the Emerald Guards in acknowledgement of its Irish character. The 14th Louisiana was of mixed nationality. Known as Lee's Foreign Legion, the regiment had initially been intended to form part of a Polish brigade, yet Irishmen were the most dominant nationality among its ranks and Civil War historian Ella Lonn reported that six of its twelve companies were predominantly Irish. The Irishmen of the 14th Louisiana had something in common with many of the Irish units already discussed and had been involved in a drunken riot at Grand Junction railway station in Tennessee the previous year.[5] Hays' brigade was bristling with Irishmen, who played a significant role at the Second Battle of Manassas.

These Louisiana Irishmen had arrived in the Manassas area with Jackson's half of the Confederate command on the evening of 26 August 1862. They were almost immediately involved in a Confederate attack on Federal trains near Bristoe Station. Piling debris on the tracks, they succeeded in derailing one train named *Abe Lincoln* before smashing the signal lights, causing another train to collide with the rear of its derailed colleague. The result was a complete blockage of Pope's railroad supply route.[6]

On 27 August, the brigade spent the day on picket duty with orders to conduct a fighting retreat should any Federal troops attempt to unblock the line at Bristoe. At about 2.00 p.m., two Federal brigades appeared and the 6th and 8th Louisiana fought a retreat into some nearby woods where they made their stand, as described by Lieutenant Ring of the 6th Louisiana:

> Taking a position in front of a fence line with an open field of about three hundred yards' width before us, we calmly awaited the approach of the enemy. General Hooker's division, or part of it, emerged from the woods and with a yell attempted a charge upon our line, but before they had passed half across the field were met by a murderous fire from our ranks that caused them to halt and after a few volleys to fall back in utter confusion.[7]

However, Hooker was able to bring more and more Federal troops upon the Louisiana men and their Georgian comrades, therefore an orderly withdrawal to Manassas was undertaken in the late evening. The 6th Louisiana Regiment suffered the most casualties of the day, leaving five dead Irishmen on the field.[8]

Hays' brigade played a support role on 28 August. They did not engage the enemy at the Battle of Grovetown and were therefore well rested when Pope's forces converged on

Jackson, prompting the Second Battle of Manassas on 29 August. In the morning, they were formed on the extreme right of the Confederate line along the railroad cutting. Their task was to reconnoitre the surrounding countryside for the approach of any Federal troops on Jackson's right flank. As such, they formed the extreme right of Jackson's position and can only have heard the fighting south of them as Federal General Milroy's brigade was repulsed from the centre of Jackson's line. Instead, they would have witnessed the long-awaited arrival of Longstreet's wing as it linked up with the far right of Jackson's line. Now the men of Hays' brigade were moved towards the centre of Jackson's line into a supporting position behind the railway cut.

Debate still rages as to whether it was Grover's or Nagle's attack that first brought the Irish of Hays' brigade into the firing line. What is certain is that they were instrumental in repairing a temporary Federal breach of Jackson's line. By the time the Irish battalion and the many Irishmen of Starke's brigade were driving Nagle's Federals back through the Grovetown woods, the Irishmen of Hays' brigade were already in the front line and had even assisted in repulsing Nagle by engaging his front while Starke and Johnson swung in on his flank and drove him through the woods. Now, as the Irishmen from Starke and Johnson's brigades moved back towards the 'deep cut' and the 'dump', the Irishmen from Hays' brigade were not quite finished fighting.

Around 5.00 p.m., Kearny's division struck Jackson's left flank, driving it back about 300 yards into the eastern edge of the Grovetown woods and towards Hays' brigade. As they were moving towards the left of the Louisiana Irish, Leasure's brigade was trampling its way through the woods and towards the front of the waiting Hays' brigade. At about 5.30 p.m., Leasure hit the edge of the embankment and made contact with the Irish of Hays' brigade. A bloody fight was soon under way, with the Confederates under severe pressure all along their left. Eventually it was a counterattack by Early's brigade that drove Kearny's Federals off and saved the Confederate line in the railway cut. However, Hays' brigade lost their commander during the fight, which meant that the Irish-born Colonel Henry B. Strong was promoted to brigade command. It was a post for which Strong may not have been fit, however, and as Early's troops moved in to rescue the hard-pressed front liners, they immediately encountered evidence of Strong's inexperience and inability to lead:

> On reaching the position General Starke wished me to occupy I found that three of my regiments ... had not followed the rest of the brigade, and I immediately sent my aide Lieutenant [S.H.] Early, to see what was the cause of it. He found these regiments engaged with the enemy in their front, Hays' brigade, under Colonel [H.B.] Strong, of the sixth Louisiana regiment, having fallen back in confusion and passed through these regiments, followed by the enemy, just as my orders were being carried out. This affair could not be seen by me from the flank on which I was and the regiments engaged in it were very properly detained by their commanding officers. I immediately marched back the rest of the brigade, and found that the enemy had been successfully repulsed by my three regiments.
>
> It is due to Hays' brigade to state that the confusion into which it was thrown was caused by an attempt of the officer in command, Colonel Strong, to change its position when the enemy were advancing, and that his want in sufficient skill in the command of a brigade caused him to get it confused, so that it could present no front, and it had therefore to fall back. The eighth

Louisiana regiment, commanded by Major Lewis, fell back in better order than the rest of the brigade, and formed in line immediately in the rear of my regiments. The rest of the brigade was soon rallied and brought back, and having been placed under my command by General Lawton, it was placed in line on the left of my brigade.[9]

As darkness fell on the battlefield, it was clear that Jackson had somehow held the line of the railway cut. A considerable number of Irishmen scattered throughout the ranks of two Louisiana brigades and their own battalion could rest happy that they had assisted 'Stonewall' in performing a task that had seemed impossible.

Skirmishing continued up and down the line as night fell over Manassas. It was a serious business, and yet compared with the fighting of a full-scale battle, it was quite mild. John Ryan of the Federal 28th Massachusetts had arrived on the field and described that night at Manassas:

After dark, it was a beautiful sight to look down along our lines to the left and see the heavy skirmish line of both armies exchanging shots. The sharp crack of the rifles and the flashes would put one in mind of looking down through a large meadow with thousands of lightning bugs. Although it was quite amusing to look at, it was just reversed to the parties engaged in it.[10]

Now that Longstreet's wing had arrived on the field unbeknownst to Pope, they would surely assist in turning the tide of battle away from the exhausted defenders of the railway cut. But as the daylight of 30 August crept over the field, the men in the railway cut, and the Irishmen among them, still had a few more hours to hold out before Longstreet was satisfied he could join in the fight.

On the morning of 30 August, the Irish battalion was deployed in reserve and awaited any Federal attack on the front line brigades of their division. A concerted attack came at about 3.00 p.m. when Major General Fitz John Porter led Pope's most grandiose attempt to break the line at the railway cut. By now, Pope knew that Longstreet had arrived but was convinced that his attacks of the previous day had forced a Confederate retreat and that he was now attacking the right of the Confederate line. However, when Porter led some 15,000 men out of the Grovetown woods and towards the 'deep cut', it quickly became apparent that he was attacking the centre of a well-entrenched Confederate army. Once again, the Irish battalion was in the very eye of the storm. Federals swept up the hill 'line after line, Brigade after Brigade' at the railway cut and thicket held by the Irishmen's brigade comrades. As the 48th Virginia was forced out of the cut, the Irish were then instructed to reinforce the position, charging into it with empty guns.

The fighting at the railway cut was even more brutal than it had been on the previous day. Confederate and Federal infantry fought hand to hand within yards of one another, and when conventional ammunition was exhausted, they once again resorted to stones as weaponry. The Irish battalion was seen to ape the stone-throwing tactics demonstrated by their Louisiana countrymen on the previous day, and those Louisiana Irish saw no reason to abandon a tactic that had served them so well. Private William A. McLendon of the 15th Alabama witnessed their vicious defence on 30 August and later described it as follows:

> On the right they were in an old field in plain view and the whole of the 15th Alabama got in some deadly work at a right oblique. They just simply jammed up against the embankment opposite the right of the 15th

Alabama and one of the Louisiana Regiments. They were so thick it was impossible to miss them ... The Louisianans ceased firing and threw cobblestones over the embankment at them. I saw them going over, landing on the heads of the Yankees just as thick as I ever saw corn go into a pen in an old time corn shucket. It was more like that than anything that I could compare it to. What a slaughter. What a slaughter of men that was. At first bomb shells, shrapnel shells and then grape shot and as they came nearer canister was pored at them which mowed them down, but still those that lived closed ranks and pressed forward.[11]

The Irish and their comrades held the cut amidst the most brutal slaughter of the Second Battle of Manassas.[12] Now came the *coup de grâce* from Longstreet.

As Porter's attackers limped back from the railway cut, Federal General McDowell feared that Porter's rout would lead to an all-out retreat. Thus he ordered Reynolds' division from Chinn Ridge into the centre of the Federal line, which opened up the floodgates for a devastating attack on the Federal flank by Longstreet's men. At 4.00 p.m., their moment came and they charged headlong into the Federal flank. It was one of the largest flank attacks of the war and its effect was devastating. Among the regiments that Longstreet moved forward was the 8th Alabama containing the Emerald Guards. Also among Longstreet's forces were the men of 1st and 19th Georgia regiments, both of which contained primarily Irish companies known as the Emmet Rifles (named for Robert Emmet) and the Jackson Guards, respectively. Both of these units were also involved in combat when Longstreet's wing had had to push its way through Thoroughfare Gap two days earlier. Now they charged into the flank of a Federal army that was once again about to be routed at Manassas. Soon, as Lee reflected on a comprehensive victory, the Federals were in full retreat towards Washington. East of the 'deep cut' and the 'dump', Ryan and the 28th Massachusetts had been briefly engaged earlier in the day. Later, he and his Irish comrades witnessed the panic-stricken retreat from Manassas:

> Infantry fell back by regiments, artillery went back on the fly, government wagons mingled with the artillerymen and everybody tried to get to the rear the quickest and nearest way. Nearby there was a creek. First would come some government wagons on the fly down the hill to this creek, then would come a battery down the hill on the fly. As soon as the leaders would strike the water, they would check up and the swings and wheelers would pile up in a heap, and the horses would run away with the limbers. Everything and everyone mingled together at this creek trying to get to the rear the best way possible. During this time, the Confederates' shells were bursting and cutting the ground in all directions, and it was nothing to see a limber coming down this incline with one horse shot and the others pulling him off ... Everything was in confusion and the Confederates following up. Our army retreated and fell back as far as Centreville where we made a stand.[13]

Joining them at Centreville, fresh from a period of rest and recuperation earlier in the month and not engaged at Manassas, were the Irishmen of the 69th Pennsylvania. They were just in time for the Battle of Chantilly.

On 31 August 1862, Lee resolved to crush the Federal army before it escaped his grasp. He sent Jackson around the left flank of the Federal army, hoping to get at their rear without being detected. They were detected, however, and on 1 September Federal troops attempting to secure a roadway junction clashed with Jackson's forces near Chantilly. The primary Irish involvement came in the form of the 28th Massachusetts, who were involved in vicious hand-to-hand combat during a charge across a cornfield. They lost twenty-five men at Chantilly, but their sacrifice assisted in holding Jackson at bay long enough for Pope to continue his retreat towards Washington.

The 69th Pennsylvania was part of the holding action at Chantilly, formed in support of an artillery battery. There they waited, under Confederate artillery fire, for about two hours until the remainder of the routed Federal army had passed them, then they fell in behind and guarded the Federal rear all the way to Washington. The regiment was not severely tested by Confederate attack on its way from the Battle of Chantilly, though they did have to support one further artillery check of Confederate infantry in the evening of 2 September. Nonetheless, acting as the rearguard brought its share of physical demands and rest was out of the question until the Federals reached the safety of the Potomac. One veteran of the 69th later described the demands of the rearguard action as follows:

As we had really no rest worth speaking of from the 30th of August until now, the 3rd of September, the men were greatly exhausted, so much so, that on the night of the second on the road back to Chain Bridge, the roads were so blocked with wagon trains that frequent halts had to be made, during which the men almost immediately fell asleep.

The effects of the severe defeat at Manassas also impacted on the 69th and men who had seen their comrades so severely routed were inclined towards panic.

During one of these shortest of halts while the troops were dozing, some cavalry men passed along the clinking of whose sabres led someone under the impression that it was the enemy, and shouted out to that effect, a stampede took place, men running every direction through the woods, many of them were easily detected the next morning as they were minus their caps.[14]

The whole Federal army was jumpy, having had a severe and comprehensive defeat inflicted upon it by a smaller and divided Confederate force. This was the second time in a little over twelve months that an Irish unit acted as rearguard for a humiliating retreat from Manassas.

With the Federal army having suffered another crushing defeat, Southern leaders began to see a light at the end of the tunnel. In the east, they had continually triumphed over superior Federal numbers and as their confidence – and the confidence of the whole army – grew, they began to think offensively. If they wanted to end the war, it would not be enough to defend their own territory – they would also have to crush the Federal army, forcing Lincoln to recognise the Confederacy. They would not yield the ground they had won, but would instead seek to continue their dominance with an invasion of Maryland. Again, the Irish on both sides would suffer.

CHAPTER 7

ANTIETAM

Having decided firmly on an invasion of Maryland, Lee's first great obstacle was the Potomac River. Between 3 and 7 September, the Army of Northern Virginia crossed the river at four different fords. Among those making the crossing was Hays' brigade and its many Irishmen, who crossed at White's Ford on 5 September, still under the command of Stonewall Jackson. They marched into Maryland in confidence, even though hunger was a serious issue for the ill-supplied Confederate troops. Their march towards Frederick was later referred to as the 'green corn march' due to their having to eat unripe corn from the fields along the way.

Reaching camp near Frederick, Lee set about attempting to portray himself as a liberator rather than an invader in the hope of eliciting some support from Maryland residents. His 'proclamation' to the people of Maryland met with little success, though: the local people did not rise up against the Federal 'oppressor'. However, Confederates still hoped that they might secure assistance, particularly from foreign powers who had suffered economically from the Federal navy's blockade of Southern ports, and consequently

Southern cotton. In 1862, the foreign power most likely to intercede on the Confederacy's behalf was the United Kingdom of Great Britain and Ireland. Only further victories could encourage the UK to join on the Confederate side, and Lee was convinced that he could provide the Confederacy with another great victory in Maryland. In order to do so, he would once again take the enormous risk of splitting his forces while they faced a numerically superior enemy.

In a letter to the President of the Confederate States, Jefferson Davis, Lee announced his intention to move 'in the direction of Hagerstown and Chambersburg'. However, he knew that the Federal garrisons at Martinsburg and Harpers Ferry would threaten his lines of supply and communication. With this in mind, Lee issued his now famous Special Orders No. 191, which detailed the division of the army into two wings, as per the Second Battle of Manassas. Stonewall Jackson's wing was to lay siege to Harpers Ferry with the intention of taking the town by 12 September. Lee would remain with the second wing, which was to march towards Boonsboro, where Jackson's wing would rejoin them having taken Harpers Ferry. Reaching his objective at Boonsboro, Lee once again divided his forces, leaving D.H. Hill's command there while moving Longstreet's forces up the turnpike towards Hagerstown.

Jackson took Martinsburg easily, as its defenders had already fled to Harpers Ferry. Laying siege to the latter town, Jackson eventually took it, but three days later than Lee had anticipated. Harpers Ferry fell on 15 September, but Lee's plans had already been fatally compromised when, on 13 September, a mislaid copy of Special Orders No. 191 was found at Frederick by Federal troops. Now McClellan, who had taken command of a combined army of his and Pope's men after the Federal disaster at Manassas, knew that Lee's

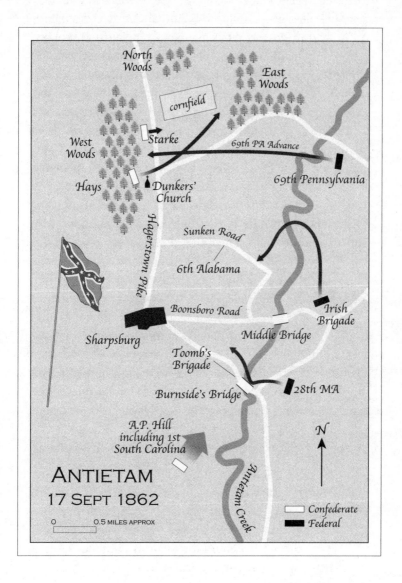

North Woods

East Woods

cornfield

West Woods

Starke

69th PA Advance

Hays

Dunkers' Church

69th Pennsylvania

Sunken Road

6th Alabama

Boonsboro Road

Irish Brigade

Sharpsburg

Middle Bridge

Toomb's Brigade

Burnside's Bridge

28th MA

A.P. Hill including 1st South Carolina

N

ANTIETAM
17 SEPT 1862

0   0.5 MILES APPROX

Antietam Creek

☐ Confederate
■ Federal

forces had been divided on either side of South Mountain.

McClellan was convinced that total victory was at hand. All he had to do was push his men over South Mountain, preventing the reunification of Lee's forces, and then rout the Confederates one half at a time. In order to do so, he would have to press through several gaps in the mountain, and those gaps were about to be filled by hastily convened Confederate forces. On Sunday 14 September, Federal forces attempted to traverse the mountain passes known as Fox's, Crampton's and Turner's Gaps and were met by Confederate forces under Hooker's command. In addition, attempts by Federal commander Burnside to co-ordinate his attacks caused enough of a delay for Confederate forces under D.H. Hill to reinforce any emerging crisis point. A successful holding action known as the Battle of South Mountain was fought in these mountain gaps. The action bought more time for Lee, whose command was now hopelessly splintered.

The 69th Pennsylvania reached South Mountain in time to offer support to their Federal comrades. However, they were not required and when the Confederates fell back they marched on towards Keedysville with the rest of the Federal army. Leading the Federal pursuit of the Confederates along the road towards Boonsboro and Keedysville was Meagher's Irish Brigade. Their chaplain, Fr Corby, described the evidence of a hasty Confederate retreat from South Mountain:

> We were in advance of all, and, as we dashed along, following the retreating Confederate forces, we saw, on every side, men and horses, dead and dying. I dismounted occasionally, and when I found men still living did what I could for them. If Catholics I heard their confessions, and if Protestants, baptized them, as individual cases required.[1]

With the Irish Brigade in the lead, the Federal Army of the Potomac pursued Lee right along the roads of Maryland to a tributary of the Potomac known as Antietam Creek. On reaching the eastern banks of the creek, they met Lee's Army of Northern Virginia drawn up along the other side. As darkness fell on the night of 15 September, a dawn attack across Antietam Creek seemed to be McClellan's most logical next step. His forces completely outnumbered Lee's, who had yet to be joined by Jackson's command as they were still at Harpers Ferry. McClellan exhibited his characteristic caution and delayed the attack, believing that Lee's 18,000 men were actually 100,000. While he delayed, Jackson arrived from Harpers Ferry and Longstreet from Hagerstown. The Confederate line was bolstered, but still far from impregnable. On the evening of 16 September, McClellan ordered the first probes across the creek and into the Confederate line. The cautious attacks allowed McClellan to form his plan, but also gave Lee some idea of what that plan may be. As darkness fell and the artillery fire died out, the stage was set for the bloodiest day in American history.

The Battle of Antietam opened with Federal artillery fire on the northern end of the battlefield soon after sunrise on 17 September. Hooker's infantry crossed Antietam Creek and advanced towards the left of the Confederate line. Fighting on the northern end of the battlefield would concentrate in an area around a little church that served as a place of worship for a small German sect that completely submerged children in water for baptism. Consequently, their church was known as the 'Dunkers' Church'. In the vicinity of that church were the two Louisiana brigades, each of them containing a high proportion of Irishmen. The first of these brigades thrown at the advancing Federals was Hays' brigade.

At daybreak, Hays' brigade emerged from the woods west

of the Hagerstown Pike and wheeled northeast towards a hotly contested cornfield. As they went, they were subjected to the most severe artillery fire they had ever encountered. One of them later wrote to his wife, 'I thought darling that I had heard at Malvern Hill heavy cannonading, but I was mistaken.'[2] Under this artillery fire, the Louisiana brigade advanced into the famous cornfield past a shattered brigade of Georgians, whom they would relieve, and on to the edge of the east woods, driving the Federals before them. A bloody stalemate developed before the Louisiana brigade was forced to retreat to the church. After only fifteen minutes of combat, 60 per cent of Hays' brigade was dead or wounded. One of the dead was the Irish-born commander of the 6th Louisiana, Lieutenant Colonel Henry B. Strong. After the battle, a famous photograph depicting his dead horse at the edge of the east woods became one of the war's more enduring images. Strong was replaced by another Irishman, Colonel William Monaghan. Later that evening, Monaghan led the remains of the brigade back to the edge of the cornfield and continued to exchange fire in a stand-off with the Federals.

Starke and his many Irishmen became engaged in the battle at approximately 7.00 a.m. They moved out of the woods, across the Hagerstown Pike and lined up along a fence facing east into the cornfield, where they encountered Federal troops of the famous 'Iron Brigade'. The Louisiana men and the Iron Brigade slugged it out at the fence for approximately fifteen minutes, with neither side able to break the other's line. Eventually the devastated Louisiana brigade was forced to fall back towards the Dunkers' Church and their Louisiana and Irish comrades from Hays' brigade. Coming towards these Irish Confederates were the Federal Irishmen of the 69th Pennsylvania.

The crossing of the creek was not a simple matter for the

The dead on the Hagerstown Pike at Antietam. Some may be men from Starke's mainly Irish Louisiana brigade.

Irishmen of the 69th, as its fast current and waist-high depth forced them to link arms and cross four abreast. Upon reaching the eastern bank, the 69th advanced towards the Dunkers' Church. Anthony McDermott of the 69th described the fighting near the church as follows:

> Here the enemy made his stand, and here the fighting was most desperate. The range of the Confederate artillery on our lines was most accurate and destructive; every conceivable article of destruction that could be used was here hurled against us – solid shot, shell, spherical case, shrapnel, grape and canister – and, judging by the tearing sounds through the air, the general opinion was that railroad iron, nails etc, were belched from the cannons mouth, so that our men jocularly claim that whole blacksmith-shops were discharged from their guns against us. In addition to the artillery fire, the lines of infantry poured in their destructive fire of musketry and the carnage became dreadful.

It soon became apparent that combat on the northern end of the battlefield was a bloody stalemate. Bodies were stacked in neat rows all along the cornfield, the Hagerstown Pike and the east, west and north woods. Hooker's Federal corps failed to make a breakthrough, but Jackson's Confederates had paid a terrible price in defending their line. Soon the fighting was moving towards the centre of the Confederate line, and the most famous Irish unit of the war advanced towards their bloodiest encounter.

The Irish Brigade had forged a reputation as the hard-fighting saviours of the Federal army in combat during the Peninsula Campaign. Whether or not they could once again sweep all before them remained to be seen. The 'damned green flag' of the peninsula now headed towards Antietam Creek. The Irishmen crossed the Antietam with Richardson's division at 9.00 a.m. They first moved northwest, then southeast, towards another famous Antietam landmark known as the 'sunken road'. As the name would imply, this road was a ready-made trench running roughly in a north–south direction, making it a difficult line for any attackers to breach. The Irish Brigade moved towards the road just as the intense fighting on the northern end of the field was dying down. The sounds of battle that they could hear ahead of them were the sounds of French's division meeting its doom at the sunken road. A tiny number (thirty at most) of Irish Confederates served in the 6th Alabama, one of the units defending this little country laneway, but this famous American landmark would always be associated with the Irish Brigade.[3]

The sunken road became a scene of carnage due to a malfunction in the Federal chain of command. As Sumner's corps advanced across the battlefield, its three divisions became scattered and the lead division (Sedgwick's) was soon out of the line of vision of the other two. Thus, as Sedgwick's division became embroiled in a fight near the Dunkers'

Church, the second division (French's) was not supporting Sedgwick. Having lost sight of his lead division, French instead swung southwest in order to engage Confederates sighted on that side. At first French's division drove the enemy before it, but their great misfortune was the sunken road into which the Confederates retreated. French's division was smashed as it attempted to break this natural trench line. Confederate units crowded the road as wave upon wave came forward from their rear. French was so overwhelmed that it looked as if the Confederates overcrowding the road could attempt a flanking manoeuvre of their own – until Richardson's division, with the Irish Brigade in the lead, arrived.

Meagher's first order sent Volunteers to attempt to remove a timber fence from the ridge above the road in order to prevent it from interfering with the advance of his brigade. This proved impossible and the few surviving Volunteers quickly retreated back down the other side of the ridge, having taken heavy musket fire from the Confederates in the road below. As the situation became more and more perilous, the brigade was given its orders to move up onto the ridge and storm the road at the double quick. Fr Corby got the men ready to make what for many would be their final attack:

> Our Brigade received orders to go in at the 'double quick,' that is on a full run. I gave rein to my horse and let him go at full gallop till I reached the front of the Brigade, and, passing along the line, told the men to make an act of Contrition. As they were coming toward me, 'double quick,' I had time only to wheel my horse for an instant toward them and gave my poor men a hasty absolution, and rode on with Gen. Meagher into the battle. In twenty or thirty minutes after this

absolution, 506 of these very men lay on the field, either dead or seriously wounded.[4]

The brigade's advance on the road soon put paid to any attempts by Confederates to leave its safety and undertake a flanking movement, but the suppression of the rebels' mobility came at a great cost – the Irish Brigade was decimated. The heroes of the Peninsula Campaign left over 500 men dead and wounded near the sunken road. The 63rd and 69th New York regiments sustained some 60 per cent casualties. Even the charismatic Meagher had the horse he had obtained during a recent recruiting trip North shot from under him and was removed to the rear in shock. Yet the colours of their country and their ethnicity were closely guarded. These men displayed huge pride in both their Irish origins and their adopted country and cause. The colours could not be allowed to drop in the face of the enemy, no matter how many had to die to ensure their survival. As the 69th New York was gradually thinned until only a few men stood around its green flags, one of the rebels in the sunken road was heard to call out, 'Bring them colours in here!' The Irishmen who held them were reported to have advanced a few steps, shaking the flags in the face of the enemy, and replied, 'Come and take them, you damned rebels.'[5] Lieutenant Colonel Fowler reported the 69th's attachment to their colours as follows:

> It is now a solace to my mind, while suffering from my wound, to testify how gallantly and promptly each officer in his place and each company moved forward and delivered their fire in the face of the most destructive storm of leaden hail, that in an instant killed or wounded every officer but one and more than one-half the rank and file of the right wing. For a moment

they staggered, but the scattered few quickly rallied upon the left, closing on the colors, where they nobly fought, bled, and died, protecting their own loved banner and their country's flag, until the brigade was relieved … As the right wing had fallen before me, I hastened to the left, where I found the major Bentley close upon the line, and Capt. Joseph O'Neill, Company A, whose company had all fallen around him on the right, now assisting the major on the left. Here also was the stalwart Lieutenant Gleason, Company H, raising and supporting the repeatedly falling colors … our colors, although in ribbons, and staff shot through, were still there, sustained at a bloody sacrifice, 16 men having fallen while carrying them … In conclusion, permit me to congratulate you that your gallant little brigade has once more crowned itself with fresh laurels, and given additional and bloody proofs of its devotion to the Constitution and the flag of our beloved country.

On seeing the 69th New York's bravery in clinging to their colours, the commander of the brigade's only non-Irish regiment, Colonel Barnes of the 29th Massachusetts, ordered another charge. Soon General John Caldwell's brigade was moving forward to support the Irishmen:

Colonel Barnes then gave the order, 'forward!' Instantly Sergeant Francis M. Kingman, the dauntless color bearer, sprang to the front, the whole regiment promptly following him. Above the noise of battle were heard the answering shouts of the brave Irishmen of the brigade, their warlike spirit gaining fresh impulse as they started forward on the charge. The crisis was over now; the bold forward movement had saved the brigade from even one blot upon its bright record of fame. The shouts of our men, and their sudden dash toward the sunken road, so startled the enemy that their fire visibly slackened, their line wavered, and squads of two or three began leaving the road and running into the corn. Now the rush of troops was heard in the rear; now the air was rent with wild yells. It was altogether too much of a shock for the enemy; they broke, and fled for the corn field. The next moment, Caldwell's Brigade, led by General Richardson in person, with Cross, Barlow and all its other heroes, came sweeping up behind the shattered lines of the Irish Brigade. The flight of the enemy was now complete. In a few moments Caldwell's men were in possession of the road, and driving the confederates through the cornfield into the orchard beyond.[6]

The division commander, Richardson, was extremely annoyed at the delay in Caldwell's support of the Irish and personally rode to the rear to move the former brigade forward.[7] The delay doubtlessly cost the Irish who held the line a considerable number of lives, yet the Irish were cool in the face of unprecedented carnage. Even McClellan noted their precise and calm military effectiveness, singling them out for particular praise in his report of the battle:

The Irish Brigade sustained its well earned reputation. After suffering terribly in officers and men, and strewing the ground with their enemies as they drove them back, their ammunition nearly expended and their commander, General Meagher, disabled by the fall of his horse, shot under him, this brigade was ordered to give place to General Caldwell's Brigade which advanced to a short distance in its rear. The lines were passed by the Irish Brigade, breaking by company to the rear, and General Caldwell's by company to the front, as steadily as on drill.[8]

As Meagher's brigade passed General Richardson on their way back from the roadway, Lieutentant Colonel Patrick Kelly reported that their divisional commander had complimented his regiment. 'Bravo, Eighty-eighth, I shall never forget you,' he was reported to have said.[9] Kelly also mentioned what was perhaps the only blemish on the brigade's record at Antietam. The commander of the 63rd New York, Colonel Burke, was not leading his regiment when Kelly sought him out and it was later established that Burke had dismounted and sought cover behind a fold in the ground before his men attacked the road. Burke was later dismissed for his cowardice.[10]

Caldwell's brigade eventually drove the Confederates from the road, but the cost of the prize was appalling. The scene of carnage on the road after the battle haunted the memories of those who witnessed it. Confederate troops lay in dense lines along the roadway, while the Federal slain lay all around. One Federal soldier believed that the bodies lay so thick along the road that he could have walked it from end to end without his feet touching the ground.[11] It was from this brutal scene of carnage that a local woman ascribed a new name to the sunken road, calling it 'Bloody Lane'. The Irish Brigade's brave stand in the face of overwhelming firepower seemed to have impressed many of those who witnessed it. Even the Confederate enemy in the sunken road was impressed, as one soldier of the 2nd Mississippi wrote:

I wish here to bear witness to the gallantry of the men of Meagher's Brigade and the superb courage of their commanding officers on that bloody day. They stood in line on their ridge, in plain view, with three flags as colors – One the Stars and Stripes, one a Pennsylvania

Bloody Lane at Antietam.

[Massachusetts] State flag and one the green flag with the Harp of Erin. Our men kept those flags falling fast, while just as fast they raised again. Several times the deadly fire of our rifles broke the ranks of those men and they fell behind the ridge, but quickly re-formed each time and appeared with shorter lines but still defiant.[12]

The heroics of the Irish Brigade at Antietam would become an important part of Irish-American history and an enormous source of pride for thousands of Irish-Americans. In the months and years that followed, the Irish often sought to remind America of the Civil War sacrifices that confirmed their loyalty and allegiance to their adopted country. In the immediate aftermath of the battle, the *Irish American* paid tribute to the heroism of these men and was at pains to emphasise that they loved two countries and that their loyalty to Ireland did not diminish their loyalty to their adopted

Bloody Lane at Antietam as it is today.

country. Referring to the Irishmen's love of General Meagher, the newspaper asserted that:

> They were high-souled, high-toned young Irish patriots, who had imbibed from his lips their passionate love of Ireland, and the hope in which they died, that some day or another they would have an opportunity to draw their swords under him, and display their soldierly skill to some purpose in the ranks of men fighting for Fatherland. At least, let us be thankful for one thing. One of the great longings of their souls has been satisfied. I am convinced that they would rather have died where they did, sustaining and supporting the honor of the Green Flag, than have died full of years, and honors and riches, gained in a strange land under strange banners. They fought and died for and loved their adopted country – but even on the red field of blood, so far away from home.[13]

Even today, the memory of the deeds of the Irish Brigade remains important to Irish-Americans. In 1997, a monument to the Irish Brigade was unveiled on the Antietam battlefield. At the unveiling ceremony, many speakers referred specifically to the sacrifices made by the brigade and the Irish ambassador to the US opined that they had 'added a glorious new chapter to the history of the Irish soldier'.[14] However, as the sun set over the Antietam battlefield on 17 September, it is highly unlikely that any of the Irish Brigade thought about their own historical legacy or that of their countrymen in grey.

One such group of grey-clad Irish had already made an enormous contribution to the Confederate cause south of where the Irish Brigade had been so viciously engaged. Far out on the right of the Confederate line, a little stone bridge over Antietam Creek was guarded by a group of Georgia rebels known as Toomb's Brigade. It was known locally as the Rohrbach Bridge, but was about to become known in history as Burnside's Bridge. The bridge itself was a beautiful limestone structure with three wide Romanesque arches. It was a relatively new river crossing, having been built in 1836, not by local slaves, but by craftsmen and labourers from Ireland. Many of them had sweated out the last of their life force in the vicinity of that bridge when a cholera epidemic struck its builders, sending many Irishmen to Maryland graves.[15] Now, a considerable number of Irishmen from the 2nd and 20th Georgia Infantry Regiments of Toomb's Brigade looked down on their countrymen's achievement from the western bank of Antietam Creek.

Perhaps the best-known Irish unit was Company K of the 20th Georgia. The company, named the Montgomery Guards after the Dublin-born American patriot General Richard Montgomery, was led by the Irish-born William Craig. Companies A and G of the same regiment also had a considerable number of Irish names on their rosters. They

Burnside's Bridge.

were charged with preventing a Federal crossing of the bridge and the ground they occupied was well suited to the task. As the sun rose on the morning of 17 September, many of them were mere hours away from their deaths.

While already attacking the left of the Confederate line in the vicinity of the Dunkers' Church, McClellan's plan was to attack almost simultaneously the Confederate line on the far right, which would mean crossing the Antietam at the Rohrbach Bridge. General Ambrose E. Burnside exercised tactical control over the area in front of the bridge, thus it was for him to secure the crossing. At about 9.30 a.m., Burnside made his first attempt to cross the bridge, but was driven back by the Georgians. Desperate attempts to cross continued, but vigorous defence led to a considerable delay for Burnside. The Georgians expended every last bullet, even using the ammunition of their dead and wounded comrades, until finally, at 1.00 p.m., they were forced to withdraw. Burnside's men crossed the bridge but delayed some two hours, re-forming their line before continuing to drive the Georgians back towards the town of Sharpsburg.

One of the regiments crossing the bridge with Burnside was the Irish 28th Massachusetts. They were not yet a part of the Irish Brigade still engaged to the north of their position, but rather served as part of the First Brigade (Christ's) in the First Division (Wilcox's) of the Ninth Corps (Burnside's). They crossed the bridge in the afternoon, just an hour after Burnside finally drove the Georgians from its eastern bank. Artillery fire was still a huge problem for crossing Federals, however. John Ryan later remembered the crossing and recounted one of those peculiar tales where compassion temporarily overtakes the cruelty of war:

> In going over the bridge you would almost step on dead bodies, the Confederates having it covered with their artillery, and they kept a continuous fire of grape and canister shots onto it. I recollect a grey horse … going over the bridge … was shot and his leg broken by a canister. The horse was in misery and I was going by at the time, and seeing the condition of the poor animal, I shot him and he rolled down the bank into Antietam Creek.[16]

Turning right, the 28th Massachusetts now moved parallel with the Antietam for a few hundred yards before their brigade formed in line of battle and attempted to advance on a nearby Confederate artillery battery, coming under a hail of canister, grape, shell and round shot for approximately thirty minutes. Eventually, when the artillery fire was directed at a Federal demonstration elsewhere, the 28th, along with two other regiments from Christ's Brigade, charged the battery, attempting its capture but instead forcing its retreat.

By now, Burnside threatened Lee's line of retreat and the fate of the Confederate army depended on the timely arrival of reinforcements, which arrived in the shape of A.P. Hill's division. Jackson had left them at Harpers Ferry, but now their timely arrival saw Burnside driven back to the Rohrbach Bridge and Lee's line of retreat secured. Among the men arriving with Hill and carrying the flag of the 1st South Carolina were Charleston's Irish Volunteers. Nine of this colour company were wounded when they struck Burnside's forces in a little rocky cornfield just outside Sharpsburg.[17] Hill's arrival summoned Burnside's retreat. That night, the 28th Massachusetts slept on their arms near the Irish-built crossing that would forevermore be known as Burnside's Bridge.

The Battle of Antietam was over. The Federal and Confederate armies had inflicted massive casualties upon one another, and by now Lee's forces had reached breaking point. Further attacks on 18 September 1862 would almost certainly have produced catastrophic results for the Confederate general. Crucially, McClellan did not know this. Indeed, the Federal commander must have been reeling from his own losses. Thus, 18 September did not produce any more attacks by either side. Instead, they faced one another in stunned silence across the battlefield. Many Irishmen had died in Hays' Confederate brigade, Meagher's Irish Brigade, Toomb's Georgians and the 69th Pennsylvania regiment. The Irish were present, and died in huge numbers, on America's bloodiest day.

Yet the Battle of Antietam was not enough to end the war. Indeed, it has been referred to as 'the longest saddest day' – long in the sense that soldiers often think their time in combat seems much longer than it actually is and sad because so many died, and yet McClellan failed to drive home his advantage and perhaps end the war, preventing future bloodshed. There would be no shortage of bloodshed in the future, and as always, the Irish would suffer their share.

CHAPTER 8

PERRYVILLE AND STONES RIVER

In the western theatre, Confederate forces were reeling from a string of devastating defeats. When their offensive stalled at Shiloh, they were forced to return to Corinth. On 7 April 1862, Confederate forces were again defeated at Island No. 10 and now the Mississippi River was under the control of Federal forces as far south as Memphis. On 18 May, New Orleans, the South's most significant sea port, fell to Federal forces. On 29 May, Corinth eventually fell to Federal forces that had made a snail-like advance from Shiloh, allowing the Confederates more than enough time to abandon the garrison city. Federal General Henry W. Halleck then divided his forces. He sent Buell to Chattanooga, Sherman to Memphis, one division to Arkansas and ordered Pope to hold a covering position just south of Corinth.

Meanwhile, twenty miles south of Corinth, the battered Confederate forces were gathering in Tupelo, Mississippi. Confederate Generals Edmund Kirby Smith and Braxton Bragg soon devised a plan to invade Kentucky, securing control of the Blue Grass State and its resources for the Confederacy. The newly created Army of Kentucky would march into Kentucky under the command of Kirby Smith, while Bragg would take his Army of Mississippi west to oppose the Federal Army of Ohio under Buell. Kirby Smith moved his army into Kentucky as planned, but Bragg changed his mind and instead of moving west towards Buell he too moved into Kentucky. Now Buell realised that two separate Confederate forces threatened both Louisville and Cincinnati. He had to place his men between the Confederate armies and these cities and so began the race to Louisville between Buell and Bragg. Buell won the race when Bragg decided to rejoin his forces with Kirby Smith's at Frankfort. On 1 October, Buell's men moved out of Louisville towards Bragg's Confederate forces encamped at Bardstown, not quite yet reunited with Kirby Smith's army at Frankfort.

When the Federal advance began, Confederate troops were moved east out of Bardstown to the small town of Perryville. Confederate pickets were set up on the roads approaching Perryville from the north and west. The three corps of the Federal army approached Perryville on three different roads. On the left, Alexander McCook's 1st Corps advanced along the Mackville Road. In the centre, Gilbert's 3rd Corps advanced on the Springfield Pike, while on the right of the Federal line on the Lebanon Road was the 2nd Corps under Thomas L. Crittenden.

The sun had taken its toll on the men of both sides and water was in short supply. As they settled into their camp on the night of 8 October, Federal troops from Gilbert's corps went in search of water. They decided to move towards Doctor's Creek west of Perryville and at 2.00 a.m. they came into direct contact with a Confederate picket on Peter's Hill. Soon the Battle of Perryville was under way and Irishmen were being sucked towards the rumble of battle rolling across a hot Kentucky night.

The battle for Peter's Hill raged through the night,

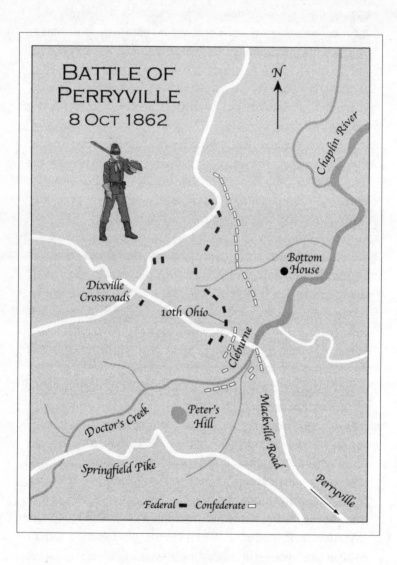

BATTLE OF
PERRYVILLE
8 OCT 1862

N

Chaplin River

Bottom
House

Dixville
Crossroads

10th Ohio

Cleburne

Doctor's Creek

Peter's
Hill

Mackville Road

Springfield Pike

Perryville

Federal ■ Confederate □

106

involving men from Sheridan's division of Gilbert's Federal corps and Liddell's Confederate brigade. The next morning, Confederate commander Polk, who temporarily replaced Bragg during his short absence from the field, formed a defensive line hoping to weather the Federal storm. Federals expanded their offensive by opening up an artillery barrage on their left. Artillery duels continued until noon, with no significant attack being made by either side. By now, Bragg had arrived on the field and immediately began planning a Confederate attack, which was due to begin at 12.30 p.m. However, further delays occurred when they could not locate the Federal flank as precisely as they desired. Bragg ordered Cheatham's division to move north along the Chaplin River in an attempt to locate and attack the Federal left. Assuming they had located the flank, they began their attack at approximately 2.30 p.m. When they began to take artillery fire from their right, it quickly became apparent that Cheatham's division was in fact attacking the Federal centre. Nonetheless, they persevered and after their initial attack was repulsed, two more brigades were called up and slowly they began pushing the Federal centre back.

Now the focus shifted south, where Confederate Brigadier General Bushrod Johnson began a confused advance towards the enemy. This disorganised advance was so disjointed that it suffered from 'friendly fire' before grinding to a halt on Doctor's Creek near the Bottom House. The beleaguered Johnson attempted to advance across the yard of Bottom House, but was quickly repulsed. It was clear that he needed assistance in bringing organisation to his chaotic attack. The man chosen for the job was an Irishman whose star was still rising in the Confederacy, Patrick Cleburne.

Cleburne's brigade was initially stationed in support of

Johnson's brigade, but when Johnson had to fall back, Cleburne moved up and once again demonstrated incredible initiative. By the time he moved his men forward, Confederate artillerists had already succeeded in dislodging some Federal defenders from the ridge that Cleburne was to attack. Cleburne moved his skirmishers into position about ten paces in front of his main attacking party. The skirmishers carried the regimental flags, so when they appeared over the ridgeline, Federal troops assumed that they were the main battle line and unloaded into them. Before they had a chance to reload, they saw Cleburne's main battle line appearing over the ridge charging straight at them. The Federals broke and ran. The Irishman fell from his horse when it was struck by a cannonball during the charge, but was seen to spit the dirt from his mouth, draw his sword and shout, 'Give 'em hell, boys' before leading the charge into the ranks of the fleeing Federals.

Cleburne was wounded twice as his brigade took the ridge and held it against several counterattacks, remaining on the field all the while, marshalling his forces.[1] The Irishman's initiative had secured an impressive victory from an attack that seemed doomed to disintegrate into failure. However, the success of Cleburne's attack was bad news for another group of Irishmen at Perryville. They were the Irishmen he had ploughed straight through, from the 10th Ohio Infantry Regiment.

The 10th Ohio was raised in Cincinnati by an Irishman called Major Joseph W. Burke. Burke was educated in military schools in Europe and had fled Ireland after the failed rebellion in 1848. When war broke out, the German population of Ohio raised several regiments from among their number. Not to be outdone, Burke placed an advertisement in the Cincinnati newspapers looking for recruits for an Irish regiment he would call the Montgomery Guards. Within a month, the regiment was recruited and the Irish population of Cincinnati had proven themselves as loyal to the Union as their German counterparts. Yet the regiment was not led by an Irishman – Burke passed over control of his recruits to the American-born and well-known member of the Cincinnati bar, William Haynes Lytle. Lytle had seen service in the Mexican War and his prominence in Democratic politics made the regiment more likely to be accepted into state service at a time when such acceptance was far from guaranteed. The Irish ethnicity of the regiment was played down somewhat by Judge Storer of the Cincinnati bar when, before presenting them with their regimental flag, he referred to Irish, Germans and Americans among their ranks. When Lytle accepted the flag, he was diplomatic enough to acknowledge the heritage of most of the men he commanded by ending his speech with the Irish Brigade's motto, '*Faugh a Ballagh*.'

Soon the Irishmen of the 10th Ohio began to display the one characteristic that seemed so prevalent among many of the Irish units of the American Civil War – they gained a reputation for drunkenness. Federal General Jacob Cox recalled that the Irishmen of the 10th Ohio were frequent lodgers in the guardhouse during their time in training near Cincinnati. They would drink too much while visiting the town and frequently returned to the camp roaring drunk. On another occasion, a member of the 3rd Ohio later recalled that he had bivouacked next to the Irishmen in the vicinity of a distillery in April 1862. Temptation got the better of the 10th and according to their neighbour, they spent the night getting 'wildly drunk'.

The Irish stereotype was being justified by Irishmen under arms all over North America, though commanding officers might often have forgiven or overlooked drunken incidents of a less serious nature. The 10th Ohio, however, proved that their ill discipline could be of a much more threatening nature. While the 3rd Ohio may have endured a little noise disturbance during their night next door to the Irish in the distillery, they seem to have endured considerably less than one other regiment that shared an encampment with the Irish. The men of the 13th Ohio had their encampment attacked by their Irish comrades when a dispute arose between the neighbouring regiments. General Cox himself had to intervene, although it was Lytle who brought the situation under control. The Ohio Irish regiment quickly acquired a reputation for belligerent behaviour off the field of battle. In the autumn of 1861, they were permitted to visit their homes in Cincinnati and their commanding officers experienced considerable difficulty in rounding them up again.[2] During the summer of 1862, the regiment once again distinguished itself as being 'extremely hard to control' and good at 'abusing the people' as Federal forces pillaged northern Alabama for food.[3] Soon, however, they were to prove equally belligerent in the face of the enemy. In an acknowledgement of its prowess in battle, the regiment soon gained the nickname the 'Bloody 10th'.[4] At Perryville, they spilled their share of blood.

The 10th Ohio served at Perryville as part of Lytle's brigade of Rousseau's division. They arrived on the field at approximately 10.30 a.m. and were immediately deployed as skirmishers for their brigade. They occupied the ridgeline through which Cleburne would attack. While an artillery duel raged over their heads, the Irishmen were afforded little cover, unlike the rest of their brigade, which remained hugging the ground on the backward slope of the hill behind the 10th. It was only when the Confederate artillery fire lifted

and Johnson's infantry began their attack that the 3rd Ohio
was ordered to fall in on the right of the Irishmen with the
15th Kentucky in support. These three regiments held the
ridge against Johnson's confused onslaught for two hours.
Indeed, in Rousseau's report of the action, he asserts that
these three regiments had 'without support struggled hard to
hold their line of battle for several hours, and were only
forced to retire after immense loss'. Even the opposing
General Johnson noted the names of the regiments he
opposed and commended them for the 'remarkable vigor'
with which they faced his command, even when they were
denied the use of any form of cover.[5]

They finally yielded the position when Cleburne's
brigade turned their right flank and the Irishmen of the 10th
Ohio were left isolated as the regiments to their right vacated
the ridge. They were the last regiment of both the 9th and
17th brigades to withdraw from the ridge that afternoon.[6]
Their gallantry, along with that of two other regiments, was
noted by the commanding officer of the 5th Indiana Artillery
Battery, who credited the Irishmen and their comrades for
buying his battery the time to withdraw without being
captured by the onrushing Confederates.[7]

At Perryville, the 10th Ohio added a reputation for hard
fighting on the battlefield to the one already acquired for the
same activity off the field, proving themselves to be the most
obstinate and courageous defenders of Rousseau's battle line.
Only the onslaught of another Irishman, Patrick Cleburne,
could dislodge these rowdy Irishmen from the ridge, which
so many of them held to their death. The 10th Ohio and
General Patrick Cleburne had both added considerably to
their reputations.

The Battle of Perryville ended as darkness crept across
the Kentucky sky. The Confederates had driven the Federal

line back, but they had not broken it. At about midnight, Bragg realised that he was outnumbered and, although he had gained a slight victory, he gave the order to retreat. Soon Bragg united his forces with Kirby-Smith's at Harrodsburg. Further skirmishes occurred, but neither side committed itself to an all-out attack.

While Buell and Bragg went toe to toe in Kentucky, Grant was still at Corinth preparing for his Vicksburg campaign. On 14 September 1862, Confederate Major General Sterling Price moved his forces towards the forces of his comrade, Major General Earl Van Dorn. The two men intended to consolidate their command and operate against Grant at Corinth. However, Grant foresaw the move and sent forces under Major Generals William S. Rosecrans and Edward Ord to attack Price and Van Dorn at Iuka. The Federals won a minor victory at the Battle of Iuka (19 September), but poor co-ordination of forces allowed Price's forces to escape a potential Federal encirclement. Price and Van Dorn now decided to ride their luck and attack the concentrated Federal forces under Grant, but tactically commanded by Rosecrans, at Corinth. On 3 and 4 October they besieged the town, which they had thought was lightly defended. However, the town contained some 12,500 Federal troops. Among the troops defending the town was another principally Irish-American regiment, known as the 17th Wisconsin. This regiment contained several companies whose names evoked their ethnicity, among them the Mulligan Guards of Kenosha, the Peep O'Day Boys of Racine and the Emmet Guards of Dodge.[8]

The Federal defenders of Corinth dug themselves in along two lines of earthworks that were initially constructed by Confederate troops before they had abandoned the town the previous June. Rosecrans planned to meet the

Confederates with skirmishers placed on the outer line about three miles from Corinth before making his final stand at the inner (or Halleck) line of earthworks just outside the town. On the morning of 3 October, as a part of Federal General John McArthur's brigade in McKean's division, the Wisconsin Irish found themselves near the extreme left of the outer line, where they were to support a Federal artillery battery. At 11.00 a.m., Federal forces to the right of the Irishmen collapsed under pressure from the advancing Confederates who were now swarming into the rear of the Federal line, dangerously close to outflanking McArthur. At this point, the Irishmen were dispatched to the right of McArthur's line. Their commanding officer, Colonel John L. Doran, later reported their movement as follows:

> About 1pm, the fight having waxed warm, I was ordered to report my command on the battlefield. Having marched to the scene of the action, the regiment, while getting into position, was greeted all along the line with as hearty a cheer as was ever raised for the sons of Erin. A fact which apparently drew from the enemy a galling fire and which was vigorously kept up until the command reached its position on the extreme right of the line.[9]

Now in position, McArthur ordered the Irish regiment to charge the advancing Confederates. This was accomplished in fine style and four Mississippi regiments were driven three-quarters of a mile before the advancing Irishmen and the three regiments that supported them (two of which did so from quite a rearward distance, according to Doran). The charge was greatly praised by many of the Federal officers on the field that day. McArthur commended their 'gallant conduct' during the bayonet charge, while McKean referred to the 'conspicuous position' of the 'brave' Colonel Doran's men during the charge.[10]

The ground gained by the 17th Wisconsin was only briefly held, however, and as more and more Confederate units stacked up against the outer Federal lines, they were eventually forced to withdraw to the inner line. The Irishmen were near the extreme left of this inner line, and as attacks went in on the centre and right on 4 October, they were not heavily engaged. The Confederates did temporarily breach the Federal line and entered the town on 4 October, but they faced far greater numbers than they had realised and were eventually forced to withdraw, having sustained heavy losses. Their attempt to relieve the pressure on Bragg's Kentucky campaign had failed.

As winter set in, the Federal government proved that their tendency for chopping and changing commanders was not confined to the east. Unsatisfied with Buell's lack of progress, and perhaps impressed by Rosecrans' performance at Iuka, they replaced the former with the latter. Rosecrans spent some time training his army at Nashville before finally moving against Bragg at Murfreesboro just after Christmas 1862 in what would become known as the Battle of Stones River. Another Irish regiment featured prominently at Stones River – the men of the 35th Indiana Infantry Regiment.

The 35th Indiana consisted primarily of Irish immigrants who had worked on the railroads and canals of Indiana. They came from cities such as Lafayette, Indianapolis, Terre Haute and small river communities like Madison on the Ohio River. Company H was raised in Dayton, Ohio, and the regiment was mustered into Federal service in December 1861, kitted out with dark green coats and green cloth caps. Lest there be any doubt about their nationality, they carried a green flag emblazoned with the motto 'Be Just and Fear Not'. The regiment had survived its share of controversy when an Irish-American Fenian, Bernard F. Mullen, was given command and John C. Walker relieved of same. Mullen had frequently resorted to Irish nationalist rhetoric when trying to recruit for a second Irish regiment in Indiana, which did not prove as popular for him as it had for Meagher and Corcoran in eastern cities. In the end, he failed to raise a regiment and his recruits were sent to Walker's 35th Indiana.

Walker and Mullen did not see eye to eye and continually sniped at one another. Walker's Scotch-Irish ancestry may well have been one reason for the conflict between the two. When Walker was eventually relieved of his command, many left the regiment in protest. It seems the Irishmen of Indiana were a little more divided in their political views than many of their Northern comrades. A look through the muster rolls of the 35th reveals a mixture of surnames. Most are typically Irish, though there are some (particularly later recruits) that are not in any way Irish, and some that could also belong to Irishmen of the Orange tradition. Some liked Mullen's republican outlook, while others disliked it so much that they would not serve under his command.

At Stones River, the 35th was part of Price's brigade of Van Cleve's division in Crittenden's corps. They crossed Stones River on the Federal left at first light on 31 December 1863, remaining east of the river for a few short minutes, facing east and awaiting an enemy that did not arrive. Soon they were ordered to return to the western side of Stones River and form their line of battle there. Unknown to them, the Confederate divisions of Major General John P. McCown and newly promoted divisional commander Major General Patrick R. Cleburne had slammed into the right of the Federal line before they had even had a chance to finish breakfast. Cleburne's and McCown's early morning attack set

115

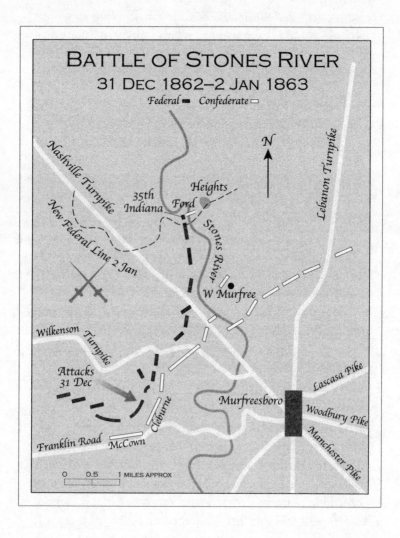

the wheels in motion for an all-out Confederate offensive that was now rolling up the right of the entire Federal line. The men of the 35th Indiana were called back across the river to assist in a desperate attempt to hold that line and prevent a disastrously disorganised retreat. Soon the ugly nature of their duty would become apparent.

Having recrossed Stones River, the Irishmen heard the sounds of battle echoing across the field from their right and it was not long before they saw McCook's battered corps heading in their direction. Mullen later described the scene that unfolded in his official report to his brigade commander:

> When in this position the action commenced on our right, and in an incredibly short space of time I found hundreds of fugitives and numerous wagons and ambulances fleeing in confusion and attempting to cross the river. Orders came from you to arrest the flight of these fugitives, and to this end I directed my men to fix bayonets and halt the panic stricken soldiers ... Two small battalions were formed and under an officer sent back to the right of the line. The confusion was great and I feel as if it was due to my officers and men to mention particularly the cool and determined manner [in which] they brought order out of the confusion.

The Irishmen had brought some stability back to the line, albeit at the point of a bayonet. The Federal line now re-formed roughly perpendicular to that which they had held in the morning, with the Irishmen anchored out on the far left near the river, from where they prevented a small force of Confederate cavalry from crossing into the rear of their line. As darkness fell, the Confederates looked back on a good day's fighting. Their early morning assault had met with overwhelming success, but some confusion in their command structure meant they had not brought their full weight to bear on the Federal troops and had allowed them to stabilise and anchor a second line of battle without being overrun. The Indiana Irish had played a key role in rallying and stabilising that Federal line.[11]

On New Year's Day 1863, Van Cleve's division, with the 35th Indiana among its ranks, crossed Stones River once again. On the eastern side they occupied the heights that commanded two river crossings, allowing for the placement of artillery. The 35th's New Year's Day consisted of companies taking their turns locking horns with Confederate skirmishers. Still, no all-out attack came, although a fairly vigorous Confederate attempt to dislodge the Irish skirmishers failed at about midnight. Daylight on 2 January brought more intermittent skirmishing, until about 2.00 p.m. that afternoon.

At that hour, a Confederate battery opened up on the Irishmen, launching solid shot and shell into their ranks for about two hours. As they fearfully hugged the ground while the lottery of artillery fire decided whether they should live or die, the Indiana Irish must have expected that an infantry assault would follow. At approximately 4.00 p.m., the artillery barrage was lifted and Confederate infantry appeared at their front. Mullen had instructed the men to lie down and fix bayonets, anticipating that his command was screened from the rebels' view. Soon his skirmishers were fleeing back towards his line, reporting the advance of several enemy brigades. Mullen cautioned his men not to fire until he gave the order. The Confederate infantry advanced towards the 51st Ohio and 8th Kentucky on the Irishmen's right and engaged them in a heavy duel of musketry. Now Mullen gave the order. The Irishmen rose with a cheer and began pouring musket fire into the flank of the surprised Confederates.

However, Mullen's position was now known to a nearby Confederate artillery battery and soon they were lighting up his ranks with as much fire as they could muster. Mullen called for support but did not receive any. Still, his command held the line for forty-five desperate minutes until the regiments to the left and right began giving way. Now the Irishmen received fire from both flanks as well as their front and were finally obliged to withdraw. Yet even then, some of them were reluctant and were consequently killed or captured by the enemy. As they retreated, the Indiana men kept up their fire. Eventually, about 400 yards behind the line and at the river, they met the remains of their now disorganised brigade. Mullen was instrumental in rallying the men to make a final stand here. By now, the Confederate advance was running out of steam and the Irishmen made a successful stand with their backs to the river. Now it was their turn to charge, and soon a mixed bag of their disorganised brigade was pushing the Confederates back up the hill. This assortment of the 3rd brigade's finest even succeeded in capturing two of the artillery pieces that had fired upon them. One of the pieces was claimed for the Irishmen of the 35th Indiana.[12]

The Battle of Stones River ground to a halt as evening fell on 2 January. On 3 January, Rosecrans received reinforcements from a Federal ammunition train. A small attack by two Federal regiments temporarily ruptured the centre of the Confederate line, but soon ran out of steam. Bragg feared the arrival of more reinforcements for Rosecrans and knew that the continuing heavy rain could raise the river enough to split his army in two. Thus, at 10.00 p.m. on 3 January, the Confederates began their withdrawal from Stones River. They travelled through Murfreesboro and began a retreat to Tullahoma, Tennessee, thirty-six miles to the south.

Rosecrans moved his forces into Murfreesboro but made no attempt to pursue Bragg. The Stones River Campaign was over and with it any hopes of Confederate control in middle Tennessee.

CHAPTER 9

FREDERICKSBURG

By November 1862, Lincoln was convinced that McClellan's indecision and failure to pursue Lee after the Battle of Antietam had cost the Army of the Potomac a possible advantage. Thus, when McClellan was replaced with Major General Ambrose E. Burnside, the new commander was under pressure to deliver a decisive victory sooner rather than later. It was against this background that Burnside planned a winter offensive against the Confederate capital of Richmond.

On 15 November, the Army of the Potomac marched towards Falmouth, Virginia, quite close to the small city of Fredericksburg. Falmouth was to be the Federal supply base for the campaign. Burnside had planned to feign movement on Culpeper Court House, Orange Court House or Gordonsville before rapidly crossing the Rappahannock River into Fredericksburg and advancing south along the Richmond, Fredericksburg and Potomac Railroad towards Richmond. When the rapid river crossing was made, it was hoped that Lee would be confused as to Burnside's intentions and thus hold the Army of Northern Virginia in position.

The Federal army arrived at Falmouth on 17 November,

but immediately their plan came unstuck. Burnside's pontoon bridges had not arrived on time and thus the river could not be crossed immediately.

While the Federal army stalled on the northern bank of the Rappahannock, Lee's forces began to gather in strength on the southern side. By 11 December, most of Lee's forces were entrenched on the high ground above the town, while a limited number of snipers remained in Fredericksburg to guard against any attempted Federal crossing. When these snipers began to take their toll on the Federal troops attempting to assemble the pontoon bridges, Burnside ordered some of his troops across the river in boats to clear the town of Confederates. These Federal troops were aided by a massive artillery bombardment. Derry-born William McCarter of the Irish Brigade graphically described the first large-scale military bombardment of a civilian town:

> At precisely eight am, our batteries opened fire. From the iron mouths of 150 cannons on Stafford Hills, nearly two miles distant from our position at that hour, flew out a constant reign of shot and shell into Fredericksburg for fully 18 hours. The noise, although at such a distance, was fearful, shaking the ground under our feet. It was deafening to those unused to the thundering of artillery.

McCarter and some of his comrades in the Irish Brigade were anxious to get a closer look at this destructive and awesome rain of death. While the whole of the Federal army lay beneath them, they climbed to the batteries on Stafford Hill. The view that awaited them was both impressive and disturbing:

> We stood a few yards in the rear of the battery. Just then we could not see farther than a few feet in front of the

guns, owing to the dense clouds of white smoke produced by their discharge. At about two p.m., however, all the artillery suddenly ceased firing, the guns being red hot. Half an hour later, the smoke having pretty well cleared away, the object of our visit was attained – a view of the beautiful Rappahannock below our feet with thousands of Union soldiers scouting and picketing along its banks, awaiting the opportunity to cross …

The once beautiful city of Fredericksburg was now on fire. Dense volumes of flame and thick, black smoke pierced the clouds above. Burning, tottering, cracking and falling evidenced the efficiency of the Federal bombardment.[1]

The artillery bombardment, combined with the crossing of infantry in boats, cleared the waterfront of Confederate snipers and the pontoon bridges were eventually laid, with the Federal troops starting to cross on the evening of 11 December. Among the first to cross were the Irishmen of the 69th Pennsylvania, who had just overcome some recent disciplinary problems when the entire regiment had managed to get drunk en masse during the movement towards Fredericksburg in early November.[2] Now, on the evening of 11 December they were engaged in some of the war's first urban combat in order to clear the town of any remaining Confederate snipers.[3]

With their countrymen of the 69th Pennsylvania already skirmishing in the town, the men of the Irish Brigade still waited for their orders to cross. No orders came and that night they camped on the eastern bank of the river. The winter was one of Virginia's worst and the stinging cold compelled Meagher to permit his men to light campfires. The fires were in the line of vision of Confederate artillery, and

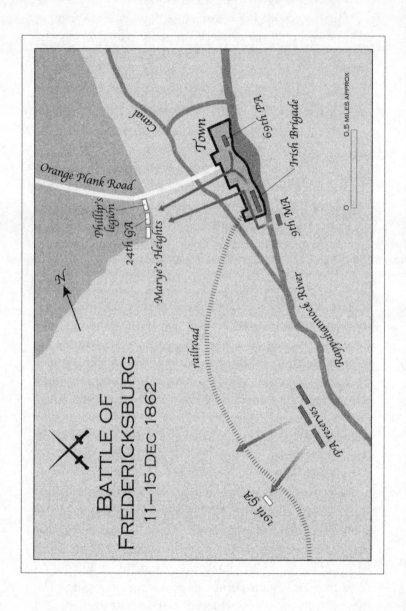

BATTLE OF
FREDERICKSBURG
11–15 DEC 1862

N

Orange Plank Road

Canal

Town

Phillip's legion

24th GA

Marye's Heights

69th PA

Irish Brigade

9th MA

Rappahannock River

railroad

PA reserves

19th GA

0.5 MILES APPROX

soon shells began falling too close for comfort. Although Meagher's men had now revealed themselves, the Confederate shelling was sporadic and did not inflict heavy casualties on the brigade. Meagher subsequently went to the trouble of expressly stating that he had not permitted fires to be lit.[4] When morning came, they once again waited for orders to cross over the icy waters of the Rappahannock, and still no orders came.

The Irishmen stood and watched as a vast portion of the Army of the Potomac streamed over the pontoon bridge into Fredericksburg. The haze of dawn gave way to a clear and cold December sun. Then, at 10.30 a.m., the Irish Brigade was ordered forward. Leaving the heights above the riverbank, the brigade lost thirteen men to Confederate shells as they descended towards the river. Then, as the bridge was not in sight of enemy artillery, they made a silent crossing into the town, losing a drummer boy to the icy water beneath. As they trudged forward, they moved closer to the Irish Brigade's most famous date with destiny.

It became clear, as Federal troops crossed into Fredericksburg, that no assault on the Confederate lines above the town would be attempted until the following day, so the army had little to occupy itself with for the remainder of 12 December. Little, that is, apart from looting the city, and it seems they set about their task with some zeal. Robert E. Lee compared the behaviour of the Federal army in Fredericksburg to that of the vandals who sacked the city of Rome. The behaviour only served to anger further the Confederate troops that waited on the heights above.

There is no reason to conclude that the Irish were above this kind of behaviour. Indeed, there is even some evidence that the Irish Brigade may have partaken of some of the spoils of the town. Private McCarter left the following account:

It was now pretty generally understood that the assault on the enemy's works would not be made until the following morning. Consequently, our men spent the interval in an endless variety of ways. Our rations being exhausted except for fat pork, our officers gave us permission to appropriate for the use of ourselves and our regiment any and everything in the shape of food found in the now uninhabited dwellings or stores near our position.[5]

McCarter noted that the Confederates had already removed many of the stores the Irishmen sought, yet they did eventually find some flour and were able to bake what he called 'army shortcake' by mixing it with pork fat. Naturally, Meagher's official report denied that his brigade had taken part in any of the looting in Fredericksburg and he proclaimed that the 'Irish Brigade scrupulously abstained from any act of depredation'. Meagher's report was written merely one week after the events that had angered many Federal superiors, so he may have been telling the truth. However, given that McCarter wrote his account long after Meagher's schoolboy-like denials were necessary to prevent the consequences of incurring anger from those in authority, his seems a more dependable account. Put simply, Meagher had reason to lie, McCarter did not.

There is further evidence of looting by the Irish Brigade in Fredericksburg. Irish-American Peter Welsh, of the 28th Massachusetts, wrote to his wife on Christmas Day and he too seemed to imply that the Irish Brigade had indulged in some looting at Fredericksburg:

I have clothing enough now we got woollen shirts here and we got plenty of towels and such things in Fredericksburg and if we could have carried it we might have tobacco enough to last us three months.[6]

Of course, tobacco was only one of the habits indulged in by soldiers. The other was one regularly associated with Irish troops on both sides, and at Fredericksburg there is some evidence to suggest that the Irish Brigade may have turned to the bottle for courage. One journalist proclaimed that Meagher had 'harangued his troops in impassioned language … and plied them extensively with the whiskey found in the cellars of Fredericksburg'.[7] This corroborates the account of a Southern soldier who alleged that he had heard of the Irishmen's behaviour from the citizens of Fredericksburg:

> Meagher's Irish Brigade passed through the city going into the fight. They were greatly applauded and cheered as they went by the masses of skulking Yankees along the streets, saying, 'Here goes the rebel batteries, in ten minutes the Irish Brigade will have them in the hills.' Meagher made them a fiery war speech, at which they lustily huzzaed, telling them that all who had tried had failed, but he knew they could take them. The Irish, half drunk with liquor, flattered by the cowardly Yankees and elated by the harangue of their leader, no doubt thought that as they entered the plain, that they would see the rebels running.[8]

They did not enter the plain on the night of 12 December, however. Instead, drunk or sober, the Irish Brigade lay on their arms in the ruins of Fredericksburg. Nearby were the Irishmen of the 69th Pennsylvania who slept beneath a blanket of freezing fog in the midst of a harsh Virginia winter.

As always, the Federal Irish were not the only Irish on the field. On the high ground above the town, right at the centre of Longstreet's corps, positioned behind a stone wall along a sunken road and at the foot of a hill called Marye's

Heights, the 24th Georgia Infantry settled in for the night. Their commander was a charismatic man from County Antrim known as Robert Emmet McMillan. His name clearly implied that McMillan was born to parents who admired revolution. Having emigrated to Elbert County, Georgia in 1831, the Irishman became a respected citizen, even serving in the state legislature. At the beginning of the war he raised a company of volunteers in Habersham County, Georgia. The company was known as the McMillan Guards and had a great many Irishmen among its ranks. Also in the ranks of the 24th Georgia Regiment were two of McMillan's sons, one of whom was also named for the Irish nationalist patriot, Robert Emmet. In the same brigade as the 24th Georgia was another unit, known as Phillip's Legion, which itself included another Irish company, known as the Lochrane Guards from Macon County, Georgia.[9] On the day that followed, the legion took so many casualties that its command devolved to Tyrone-born Captain Joseph Hamilton. These men slept beneath the same sky as the Irish Brigade, but none of them knew that soon they would meet in battle.

The morning of 13 December began with an attack on the far right of the Confederate line (Jackson's corps) by three divisions under the command of Major General Franklin. One of those divisions was that of Major General George G. Meade. Meade's division was composed of three brigades of Pennsylvania reserves along with four artillery batteries. The Pennsylvania reserves were made up of men from all over the state of Pennsylvania, and though none of the regiments were exclusively Irish, a large number of Irishmen served in their ranks. Indeed, the 2nd Pennsylvania reserves in Meade's 1st brigade contained a number of 'solidly Irish' companies raised in Philadelphia.[10] It seems these Philadelphia Irishmen clashed with an Irish colour company of the 19th Georgia during their initial advance into the Confederate line. Lieutenant John Keely served with the Irishmen of the Jackson Guards, colour company of the 19th Georgia Regiment, and wrote in his diary:

> The enemy found a weak place in our line on our left, and Meaghers Brigade of Irish troops charging it with empty muskets and fixed bayonets and were upon us before succour could reach us.[11]

But Keely was wrong – Meagher's men did not attack anywhere near the 19th Georgia. They were about to march into infamy some two miles north of that position. As historian Kelly O'Grady has suggested, it is likely that Keely heard the Irish accents of those who charged into his regiment and assumed they were of Meagher's brigade, when in fact they were the Irishmen of the Pennsylvania reserves. O'Grady also credibly theorises that the recognition of their fellow countrymen in the 19th Georgia might well have been the reason that Federal troops pleaded for surrender before overrunning the position. It might also have been the reason for the reported affable handshakes between Federal captors and their Confederate prisoners.[12] At any rate, the 19th Georgia came under artillery fire at 12.00 p.m. and was overrun by infantry at approximately 2.30 p.m. By then, the Irish Brigade was already involved in some of their heaviest fighting and the focus of the battle had turned eastwards.

With the day's action beginning west of Fredericksburg, the Irish Brigade had had a quiet start to what would become their most memorable day. The men woke before dawn, feeling the effects of the cold Virginian winter. Peter Welsh described waking up on the boards he had placed between him and the muddy street and finding his blanket 'thick with frost'.[13] On the hills above the town, some Confederate troops

129

lay dead from exposure to the freezing fog of the previous night. The Irishmen each cooked their breakfasts and many ate what would be their last meal, awaiting further orders. At 11.00 a.m. they heard the scattered musket fire that drove the Confederate pickets back towards the safety of the heights. Among the men driven back were the pickets of McMillan's 24th Georgia.

As the morning turned to afternoon, the sound of firing on the heights grew at a steady rate. The smell of burned powder lay thick on the air as the morning fog began to clear. French's division was storming the Confederate line along the stone wall. If he failed to break through, the Irish Brigade knew that, as part of Hancock's division, they would be among the next to try. Soon the firing died away and the cheering of Confederate troops could be heard in the town. Word began to spread that French's men were beaten and the Irish Brigade readied itself for the fray.[14] They were drawn up in columns along the streets of the town and Meagher soon appeared on horseback. The general ordered that each man of the Irish Brigade be presented with a little piece of green boxwood shrub to place in his cap. As the new regimental flags had not arrived from New York, the boxwood would serve as the brigade's Irish emblem at Fredericksburg.[15] By now, the 28th Massachusetts had joined the Irish Brigade, replacing the non-Irish 29th Massachusetts. They would be the only regiment to carry a green flag into battle.

At 2.00 p.m., the men were ordered to shoulder their arms and marched on the double quick along Hanover Street and out of the town. Upon leaving the cover of the buildings, they were immediately under Confederate artillery fire, some of which came from a Confederate artillery battery known as the Washington Artillery of New Orleans. Among the ranks of that battery, quite a few Irishmen loaded and fired the cannon at the advancing Federal infantry.[16] Moving out of the town, the men faced a daunting task. Confederate gunners had boasted that if a chicken moved on the field, they could kill it and Longstreet himself had stated that his position was so perfect for defence that he could hold the line against every man in the Army of the Potomac. It was little wonder the Confederates felt so confident.

As they emerged from the streets of the town, the Irish Brigade faced an 800-yard march across the Confederate field of fire. The first 200 yards sloped gradually downwards until reaching an old disused canal that the brigade had to cross over on hastily improvised planks in single file, while still under fire. As the Irish Brigade struggled through the murderous artillery fire, many men simply jumped into the canal and waded across its icy shallow waters. Having crossed the canal, the brigade was afforded some cover by the ground, which once again started to rise. Under this brief cover they swung right and left, forming themselves into a line of battle.

As the only regiment with its own green flag, the dubious honour of being the centre regiment of the brigade's line of battle fell to the 28th Massachusetts. To the immediate left of the 28th Massachusetts was the 88th New York, while on their left the core regiment, the 69th New York, made up the far left of the brigade's line. To the right of the 28th stood the men of the 63rd New York, while the 116th Pennsylvania, also a new addition to the brigade, was on the far right of the line.

They listened to the gunfire that mowed down Zook's brigade and soon had the order to fix bayonets. As the Irishmen advanced over the shallow ridge that had afforded them some cover, they stepped back into a hail of artillery fire from their front and flanks. Meanwhile, Meagher made his way back towards the canal. The general later explained

131

that he was unable to lead his brigade that day due to 'a most painful ulcer in the knee joint, which I had concealed and borne up against for days'.[17] It is worth pointing out that Meagher was not on horseback and had walked out of the town and across the canal under heavy fire with his men. His reasons for deciding that his knee could not effectively bear him up as the brigade attacked the heights are still debated.

With Meagher making his way towards the rear, the men of the Irish Brigade marched towards the heights, picking their way over the bodies that were already strewn along the slope. Behind the stone wall, at the base of the heights, the Irishmen of the 24th Georgia and Phillip's Legion awaited their arrival. They were well disciplined, cool and calculating, having dispelled brigade after brigade already that morning. McMillan gave the orders to the 24th, urging his men to hold their fire until the Irish Brigade came within range. Did McMillan know that it was Irishmen who came against him? It is quite likely that he spotted the green flag of the 28th as many other Confederate troops did and it is also possible that he noted the green boxwood in their caps as they came closer. In the months that followed, one report alleged that McMillan commented, 'That's Meagher's brigade, give it to them now, boys! Now's the time. Give it to them!'[18] Nonetheless, he made no mention of the Irish Brigade in his official report.

Some of his men were reported to have noted the approach of their fellow Irishmen with the words, 'Oh God what a pity, here come Meagher's fellows.'[19] But on the heights outside Fredericksburg on that cold December afternoon, there was no further room for sentiment. McMillan walked the line behind the stone wall to and fro, clearly exposing his head to Federal fire, constantly urging the men to hold their fire until his order was given. He wanted the Irishmen close enough for his regiment's smooth-bore 'buck and ball' muskets to do the most damage. As the Irish Brigade moved ever closer to McMillan's line, it almost seemed that they might overrun it. Then as they passed beyond the point of the most advanced Federal fallen, McMillan opened up with devastating effect, stopping the advance of the Irish Brigade in its tracks and shattering its ranks within yards of the wall. The men tried to rally and held their line, blazing away at the wall. Confederate General Pickett later wrote to his fiancée:

> Your soldier's heart almost stood still as he watched those sons of Erin fearlessly rush to their death. The brilliant assault on Marye's Heights of their Irish Brigade was beyond description. Why, my darling, we forgot they were fighting us, and cheer after cheer at their fearlessness went up along our lines.[20]

It is obvious that the deeds of the Irishmen at Fredericksburg left a mark on the flamboyant Confederate general, who six months later would lead the most famous charge of the war. Perhaps the similarities between the Irish assault at Fredericksburg and the assault he was ordered to perform at Gettysburg may have occurred to him in July 1863. Pickett's division was stopped in its tracks at Gettysburg, much like the Irish Brigade was in front of Marye's Heights.

The commander of the 28th Massachusetts, Colonel Richard Byrnes, described his regiment's advance as follows:

> On arriving at the crest of the hill, the firing was so severe and concentrated that the men were compelled to take shelter by lying down and many endeavoured to hold their position by piling wood, to form a barricade, in rear of a brick house on our right, behind which they did good execution …[21]

The brigade was now stuck in the firing line of Confederate muskets. The men who were not lucky enough to find limited cover behind the brick house retreated to where a small indentation provided extremely limited cover when one could lie flat on the ground. Others piled the dead bodies that lined the slopes in front of themselves. There was no going back and there was certainly no going forward. To attempt either would have exposed the men to murderous musket fire. All they could do was wait for Federal reinforcements to overrun the Confederates at the stone wall or for the veil of darkness to conceal withdrawal.

By now, William McCarter was badly wounded. He had received a wound in his ankle from artillery fire as he left the town. He was then hit in the shoulder as he lay between the canal and the ridge. Still, he stayed with his regiment as they advanced on the heights. As he blazed away at the men behind the wall, a musket ball smashed into his arm, inflicting a very serious wound and heavy bleeding. He quickly experienced dizziness and dropped to the ground, unconscious. He regained consciousness some minutes later, and many years after the events he described the scene to which he awoke:

> But where was I? Left all alone in my glory if such it really was. Lying among heaps of my wounded, dying and dead companions. Cannon to my right, cannon to my left, cannon in front and cannon behind volleyed and thundered to the music of thousands of minie balls flying about in all directions. To rise up and run was impossible … To get aid or even to expect it from any of our own men was out of the question. No one could get near me except at the risk of his own life.[22]

As the men of the Irish Brigade lay pinned down on the

slopes in front of the wall, the scene around them grew more and more piteous. The next brigade flung at the heights was Caldwell's. They too were quickly cut down, sustaining even higher casualties than the Irish. As afternoon turned to evening, the Federal brigades continued to roll up the hill towards inevitable slaughter. The three brigades of Howard's division were the next unfortunate victims flung at Marye's Heights. The Irishmen of the 69th Pennsylvania served in the second brigade of Howard's division and they advanced towards their fellow Irishmen pinned down on the slope. However, the 69th Pennsylvania could not quite make it as far as the Irish Brigade and took cover lying flat on the ground about 25 yards to the rear of their countrymen. Two companies of sharpshooters were sent forward in the direction of the Irish Brigade in order to provide cover for the evacuation of Federal units. The rest of the regiment remained pinned down on the slope. Like the Irishmen in front, they waited for darkness.[23]

More of their countrymen were about to join them. At 3.30 p.m., the men of Griffin's division were moved towards the slaughter. Among them were the men of Boston's 'Irish 9th'. As they crossed the pontoon bridges into the town, they met a lucky few from the Irish Brigade who had somehow managed to retreat from the hill. 'They shook their heads in rueful and not assuring manner,' reported Daniel Macnamara. 'One wounded veteran captain of the 28th remarked that it was the toughest place he had ever been into and he was sorry to see us going in.'[24] The Irish 9th were spared the carnage experienced by their Irish comrades, however. They were advanced some distance across the plain and took heavy artillery fire, but their commanding officer, Colonel Patrick R. Guiney, recognised the futility of attacking the wall and refused the order of a staff officer to do so, stating that he would only obey orders from his own immediate superiors. Mercifully, darkness intervened before any such order was given and the 9th sustained comparatively light casualties, with only one man killed and twenty-six wounded.

Inside the wall, the Irishmen of the 24th Georgia rested on their arms that night. McMillan's official report expressed satisfaction at their having repelled wave after wave of Federal troops 'with great slaughter'. Outside the wall, the Irishmen were feeling the effects of that slaughter and the dangerous withdrawal was beginning. William McCarter still lay wounded in front of the wall and later described the eerie scene on the field as darkness crept over the Confederate and Federal Irish.

> Here I must say a word with regard to the appearance of the Rebels and the interval firing at night. I still laid on the ground directly in their front, awaiting a safe opportunity to rise up and get out of the range of their fire. Such an opportunity, however, had not yet arrived. About every ten minutes a storm of bullets came from Cobb's brigade [now commanded by McMillan] behind the stone wall, only 50 paces to my front. The sudden flashing fire of their muskets in the darkness for a second of time so illuminated the faces of this part of the Confederate army that the men looked strangely red and savage – more like devils than human beings. Then the blackness and darkness of night covered them. The only sounds heard were the shrieks and groans of our wounded and dying, strewn on every side like scattered seed. Truly, war is sad.[25]

McCarter, although in severe pain, eventually managed to stand up and walk to the rear, doing so immediately after one of the Confederate volleys in order to give himself the maximum time before the field was once again illuminated. Many of the wounded were not so lucky. Peter Welsh was pinned down at the stone wall as darkness fell and later wrote to his wife, telling her of his night at Marye's Heights:

> Some went out but a great many remained in front as in going out they would again be exposed to the raking fire of the enemys batteries and by remaining in front we had only the fire of enemy infantry and sharpshooters to bear our position was beside a fence and a house and yard which was in our line a great number of our wounded were carried into that house and some of them had to remain there untill Sunday night as our ambulance wagons could not be brought up there and those who had no friends to carry them out at night had to remain until men were sent from the different regiments to bring them out I remained in front untill dark and then brought out some wounded belonging our company I went over the battlefield again before daylight to see if I could find any more of our men and the sights that were to be seen there were hard enough I slept about an hour that night in the house which was being used as a hospital in which I left the wounded that I brought ought [out] ...[26]

13 December had seen Irishmen kill Irishmen at Marye's Heights outside of Fredericksburg. The night and morning of 14 December saw those men lying wounded, helpless, dead and dying on the spot where they had fallen. Yet there was one final irony that ensured Fredericksburg would live forever in the minds of all Irish-Americans: literally, it was the ground beneath their feet. John Edward Dooley was born of Irish parents who settled in Virginia. He served with the

1st Virginia Infantry and later wrote of Fredericksburg's Irish irony:

> The field on which they fell was at the foot of Marye's Hill , and was the property of Colonel Marye, an officer in our brigade. In 1848 or '49 when famine was inflicting such distress in Ireland, the whole crop of corn raised in this identical field had been sent in contribution for the relief of that starving and oppressed people.[27]

Thus, the dead, dying and wounded Irishmen now lay on American soil that may once have fed them or their countrymen. The life force they may once have taken from that very ground was now being returned to it. They waited for the morning and possible evacuation for those who remained.

Yet when morning came, there was no rescue for the men who lay at Marye's Heights. Burnside still dithered, toying with the idea of further attacks while his men wasted away on the heights. Eventually, on 15 December, the Federal leader sought a truce with Lee in order to attend to his dead and wounded. Lee graciously agreed and help finally reached the men who were still alive in front of the stone wall. One of the men of the 28th Massachusetts, upon reaching the heights to attend to the dead and wounded, noted that many of the former had had their clothes removed from them by desperately ill-provided Confederate troops.[28]

Evacuating the wounded first, the Army of the Potomac withdrew across the Rappahannock on the night of 15 December, lifting the pontoon bridges as they went. The Battle of Fredericksburg was over, but the legend of the Irish Brigade's participation was only beginning to take shape. Soon after the battle, the correspondent for the London *Times* carried the story of the brigade's exploits across the Atlantic with an article that added to their growing reputation:

> Never at Fontenoy, Albuera or at Waterloo was more undaunted courage displayed by the sons of Erin than during those six frantic dashes which they directed against the impregnable position of their foe. That any mortal men could have carried the position before which they were wantonly sacrificed, defended as it was, it seems to me idle for a moment to believe. But the bodies which lie in dense masses within forty yards of the muzzles of Colonel Walton's guns are the best evidence what manner of men they were who pressed on to death with the dauntlessness of a race which has gained glory on a thousand battlefields, and never more richly deserved it than at the foot of Marye's Heights on the 13th day of December, 1862.[29]

Such reports had the immediate effect of adding to the growing disillusionment with the war among the Irish in the Northern states. Some felt that Irishmen were being overused and sacrificed where American units would not be, though of course American units were also flung hopelessly at Marye's Heights. However, in the immediate wake of the carnage at Antietam, some Irish-Americans began to feel that immigrants were doing a disproportionate amount of fighting. Such feelings would make further recruitment of Irishmen increasingly difficult for the Federal authorities.

Yet as the years passed by, Fredericksburg and Antietam became important sources of pride for Irish-Americans. The sacrifice of Irishmen who fought under the Stars and Stripes was celebrated by Irish-Americans to a greater extent than the sacrifices of those who had fought under the rebels' 'Stars and Bars'. Romantic tales surrounding the Irish at Fredericksburg were often told and repeated, gaining increasing acceptance with each telling until they were unilaterally accepted as fact. One such tale revolved around the flag of the Irish Brigade at Fredericksburg and was repeated in the *Freeman's Journal* of 28 March 1914. The story told of a Confederate Irishman called Michael O'Sullivan who sneaked out from the Confederate lines at Marye's Heights to retrieve the flag of the Irish Brigade, which had fallen on the field in front of him. Having done so, O'Sullivan was wounded by Confederate pickets who assumed he was deserting as he made his way towards the Federal line. The wounded O'Sullivan now swam across the icy Rappahannock to return the flag to General Meagher himself. Meagher's surgical staff tended to his wounds and Meagher offered him a place in the Irish Brigade. The loyal O'Sullivan refused and made his way back to his own regiment on the Confederate side. The story is beautifully romantic, but O'Grady has thrown a few spokes in its wheels with some dispassionate historical research. Firstly, it appears that nobody of that name served in any of the units anywhere near the stone wall, and secondly, the likelihood of a wounded man swimming 100 yards across an icy river, quite possibly under fire from both sides, has to be questioned.[30]

Unfortunately, there were no romantic Irish stories at Fredericksburg. There was much bravery, valour and courage, but also much savagery and death. No doubt growing increasingly immune to the horrors of war, the Irishmen of both sides settled in for a cold winter on either side of the Rappahannock.

Chapter 10

Chancellorsville

As the snow continued falling through the Virginian winter, the armies on either side of the Rappahannock became increasingly familiar with each other. It may have been here that two Irish picket guards allegedly encountered one another across the dark divide of a black night. Upon asking the Federal Irishman how he could fight for the Northern oppressor, the Confederate son of Erin got the reply, 'I am fighting for thirteen dollars a month, I hear you only get eleven!'[1] Whether or not this happened at Fredericksburg or if it happened at all, we simply do not know. Nonetheless, the story offers an insight into the unpatriotic motivation of many Irishmen who fought in blue and in grey. The story seems to fit Fredericksburg better than any other time or place in the war because of the familiarity and comradeship that developed between the two opposing armies that winter. 'While burying their dead I was particularly struck with the good feeling that seemed to prevail among the troops of both armies … as if they never had been enemies,' one soldier wrote.[2]

The men of the Irish Brigade were regular trading partners with their Confederate counterparts and they may well have managed some trade across the river that winter. The Irish pickets regularly stuck their muskets in the ground, bayonet first, in order to alert Confederate pickets that they were open for business. The Confederates would do likewise and a trading session involving quantities of coffee, sugar, whiskey and tobacco would ensue. Sometimes Irish immigrants from both sides would use the opportunity to exchange news of family and friends on either side of the divide. The trust of the opposing pickets was so important to the Irishmen of the 116th Pennsylvania that they even developed a warning system for their Confederate friends: when they were due to be replaced on picket by another regiment, they would shout the phrase 'hardtacks' across to their Confederate counterparts. This was intended to alert Confederates that they should not attempt any form of truce or trade with the 'hardtacks' of the new regiment.[3]

With the quiet of the winter by the Rappahannock, such activities may have been attempted depending on whether the natural river obstacle could be overcome. A general lack of military discipline continued to affect Irish units, and by March 1863 two of them (the 69th Pennsylvania and 88th New York) were so lacking in discipline that all officers' leave was cancelled until they could get their regiments back into order.[4]

The quiet downtime of that winter also afforded the Irish some time for activities that stretched beyond the confines of that particular war and back to another conflict with which some were at least partially intellectually engaged. There were many Fenians in the ranks on both sides and it seems that they held a meeting or meetings in the vicinity of Fredericksburg that winter. One such meeting, the monthly meeting of the Fenian Brotherhood's Potomac circle, was held in the hospital tent of the Irish Brigade, while another Fenian meeting in the vicinity of Fredericksburg may even have been attended by Confederate Fenians. The story goes that the Confererate and Federal leaders, Lee and Hooker, agreed that the Irishmen could meet in secret provided that nothing about the current conflict was discussed.[5] It is difficult to understand why the supreme commanders of both armies would have permitted such a meeting, but we must consider the account of one Irishman who claimed to have been in attendance as some evidence of its occurrence. If the meeting did occur, it is difficult to guess what might have been discussed. However, we should bear in mind that the Fenians did initiate a series of raids into Canada a year after the conclusion of the American Civil War, and that many of the men involved in those Fenian raids were veteran soldiers of the American Civil War and may have been in camp at Fredericksburg in the winter of 1862–63. John O'Mahony, who led the first of these raids, served as a colonel in the Irish Brigade at Fredericksburg.

The only attempt at an offensive movement that winter came in late January with Burnside's disastrous 'mud march'. The plan involved moving huge numbers of Federal troops up the Rappahannock in order to cross upstream and flank Lee's forces. Unfortunately for Burnside, the winter rains were particularly heavy and turned many of the Virginian roads to mud. Men sank up to their knees in mud in some places, and if men were bogged down, then artillery was even more so. Although the Irish Brigade was not involved in the march, one of their number later described the operation as 'one half of the army trying to pull the other out of the mud'. Eventually Burnside abandoned his plan and the troops returned to camp. It was the final operation that Burnside commanded and once again the Federal army changed its leader. This time, General Joseph Hooker, or 'Fighting Joe', took command. As the *nom de guerre* suggests, Hooker was a man of action. The armies would soon be on the move again and the Irish on both sides could expect some action.

On 26 April 1863, Hooker split his forces, sending four corps marching stealthily northwest. His plan was that they would turn south and cross the Rappahannock and Rapidan rivers before turning east and slipping behind the rear of Lee's forces. From here, cavalry raids would cut Lee's supply routes. Meanwhile, those corps retained opposite Fredericksburg would strike again through the town, ensuring that Lee was attacked from two sides with no prospect of retreat or reinforcement. As part of Couch's corps, Hancock's division, the Irish Brigade made the stealth march northwest.

The Federal troops crossed the rivers near Chancellorsville on 27 and 28 April. By 1 May, Lee had noted the threat to his rear and moved 40,000 troops to confront the 70,000 Federals at Chancellorsville. He left approximately 12,000 at Marye's Heights to deal with any threat coming from Fredericksburg.

The Battle of Chancellorsville began when Hooker's men advanced out of Chancellorsville and clashed with the approaching Confederates on 1 May. They had forced their way out of the dense forestry that characterised the area and out into the open, where artillery could be effective. However, Hooker did not want to fight an offensive battle – he wanted Lee to attack him. He knew that Lee could not sustain the losses that the attacking Federal army had sustained at Fredericksburg and hoped that any attack by Lee on his superior numbers would result in such losses. Thus, on the evening of 1 May, he ordered the retreat of the Federal army back into the forestry, known locally as 'the Wilderness'. Lee took the bait and planned an attack for 2

May. However, once again, he and Jackson took the enormous risk of splitting their forces in the face of a numerically superior foe. Jackson took 28,000 men off to the west, then marched north and approached the Federals from their western flank. Among the units surprised by the arrival of Jackson were the remnants of the Irish Brigade.

By the morning of 2 May, the Irish Brigade was camped at a place called Scott's Mills. They spent the day quietly fortifying their position by cutting timber and placing it at their front. They could hear the rumble of battle as skirmishing continued with Confederates advancing from Fredericksburg. It was when they heard the sounds of battle to the west that they were most surprised, as there should not have been any enemy troops on the Federal flank. However, by 5.00 p.m., that is exactly where Stonewall Jackson was. As the Irish Brigade continued to perfect its fortifications, he was driving Howard's Federal corps through the woods to their right. Soon, to the astonishment of the Irishmen, a startled deer came darting out of the woods and through their line. Immediately following the deer came a few startled Federal troops, then a few more, and then a few hundred more. Howard's corps was in headlong retreat and had run into the Irish Brigade. Meagher, in a move that may have run contrary to his own alleged cowardice, ordered his depleted brigade to fix bayonets and halt the retreat. The panic-stricken men were forced to the rear of the line and those that were still fit made their stand with the Irishmen, awaiting the arrival of Confederate troops from the woods. No such troops appeared that night, as darkness impeded Jackson's advance. Lost in Jackson's devastating thirty-minute attack was Sergeant Peter Gavan of the 19th Georgia's Jackson Guards, a young Irish-American who perished in a bush fire triggered by the continuous firing. His charred remains were

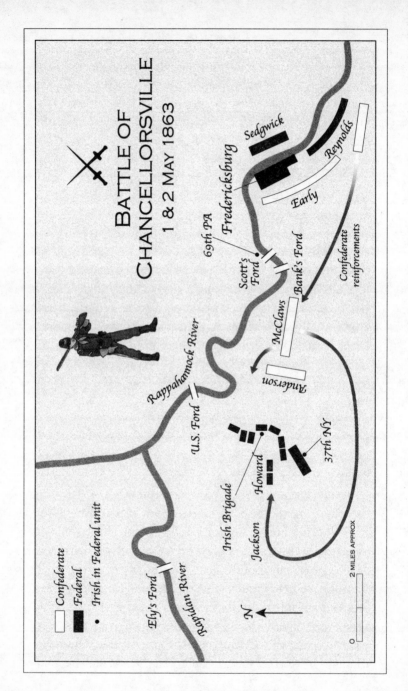

BATTLE OF CHANCELLORSVILLE
1 & 2 MAY 1863

Sedgwick

Reynolds

Fredericksburg

Early

69th PA

Scott's Ford

Bank's Ford

Confederate reinforcements

McClaws

Anderson

Rappahannock River

U.S. Ford

Ely's Ford

Rapidan River

Irish Brigade

Howard

Jackson

37th NY

N

Confederate
Federal
Irish in Federal unit

0   2 MILES APPROX

found still clutching his musket. His Irish-born mother died of a broken heart two weeks after her son.[6] The most notable death at Chancellorsville was that of General Jackson. That night, as he returned to his own lines following a reconnaissance mission into the darkness, Stonewall Jackson was shot from his horse by his own men. He was removed to a hospital and his arm was amputated, but the famous general died of pneumonia on 10 May, depriving Robert E. Lee of one of his most able commanders.

On the morning of 3 May, Hooker began withdrawing his troops to a more defensible position nearer the river. As new men now came to occupy the position of the Irish Brigade, the Irishmen were able to move towards the Chancellorsville clearing, where the rest of their division was engaged in covering further tactical withdrawals. As they moved forward through the wounded and retreating men, they were often cheered along the way.[7] Perhaps there were still many who remembered their heroics in the Peninsula Campaign. There were certainly many who remembered their heroics at Fredericksburg.

Deployed on the edge of a clearing, the Irish Brigade was ordered to support a battery that covered the Federal withdrawal. Soon, however, the Confederate advance became too much for the brigade to bear and they were beating a hasty retreat through the woods, along with the remainder of their Federal comrades. For one unlucky Irish regiment, however, there was to be no easy retreat. The 116th Pennsylvania was ordered to save the battery's guns regardless of the risk to themselves. They were assisted by some men from the other Irish regiments, but by only one of the men attached to the battery, as the remainder of his comrades had been killed or had taken flight. Once again, it was the Irish who seemed willing to take risks when other regiments thought it far too dangerous to do so. Major St Clair

Mulholland commanded the saving of the battery and reported the actions of the Irishmen under his command as follows:

> When the battery had been engaged with the enemy about one hour, all the officers and [men] belonging to it had either been killed, wounded, or had abandoned their pieces, with the exception of one man, Corpl. James H. Lebroke, and all the guns were silenced except one. About this time, Major Scott, of General Hancock's staff, rode up to me, and requested me to bring out a sufficient number of men to haul the abandoned guns off the field, as they were in great danger of being captured by the enemy. My regiment at this time occupied the left of the brigade line, and was nearest the battery. I at once, at the request of Major Scott, led my men toward the abandoned battery, and ordered them to haul the guns up the road. My men obeyed with alacrity, and removed three of the guns off the field, and to the rear. After taking off the last piece, I followed my men up the road, and found another gun in possession of one of my lieutenants L.J. Sacriste, of Company D. This piece he had taken off without my knowledge, and made, in all, four pieces saved by my command. The fifth piece taken to the rear was taken off the field by some men of the One hundred and fortieth Pennsylvania Volunteers, and was by them taken up the road about 100 yards. There they were forced to halt, not having enough men to move the piece farther. I at once sent some men of my command to assist them, and the piece was brought off successfully. I found it necessary, in removing the guns, to order the men to leave their muskets, as they could not work with them in their hands. Seventy-three of my

men did so. When the last gun was brought off, I went back to the left, to ascertain whether any more remained. I then found 8 or 10 of my men coming up the road, and ordered them back to gather up as many muskets as they could carry off. I do not think they succeeded in saving any.[8]

The action cost the Irish Brigade a further 100 casualties, which was approximately 20 per cent of the number they had brought to battle. The brigade was by now a brigade in name only and was far too small to function realistically as such. Meagher had failed in his attempts to organise further recruitment drives for his brigade. Indeed, the Irish Brigade's leader was proving more and more controversial with each passing day. His antics during, or absence from, battle, as well as his frequent bouts of heavy drinking, were beginning to grate on his superior officers. Soon he tendered his resignation and the brigade lost its only brigadier general. Nonetheless, the Irishmen continued on as a fighting unit, though they would never again play the major roles in significant battles that had once made them one of the most renowned and feared units in the Federal army.

Other Irish units had also forged reputations, and some of them were in action at Chancellorsville. The 37th New York Infantry Regiment, or 'Irish Rifles', was one such unit and they too saw action at Chancellorsville. As part of Sickle's division, the Irishmen of the 37th New York fought to the west of the Irish Brigade as Stuart's Confederates closed in from that side. They fought a rearguard action that day and came under particularly heavy fire, reporting 222 men killed, wounded or missing by the day's end. In fact, only four other Federal regiments reported more casualties than the 37th New York. Many of the regiment's officers had fallen, leaving it leaderless on the field. They lost three captains, three lieutenants and a colour sergeant, a substantial loss in leadership for any regiment. The lack of leadership added to the confusion of battle and the regiment was separated from its brigade. As such, the regiment's commander, Lieutenant Colonel Gilbert Riordan, withdrew it from the line of battle and made towards the safety of the rear. While nobody could argue that the 37th had not done much of the fighting and taken its share of the casualties, some senior Federal officers did express disappointment at how hastily the regiment was withdrawn from the field. The colonel of their brigade, S.B. Hayman, himself of the 37th New York, reported that he did not deem the loss of the officers 'sufficient excuse' for Riordan's withdrawal of the regiment three miles to the rear. Nonetheless, he also complimented Major William DeLacy and Captain Phillip Doherty for rallying portions of the 37th and returning them to the front, while mentioning Lieutenant Lawrence Murphy's personal capture of two Confederate prisoners.

Meanwhile, back at Fredericksburg, it was the Confederate Irish who were being called into action. With Lee's unexpected success at Chancellorsville, Hooker soon ordered Sedgwick to lead his troops through the Confederate lines on the heights above Fredericksburg and come immediately to his assistance at Chancellorsville. The Federal troops swarmed over the pontoon bridges and into Fredericksburg and once again stormed the Confederate position on the high ground west of the town, but now there was one key difference. This time, the Confederates had deployed most of their army to the west in the Chancellorsville region, and now their line at Fredericksburg was only lightly defended by one division under Major General Jubal Early. Under Early's command that day was Hays' Louisiana brigade and the substantial number of Irishmen it still contained. As

Federal forces built up in the town, Hays' brigade was ordered to the extreme left of the Confederate line, with the 6th Louisiana regiment detached from it and placed at the foot of Lee's Hill just behind Marye's Heights. Here they would link up with another group, which contained a small number of scattered Irishmen, the Washington Artillery of New Orleans. The large numbers of Irishmen in the 6th would provide support for their few fellow Irishmen of the artillery battery.

For days, the crafty Confederates had sought to deceive the Federals across the river, lighting hundreds of campfires at night and cheering the arrival of imaginary reinforcements by day, as well as constantly moving regiments and brigades along the line. When Hays' brigade was initially ordered to the left of the line, they had just arrived at the five-mile-distant Hamilton's Crossing. They immediately turned around and marched back to where they had come from, this time under heavy Federal artillery fire. On the morning of 3 May, however, the Federals were to employ a controversial tactic of deception. Two independent Confederate sources alleged that when early Federal attacks on the heights failed, they approached the Confederate position under the flag of truce. While retrieving their dead they made a quick recon-naissance of the Confederate line, noting its weaknesses. Twenty minutes later, they were on an all-out offensive, exploiting those very positions.[9] In the eye of the storm were the 6th Louisiana and the Washington Artillery.

It was about 11.00 a.m. when the Federal troops stormed Marye's Heights and Lee's Hill. The 6th Louisiana was commanded by the Irish-born Colonel Monaghan. They had already been involved in heavy skirmishing with Federal units trying to cross the river on 28 April, which had cost them a whole company and a lieutenant colonel, Joseph

Hanlon, all taken prisoner by the Federals.[10] Thus it was a weakened 6th Louisiana that faced the Federal onslaught at Lee's Hill. They were soon retreating from the position, having had some luck in not being entirely surrounded and captured. Some men from the Washington Artillery were captured. One of them was H.D. Coleman, although we do not know whether or not he was born in Ireland. The 6th Louisiana's orderly retreat from Lee's Hill along the telegraph road was praised by their divisional commander, Early. Using their example, he was able to assemble a makeshift force that fought a tactical retreat along the telegraph road. Eventually, Sedgwick's Federals broke off the pursuit and followed their own orders to drive towards Chancellorsville. By the morning of 4 May, Lee had the situation at Chancellorsville under control and was able to dispatch two divisions, McClaws' and Anderson's, in Sedgwick's direction. Early retook the heights above Fredericksburg, preventing retreat back towards the town. With McClaws' division approaching from the west and Early's men to the east and moving south to join with Anderson's, Sedgwick's division was being boxed in on three sides, while on the fourth side, the Rappahannock formed a natural barrier to retreat.

By 5.30 p.m. the Confederates had Sedgwick's corps surrounded and started their attack. Hays' brigade moved with Early's division from the east. They attacked in a ball of Louisiana and Irish fury uphill against a Federal enemy that had had time to dig in and place its artillery. They stormed through the first enemy line with such force that the opposing commander imagined he was being attacked by 'the whole of Longstreet's Corps'. The brigade they cut through took 1,000 casualties at the hands of Hays' brigade. Still running furiously, the men from Ireland and Louisiana soon smashed through the second Federal line. Federal

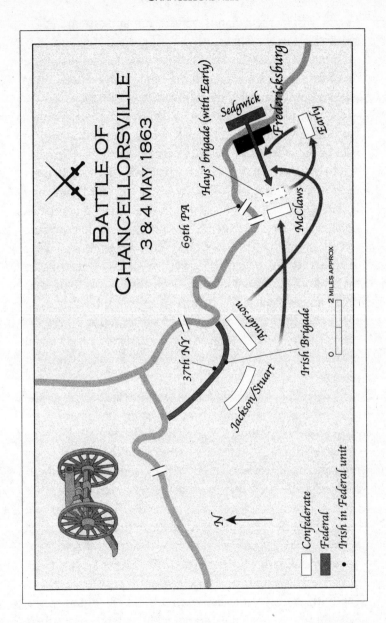

BATTLE OF
CHANCELLORSVILLE
3 & 4 MAY 1863

Fredericksburg

Sedgwick

Hays' brigade (with Early)

Early

McClaws

69th PA

Anderson

37th NY

Irish Brigade

Jackson/Stuart

2 MILES APPROX

N

☐ Confederate
■ Federal
• Irish in Federal unit

troops threw their hands in the air and attempted to surrender, but as soon as they had appeared, Hays' howling mob had disappeared. They had no time to take prisoners, no time to break the momentum of their charge. Even Early, who had been critical of the Louisiana and Irish men's looting in the past, was jubilant. He was alleged to have thrown his hat on the ground and declared, 'Those damned Louisiana fellows can steal as much as they please now.'

Exhaustion was now becoming a factor for the charging mob of Hays' brigade. They reached the third and final Federal line but were quickly stalled by the ferocious resistance of dug-in Federals. As a North Carolina brigade closed in from the rear, Hays' men soon began taking 'friendly fire' from their comrades who mistook their backs for those of running Federals. Soon the grand charge was staggering exhaustedly back down the hill it had so spectacularly charged. So confused and exhausted were the men of Hays' brigade that many of them were later taken prisoner, as they had been unable to retreat with sufficient haste.[11]

While Early's division had pressed their attack from the east, Anderson's and McClaws' divisions had made little progress in the south and west. That night, Sedgwick's corps was able to retreat under the cover of darkness over Scott's Ford and back to the safety of the Rappahannock's northern bank. On the way, they passed the Irishmen of the 69th Pennsylvania, who had had a quiet Chancellorsville campaign, assigned as they were to guard the pontoon bridge at the ford. When Sedgwick's troops had trudged across the bridge and into the blackness of the night, the Pennsylvania men followed suit, bringing up the rear of the defeated corps. The 69th Pennsylvania had played but a small part in the Battle of Chancellorsville, though within a few months their name would go down in American history, as they were central to the most famous incident of the Civil War.

To the north, it took Hooker another day to order his hemmed-in forces, the Irishmen of the 37th New York and Irish Brigade among them, back across the Rappahannock. Another large-scale Federal assault had ended in complete failure. The armies were back where they had begun, camped on either side of the Rappahannock near Fredericksburg.

CHAPTER 11

GETTYSBURG

With high morale prevailing throughout the ranks of Lee's Army of Northern Virginia, the time had come for the Confederates to push their advantage. Once again, they had snatched a most unlikely victory from the jaws of near certain defeat. The war had entered its third summer and the skill of Confederate officers, along with the ferocious fighting of their rank and file, had not only prevented the numerically superior and better-equipped Federal army from crushing them, but had even created an opportunity for the Confederacy to win its independence.

From a Confederate perspective, the war in the west was not proceeding well. The Federal General Ulysses S. Grant was poised at the gates of Vicksburg and his army seemed certain to prevail. Lee knew that should his army win a major victory over the Army of the Potomac on its own soil and threaten the Northern cities of Washington, Philadelphia and Baltimore, peace would be an increasingly attractive option for the besieged President Lincoln.

With that in mind, Lee ordered his army north, with the first elements leaving camp near the Rappahannock on 3

June 1863. By now, Lee's army was reorganised into three corps. Lieutenant General Richard S. Ewell's corps began crossing the Potomac on 15 June, and on 24 and 25 June the corps of Hill and Longstreet followed suit. The Federal army made their crossing from 25 to 27 June. On 29 June, Lee learned that the Federal army was in pursuit. As was typical of an army on the march, the Confederates were moving along parallel roads through Pennsylvania. The threat of a Federal army in close proximity meant that Lee would have to concentrate his forces immediately. He ordered that no engagement of any Federal force should take place before his entire army was concentrated. However, on 30 June, such an engagement almost occurred when a Confederate brigade in search of shoes moved out of a place called Cashtown towards a little town eight miles to the east. That town's name would become one of the most famous in American history. That small Pennsylvania town was Gettysburg.

Upon approaching Gettysburg on 30 June, Confederates under Brigadier General J. Johnston Pettigrew noticed Federal cavalry arriving to the south of the town. Pettigrew was still under orders not to engage, so he withdrew his brigade and reported the sighting to his superior officers. His corps commander, A.P. Hill, did not believe that any significant Federal force was in the area and decided to mount a reconnaissance in force on the morning of 1 July.

On that fateful morning, two brigades of Heth's division, Hill's corps, moved through Gettysburg and about three miles east of the town met with resistance from dismounted Federal cavalry. For approximately three hours, the Confederate troops pushed this small Federal force gradually eastwards until Federal reinforcements arrived and forced the Confederates back. As morning turned to afternoon, the engagement escalated as increasing numbers of troops arrived in the Gettysburg area. Coming in from the north of the town as part of Ewell's corps were Hays' Louisiana brigade and the substantial number of Irishmen still in its ranks. They were engaged at 2.00 p.m. by Howard's Federal corps just north of Gettysburg. The Louisiana men succeeded in driving the Federal opposition before them and through the streets of the town.

To the west, the Confederate attacks had once again gained momentum and were also driving the Federal troops towards the town. With Federals now in general retreat through the town from the north and west, the day was turning out to be a good one for Lee's forces. However, the veteran fighters of the Louisiana brigade knew that further gains could be made before nightfall. As Federal troops retreated onto the high ground south of the town, the divisional commander of Hays' brigade, General Early, sought permission to continue his attack onto the lightly defended hills before the Federal troops had a chance to dig in. However, Early was unable to secure that permission from corps commander Ewell, so as night fell the Irishmen of the Louisiana brigade remained in the town looking southwards at the hills they knew they could have secured. Through that still night they listened to the sounds of pickaxes, shovels and spades echoed along the plain from the hills and ridges to the south as the Federals dug in along their line. Federal General Winfield S. Hancock referred to the position on which they would build their line as 'the strongest position by nature upon which to fight a battle that I ever saw'. It would take some effort to move them.

With the Confederate army gathering numbers off to the north, the Federals constructed their line along a series of hills and ridges south of the town. The line was in the shape of a fish hook running north–south along Cemetery Ridge before looping east–west between Cemetery Hill and Culps Hill. South of Cemetery Ridge were two hills known locally as Big and Little Round Tops. The Federal line did not extend onto those hills on the evening of 1 July and Robert E. Lee planned accordingly.

On the morning of 2 July, Lee planned to attack both of the Federal flanks, hoping to move his forces around the rear of their line. The morning passed without engagement as Confederate officers manoeuvred into position to make their attack. Meanwhile, in one of the most controversial decisions of the entire war, Federal Major General Daniel Sickles moved his entire corps forward from the Federal line. Sickles was not satisfied with his position and, sighting higher ground at his front, he moved his corps onto it without orders from any superior officer. The difficulty with Sickles' move was that it left a weakly defended point on the Federal line in an area which would become known as the Wheatfield and the Peach Orchard. When Confederate troops eventually began their attacks along various points of the Federal left, this section would have to be reinforced, and one of the units called upon to reinforce the area was the Irish Brigade.

By now the Irish Brigade was a shadow of its former self. In reality, it was not nearly big enough to be considered a brigade and might just about constitute a regiment. Indeed, its officers had requested that the old regimental numbers be retired and the brigade reorganised into a single regiment with a new designation, though nothing had come of their request. Meagher had left the brigade in May, stating that he could no longer remain in command of a 'poor vestige and relic of the Irish Brigade'.[1] The controversial Irishman had raised some hackles in Federal circles and rumours of his drunkenness and cowardice in battle continued to circulate throughout the army. A few weeks after his departure from command of the brigade, his attention seems to have turned back to the politics of his birthplace and he was sworn into the Fenian Brotherhood during a meeting with Jeremiah O'Donovan Rossa and John O'Mahoney.[2] In the aftermath of the war, Meagher served as governor of the territory of Montana. In that capacity, he was involved in mustering the state militia to campaign against Native Americans who had allegedly murdered white settlers, but the militia failed to find the alleged offenders. The controversial general's life ended in mysterious circumstances when in 1867, while still serving as governor of Montana, he fell from a steamboat into the Missouri River. His body was never found and he was presumed drowned. Speculation as to whether he committed suicide, fell overboard having consumed too much alcohol or was murdered by political opponents continues to this day. Statues in honour of Meagher were erected in the Montana towns of Billings and Helena. Meagher County, Montana, was also named in honour of the Irish Brigade's first commander.

By the morning of 2 July 1863, this 'poor vestige' of Meagher's once-celebrated Irish Brigade was under the command of Galway-born Colonel Patrick Kelly and positioned to the right of Sickles' former position at Cemetery Ridge. When Confederate attackers swarmed all over Sickles' isolated corps, the Irishmen were quickly moved forward in an attempt to prop up the line. Before they moved out that morning, one of the war's most famous incidents took place when Fr Corby offered the men general absolution. The scene was later described by Major General St Clair Mulholland of the 116th Pennsylvania:

> There are yet a few minutes to spare before starting, and the time is occupied by one of the most impressive religious ceremonies I have ever witnessed. The Irish

Brigade ... whose green flag had been unfurled in every battle in which the Army of the Potomac had been engaged from the first Bull Run to Appomattox, and was now commanded by Colonel Patrick Kelly of the Eighty eighth New York, formed a part of this division. The brigade stood in column of regiments, closed in mass. As a large majority of its members were Catholics, the Chaplain of the brigade, Rev. William Corby, proposed to give a general absolution to all the men before going into the fight. While this is customary in the armies of Catholic countries in Europe, it was perhaps the first time it was ever witnessed on this continent ... Father Corby stood on a large rock in front of the brigade. Addressing the men he explained what he was about to do, saying that each one could receive the benefit of the absolution by making a sincere Act of Contrition and firmly resolving to embrace the first opportunity of confessing his sins, urging them to do their duty and reminding them of the high and sacred nature of their trust as soldiers and the noble object for which they fought ... As he closed his address, every man, Catholic and non-Catholic, fell on his knees with his head bowed down. Then, stretching his right hand toward the brigade, Father Corby pronounced the words of the absolution ... Near by stood a brilliant throng of officers who had gathered to witness this very unusual occurrence, and while there was profound silence in the ranks of the Second Corps, yet over to the left, out by the peach orchard and Little Round Top ... the roar of battle rose and swelled and re-echoed through the woods ... I do not think there was a man in the brigade who did not offer up a heart-felt prayer. For some, it was their last; they knelt there in their grave clothes.[3]

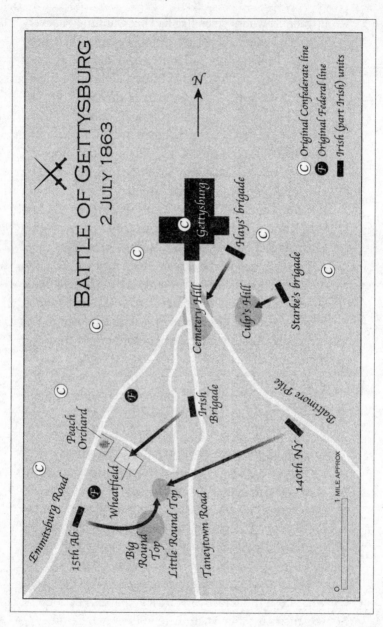

BATTLE OF GETTYSBURG
2 JULY 1863

N

© Original Confederate line
Ⓕ Original Federal line
▬ Irish (part Irish) units

Gettysburg

Hays' brigade

Culp's Hill

Starke's brigade

Cemetery Hill

Baltimore Pike

Irish Brigade

140th NY

Peach Orchard

Wheatfield

Emmitsburg Road

15th Ab

Big Round Top

Little Round Top

Taneytown Road

1 MILE APPROX

Watching this memorable scene were the men of the 140th Pennsylvania. The great bulk of this Pennsylvania regiment were Presbyterians and their regimental historian described their Scotch-Irish descent. One of their number, Private Robert Laird Stewart, who would become a Presbyterian minister, later described Corby's actions:

> The next command was delayed for a few moments and during that interval we were witnesses of an unusual scene which made a deep impression upon all who witnessed it. The Irish Brigade whose green flag had been unfurled on almost every battlefield from Bull Run until this hour, stood in column of regiments in close order with bared heads while their Chaplain priest, Father Corby, stood upon a large boulder and seemed to be addressing the men. At a given signal every man of the command fell on his knees and with head bowed low received from him the sacrament of extreme unction. Instinctively every man of our Regiment took off his cap and no doubt many a prayer from men of Protestant faith, who could conscientiously not bow the knee in a service of that nature, went up to God in that impressive and awe inspiring moment.[4]

If Stewart's account is to be believed, the second day at Gettysburg saw Ireland's green and Orange traditions pray and fight in union with, and respect of, one another. Corby's general absolution of the men of the Irish Brigade left a lasting impression on American history. Today, the reputed site of the ceremony is marked by a statue of Fr Corby standing atop what some claim is the self-same rock from which he gave the absolution on 2 July 1863. However, it has been argued quite convincingly that the absolution was more likely to have taken place several hours before the brigade moved out and at the site of the present-day Pennsylvania memorial, located some 500 yards to the right of the Corby statue.[5]

As the Irish Brigade moved southwest towards the Wheatfield, they were showered with shot and shell by Confederate batteries positioned near the Peach Orchard and could hear all of the noise of the vicious battle that had erupted to their right, but still they went onwards. Upon reaching the Wheatfield, they marched through it and towards Stony Hill on the southwest side, where they engaged and defeated Confederates positioned behind the natural cover of a number of boulders strewn around. The Brigade succeeded in temporarily stabilising the Federal line, but as the situation in the Peach Orchard became increasingly serious, the

Irishmen had little time for rest before they were once again in the midst of a fight for survival. Confederate troops had already broken through at the Peach Orchard and were swarming along the rear of the Federal line. The Irish Brigade was almost cut off, but succeeded in fighting their way out of the jam. With Confederates moving in from both sides, the Irishmen fell back through the 'alley of death' that was

The monument for the New York regiments of the Irish Brigade at Gettysburg.

164

the Wheatfield. St Clair Mulholland, commander of the 116th Pennsylvania, admitted that his regiment had 'encountered the full sweep of the enemy's fire'. In all, the Irish Brigade's hurried retreat through the 'alley of death' cost them almost 200 casualties,[6] approximately 40 per cent of the number they had brought to battle. It was another bad day for the remnants of a once-celebrated brigade. They were not the only Irishmen who met with tragedy near Gettysburg. All around them, a huge battle was now fully under way, and a large number of Irishmen were dying in it.

When the Irish Brigade was beginning their fight in the Wheatfield, further reinforcements were soon dispatched to assist the Federals in combat there. One of the regiments sent to the Wheatfield was the 140th New York Infantry, which had been raised in upstate New York in the city of Rochester. Rochester's Irish population was significant throughout the nineteenth century and by 1850 accounted for approximately one-quarter of the city's total population. Most Irish immigrants in Rochester lived in a tough but affectionately remembered neighbourhood known as Little Dublin. Thus, when recruitment for the 140th New York began in Rochester in 1862, it is hardly surprising that a large number of the men who thronged its ranks were Irish, or second-generation Irish. The regiment even had two specifically Irish companies, C and K, and was led by Cavan-born Patrick O'Rorke. O'Rorke had finished first in his class at the famous West Point military academy and was a respected military strategist. One of O'Rorke's contemporaries even speculated that he would be the future commander of the US army. At Gettysburg, any chance of the Cavan native rising to that position was lost, but his regiment was about to write itself into the annals of America's bloodiest battle.

The 140th New York arrived at Gettysburg on the morning of 2 July. Before going into battle, O'Rorke had given his

Patrick O'Rorke of Gettysburg fame.

regiment a very rare address. He was not known for rallying his men with inspirational speeches, but at Gettysburg he did, calling on 'the file closers to do their duty, and if there is a man this day base enough to leave his company, let him die in his tracks – shoot him down like a dog'. It was with those words ringing in their ears that Irish, German and American men of the 140th went into action on the afternoon of 2 July.

When Sickles' corps moved forward towards the Wheatfield and Peach Orchard and weakened the Federal line considerably, they also left two strategic hills undefended. Those hills were the highest in Adams County – Big and Little Round Tops. Big Round Top was densely wooded and as such was of little use to artillerists on either side. However, Little Round Top was partially clear of trees and the side that could place its artillery on that hill would be in the ideal position to command the entire Federal line. With Longstreet's corps launching a series of staggered attacks all along the Federal left, it was only a matter of time before the Round Tops came under attack.

The first to notice the impending danger on the lightly guarded Round Tops was Brigadier General Warren, the Federal army's chief engineer. He quickly dispatched Vincent's brigade to the smaller hill. Their arrival on its crest came not a moment too soon. Confederate forces were already rolling in from the south, having swept up over Big Round Top. Vincent's brigade managed to halt the Confederate advance. They had the considerable advantage of the high ground but were still under sustained attack from determined Confederates. Warren judged their position to be in

The O'Rorke Monument on Little Round Top at Gettysburg.

need of further reinforcement and quickly found it in the form of O'Rorke's 140th New York, by now on its way to the bloody fight in the Wheatfield. Warren immediately requested the assistance of O'Rorke's regiment. However, O'Rorke was reluctant to follow the chief engineer, as he had other orders from his own direct superiors to follow the rest of his brigade to the Wheatfield. He was under no obligation to take orders from Warren, but he seemed to recognise the seriousness of the situation and after some further coaxing from Warren, he moved his regiment in the direction of Little Round Top's wooded, rocky, eastern slope, arriving just in time.

Just as Vincent's brigade was about to break, O'Rorke's men came out of the woods behind them and positioned themselves along the southern crest of the hill. There was a brief pause for the breathless men on the crest before O'Rorke noticed that the 16th Michigan in front of them was at breaking point. 'Down this way, boys!' he was heard to shout as he dismounted his horse and charged towards the weak point of the line. Moments later, the young Irishman with such a promising military career ahead of him lay dead on the slopes of Little Round Top.[7] Although at severe cost to itself, his regiment halted the advancing Confederates and was soon forming itself up to continue the defence of Little Round Top. Off to their left stood the man who would make the defence of Little Round Top resonate through American history.

O'Rorke's use of his own initiative in answering Warren's request for assistance on Little Round Top may well have saved the hill from Confederate occupation, but it was Colonel Joshua Chamberlain and his 20th Maine Infantry that would always be most associated with the hill. The 20th Maine became one of the Civil War's most celebrated units, primarily because of Chamberlain's extensive writings after the war. Their defence of Little Round Top remains their most famous action and was featured in Michael Shaara's Pulitzer Prize-winning novel *The Killer Angels*. The film *Gettysburg* was based on Shaara's novel and the action of the 20th Maine also featured significantly in the film. One of the lead characters in both the film and the book is an Irish sergeant of the 20th Maine known as Buster Kilrain, but Kilrain is the only major character of Shaara's story who did not exist. He is a composite of a number of real men who served in the 20th Maine. The most significant Irish presence on Little Round Top were the very real Irishmen in the ranks of the Federal 140th New York and the Confederate 15th Alabama.

The 15th Alabama was commanded by Colonel William C. Oates, who described Company K of his regiment as 'an Irish Company'. Perhaps his own Irish heritage led to Oates' expression of some pride in the fighting prowess of this company, a large part of which were Irish-born labourers, with only a few second-generation Irish completing its make-up. When war broke out in April 1861, some ninety Irish immigrants who had settled in towns along the Chattahoochee River enlisted in Company K. The company was notoriously unruly and several of its commanding officers had resigned, having failed to control the Irishmen. At Gettysburg, they were led by Lieutenant William J. Bethune, who experienced less difficulty in exercising his authority, often resorting to the use of his fists to control his command.

On the far right of the Confederate line, the 15th Alabama began its advance towards the Federals in the afternoon, advancing through Federal sharpshooters positioned behind a stone wall at the base of Big Round Top. Passing over the top of that hill, the Alabama men and their Irish comrades continued down and towards the steep incline of Little Round Top. Here, at the base of the smaller hill, they met with severe resistance from Federal troops using the natural cover of the huge boulders strewn across the terrain. The Alabama men tried several charges up the steep slopes of the rocky hill, with the Irishmen shouting their 'gaelic war crys'. Under a baking hot summer sun, the vicious fighting continued into the evening. As fighting intensified and the impregnability of the Federal position began to sink in, one Irishman, Private John Nelson, had had enough. Nelson attempted to flee to the rear, but Oates had already ordered Company Sergeant Michael O'Connor to 'hold Nelson to his work'. As the 23-year-old Irishman attempted a personal retreat, his burly countryman 'collared him and held him to his place until he was killed ... as O'Conner let him down he said "now I guess you will not run away".' O'Connor was in fighting mood on Little Round Top and was also reported to have pushed his bayonet through the head of a misfortunate Federal soldier who had attempted to wrestle the regimental flag from a comrade of the Irish sergeant.[8]

Having repeatedly attempted to charge up the rocky and wooded slopes through the murderous Federal fire and under the heat of a blazing sun, the Alabama men eventually grew tired and demoralised. Yet they still managed to withstand five separate bayonet charges before they were finally forced to flee when the Federals broke the line to their left.[9] Company K and the rest of the 15th Alabama had failed to turn the Federal left-hand flank and retreated back towards the town of Gettysburg, the slopes of Big and Little Round Tops littered with their dead. They had come into direct contact with the most famous defenders of Little Round Top, Colonel Joshua Chamberlain's 20th Maine Infantry.

While the 15th Alabama were attempting to fight their way around the southern flank of the Federal army, another group of Irishmen were attempting to do the same on the northern flank – the Irishmen of Hays' Louisiana brigade, fresh from their victory of the previous day. At 2.00 a.m. on the morning of 2 July they had been stirred from their slumber in the town and marched through the dark of night to a gentle slope near the farm of William Culp. There they lay down as flat as possible, hoping that the slope would provide cover from any fire the dawn might bring. Federal forces were still digging in on Cemetery Hill about 600 yards away from their position. These were the hills they had wanted to take on the previous evening. Now, as they lay awaiting daylight, they could still hear the Federal defenders digging in for a fight.

When the sun's first rays drifted across the sky, they cannot have been encouraged by the sight of the fortifications that had been constructed on the high ground. The hills now bristled with the bayonets of Federal troops waiting in rifle pits behind the stone walls of the slope. They had expected to attack at dawn, but their expectations were a little optimistic. Lee had instructed his troops not to begin any attack on the Federals' right until Longstreet had begun his action against the left, in the vicinity of the Round Tops and the Peach Orchard. As Longstreet manoeuvred his whole corps into position in the south, Hays' brigade lay pinned to a slope under the watchful eye of Federal gunners for the entire day. They could not eat or attend to bodily functions and dared not even raise their heads. Their commanding officers could not withdraw them without exposing the men to Federal fire. They simply waited under the baking July sun for the cannon fire that would signal the opening of Longstreet's attack to the south. That cannon fire was not heard until 5.00 p.m.

The men of Hays' brigade continued to hug the ground while their own artillery batteries opened fire on Cemetery Hill. It was only a matter of time before the Federal cannon began to respond, and as the men still lay as flat as they could, a great artillery duel went back and forth over their heads. Eventually, Federal gunners were able to bring their superior firepower to bear on their Confederate counterparts, and as the Confederate artillery withdrew, the time had come for Hays' brigade to begin their assault on Cemetery Hill.

As the sun began to sink in Pennsylvania's July sky, the weary men of Hays' brigade lifted themselves from cover and stretched their stiffened limbs before advancing resolutely on Cemetery Hill. They moved but a short distance before coming under intensive artillery fire from Federal gunners now positioned all along the heights south of the town. The fading light had its advantages: the Federal artillery fire did not prove as disruptive as it might otherwise have done. Federal infantry were not nearly as inconvenienced, however. Soon the Louisiana brigade and its many Irishmen crashed into the first Federal line at the base of the hill. The Federals fired one volley into the face of the onrushing Confederates, but quickly fled as Hays' brigade cut through their line and on up the hill. The second Federal line, positioned behind a stone wall, offered little resistance to the screaming rebels hollering their way towards the top. The German Federals whom they had already beaten through the town the previous day once again fled before them. More Federals simply cowered at the wall while the Louisiana and Irish men climbed over and continued their uphill advance. They cut through the third line of Federal infantry, in rifle pits about 50 yards from the crest of the hill. By now the brigade had taken some casualties but incredibly was still on the move towards the Federal batteries that crowned the summit.

The Federal gunners at the top of the hill proved more difficult to dislodge. As the Confederate fury approached, they caught up whatever weapons they could find and engaged in a fierce hand-to-hand struggle. By now, the Louisiana brigade had been mixed with a brigade from North Carolina, which had also participated in the attack. One of the attackers later remembered the confusion of the melee:

> While advancing on the main line of works I saw one of our color-bearers jump on a gun and display his flag. He was instantly killed. But the flag was seized by an Irishman, who, with a wild shout, sprang upon the gun, and he too was shot down. Then a little bit of a fellow, a captain, seized the staff and mounted the same gun; but as he raised the flag, a ball broke the arm which

172

held it. He dropped his sword, and caught the staff with his right before it fell, waved it over his head with a cheer indifferent to the pain of his shattered limb and the whizzing balls around him. His third cheer was just heard when he tottered and fell, pierced through the lungs.[10]

The disorganised and furious fight continued until the unthinkable occurred and the Confederate infantry captured the summit of Cemetery Hill. As the Irish, primarily from the 9th Louisiana's two Irish companies, and their Louisiana and North Carolina comrades milled around the spoils of their magnificent conquest, they must have expected that support would soon arrive, enabling them to defend their newly won position. Through the darkness they soon heard troops approaching, though with visibility now limited, they could not tell whether these troops were friend or foe. Three successive volleys convinced them that the men approaching were of the latter variety, and the Confederates were ordered to fire. Upon doing so, the flashes of musketry fire soon offered dim lighting to the lower recesses of the hill. Hays knew the game was up when he saw two further lines of Federal infantry approaching him. As the first wave descended, they delivered a volley only twenty feet away from the faces of Hays' men. Having done so, they seemed to melt away in the darkness before the next and substantially stronger Federal line emerged from the gloom. Hays was now outnumbered and unsupported and had little option but to relinquish his hard-won prize.[11]

On nearby Culp's Hill, another Confederate attack was already failing. To the forefront of that advance was the 10th Louisiana and the three Irish companies it contained. Although this regiment made greater gains than any other, they could not dislodge the Federal defenders. Among their losses that night was Colonel Michael Nolan, one of the leaders of the stone-throwers at Manassas.[12]

As the Confederates made their hasty retreat back down the slopes of Cemetery and Culp's Hills, they were left to ponder what might have been. Had the Confederates held Cemetery Hill on 3 July, the final day of battle would inevitably have been very different. Confederate artillery on that hill would have been able to deliver a devastating barrage all along the length of the Federal line. However, Hays' brigade and his North Carolina comrades were not supported and when the sun rose above Gettysburg on the third and final day of battle, Federal forces still held the high ground south of the town. Lee's attacks on both Federal flanks had failed to meet with their objectives and Irishmen had died at either end of the Federal line. Yet the devastating losses of Gettysburg's second day of battle did not bring the curtain down on Irish involvement; there was still one final day of battle to contest. This time, it was the Irishmen right in the centre of the Federal and Confederate lines who would bear the brunt.

Lee was still optimistic that he could inflict a definitive defeat on the Army of the Potomac at Gettysburg. Confederates could still see a clear road to several Northern cities if they could only break the Federal army and inflict upon it what might prove to be its final defeat. Thus, the Civil War's greatest general was not ready to leave the Federals in command of the field. He began the third day with the same basic plan of attack as the second, planning to attack on both ends of the Federal line once again. However, Federal artillery quickly changed his plans when they opened up a dawn bombardment of Confederates at Culp's Hill. The second battle for Culp's Hill ended at 11.00 a.m. with the Confederates beaten from its crest. Most of the Irish

Confederates in the 33rd Virginia's Emerald Guard were captured.[13]

Lee was forced to change his plans. Now, under the conviction that Meade would have reinforced both sides of his line, Lee planned to attack the centre, which was where he surmised the Federal army was now at its weakest. He believed that one determined push through the centre would breach their lines, divide their forces and allow the Army of Northern Virginia to defeat the Army of the Potomac one half at a time. That was the plan, and in order to execute it Lee chose the only fresh men he had left at his disposal. Those men were the 12,500 of Pickett's division and six brigades from Hill's corps, with the Irishmen of the 1st Virginia standing among them. What unfolded over the coming hours was to become the most famous event of the American Civil War.

At about 1.00 p.m., between 150 and 170 Confederate cannon opened up on Cemetery Ridge just right of centre on the Federal line. Among the batteries pounding the Federal troops was the 1st North Carolina Artillery, under the command of a burly Athlone man, Captain James Reilly. Reilly was nicknamed 'Old Tarantula' as he was 'rough, gruff, grizzly and brave'. He was a veteran of the Mexican and Seminole Wars and ended his military career in a Federal prison after his capture at Fort Fisher in early 1865.[14] As Reilly and his comrades showered Cemetery Ridge with a blizzard of death, the infantry waited in the woods behind the batteries. At 3.00 p.m., the Confederate artillery batteries were running low on ammunition and their fire subsided. As it did, the infantry stepped out from the trees behind them, unit by unit, and began forming up on the field.

Across that field, the Federal Irishmen of the 69th Pennsylvania looked on in awe. One of them later remembered that the appearance of Confederate infantry was actually a relief, as it signalled the end of the intensive artillery barrage and the possibility that the Irishmen of the 69th would be 'plowed into shreds or torn to fragments by the solid shot or bursting shell that had so thickly filled the air a few moments before'.[15] As they looked out at that Confederate infantry forming up, they would not have been aware that the Irishmen of the 1st Virginia's Montgomery Guards were stepping out of the trees as part of Kemper's brigade, Pickett's division. They were close to the right and front of two Confederate lines, consisting of nine brigades stretching for approximately a mile across the field. The Irishmen of the 69th Pennsylvania were ahead and to the left of the advancing Montgomery Guards. Looking out across the field as the Confederate infantry began their advance left quite an impression on one of the 69th's personnel.

> On came those two lines of battle with the precision of troops on parade and the cool, steady marching of veterans, which they were. While the enemy was advancing across the plain towards us, Col. O'Kane, commanding the regiment, ordered the men to reserve their fire until they could plainly distinguish the whites of their eyes; he also reminded the command of their being upon the soil of their own state, concluding his remarks with the words, 'And let your work this day be for victory or to the death.'[16]

The ground across which the Montgomery Guards marched was slightly undulating, which allowed temporary cover from the Federal artillery fire now raking the field. However, no sooner had they marched into a dip than they had to march out again and continue forward into the galling fire. As the gunners poured shell, solid shot and canister fire into the advancing Confederates from the high ground all along the two-mile Federal front, the ranks quickly thinned. The Confederate line narrowed to less than half a mile in width as men closed in the gaps created by fallen comrades. Then, as they passed over the Emmitsburg Road, Pickett's division, with the Montgomery Guards still among them, made their planned manoeuvre. Still the Irishmen of the 69th Pennsylvania looked on, waiting for their chance to greet the Confederates with a hail of musketry. Anthony McDermott of the 69th remembered watching Pickett's division make their turn towards death:

> After Pickett's lines had crossed the Emmitsburg pike, their direction was changed, marching obliquely 'to the left' until they overlapped our right and the 'Angle.' At this juncture two of Cushing's guns were brought from the crest of the ridge in the rear to the wall, and placed in position between the men of Company I – the first company – and commenced firing upon the advancing lines, until their ammunition became exhausted. The gunners then retired leaving their guns at the wall with this regiment.[17]

Pickett had executed this left turn in order for the whole Confederate force to be brought to bear on one part of the Federal line. That part was marked by a small grove of trees, near which the men of the 69th Pennsylvania were situated. Pickett's left oblique was now leading the Irishmen of the Montgomery Guards in the direction of the Irishmen of the 69th Pennsylvania.

As the 1st Virginia and the rest of their brigade made the left turn, their right flank was exposed to withering fire from the Federal line. This was the point at which they began taking their heaviest casualties. Men were cut down like corn before a scythe. John Edward Dooley of the Montgomery Guards later recalled the horrific events as if he were still there that fateful day:

> Here is the line of guns we must take – right in front – but how far they appear! … Behind the guns are strong lines of infantry. You may see them plainly and now they see us perhaps more plainly … Volley after volley of crashing musket balls sweep through the line and mow us down like wheat before the scythe.

Dooley himself was a casualty and heard only the sounds of the final attack as he lay, shot through both thighs, in front of the Federal works.[18] Still, his comrades continued the advance as best they could and soon the chaos resulted in the merging of disorganised brigades. As such, any 1st Virginia Irishmen still standing may have been joined by the remnants of a partially Irish company in the 19th Virginia.[19] On they went towards the little stone wall in front of the grove of trees. At that point, the wall turned inward, creating the 'Angle' that McDermott referred to. The guns of Cushing's battery that had been left in the care of the Pennsylvania Irishmen were quickly captured by onrushing Confederates. In order to make room for these guns, the greater part of the 71st Pennsylvania had been withdrawn from the wall and the two remaining companies were now faced with the overwhelming convergence of Pickett's charge and quickly withdrew. This created a peril for the Irishmen of the 69th, as McDermott remembered:

> When within 20 or 30 paces of the wall the direct march was resumed by the enemy, and shortly after this regiment received the command to fire, and a destructive fire was poured into the ranks of the foe, which staggered him and threw his ranks into disorder.

The fight now became desperate and destructive. For some reason or another the troops on the right of this regiment, and between it and the angle, abandoned their position. The rebel commander Gen. Amistead, perceiving this passed through the ranks of his men, and ran the gauntlet of fire of the first two companies of this regiment, I and A, and passing a short distance beyond the right of the sixty ninth, he stepped over the wall and pushed towards the crest of our ridge and to the rear, followed by his men, who were in front of the abandoned part of the wall, thus imperiling our right and our rear, to protect which the first three companies, I, A and F, were ordered to change front and face these flankers. The first and second companies executed the order. The commander of Company F, George Thompson, being killed before he could give the command to his men, they remained at the wall with the regiment. This left a space at the left of A and the right of F, through which the enemy poured enveloping the latter company and forcing almost all of their men over the wall and into the lines of the Confederates in front, making them prisoners. The adjoining Company, D, having more time, were enabled to turn upon and hold the enemy at bay, using their muskets as clubs, the enemy doing likewise.[20]

This very point in the American Civil War is often referred to as the 'high water mark' of the Confederacy. The battered troops of Pickett's charge had breached the Federal line and victory was glimpsed, however fleetingly. This was the point of the Confederacy's greatest power. Had they driven on from here, they may well have won the war and the world today would be a very different place. However, the Confederate ranks were thinned. Although they had breached the line, they simply did not have the numbers required to drive home their advantage. Soon, Federal reinforcements were rolling in from all sides, and right in the middle of the melee, checking the high-water mark of the Confederacy, was a regiment of Irish immigrants from Pennsylvania. McDermott explained how Amistead led his men into an alley of fire, with the 71st Pennsylvania on one side and the Irish 69th on the other. He also remembered the brutal hand-to-hand combat and the moment the 69th and 71st Pennsylvania regiments turned the tide:

> Corporal Bradley, of this company, a powerful man, was using his piece as a club very effectively, but was overpowered by numbers and had his skull crushed by a blow from a musket in the hands of a rebel. During the mêlée at this point, the other two companies of the right, together with the Seventy first at the rear angle of the wall opposite, kept a destructive fire crossways until the rebel Gen Amistead at this point fell mortally wounded, close to one of Cushing's guns, the muzzle of which he tried to grasp in his fall, but failed. With the fall of this leader the fighting here ended and the enemy surrendered.[21]

The Confederacy had reached its high-water mark and those who had not been taken prisoner now limped dejectedly back through the bodies of their slain comrades and toward the line from which they had started, hearing Federal taunts ringing in their ears as they left, with chants of 'Fredericks-burg' echoing from several points on the Federal line. The Irishmen of the 69th Pennsylvania, who had spilled much of their own blood at Marye's Heights, were likely to have joined in the chorus.

For the Irishmen of the 1st Virginia's Montgomery

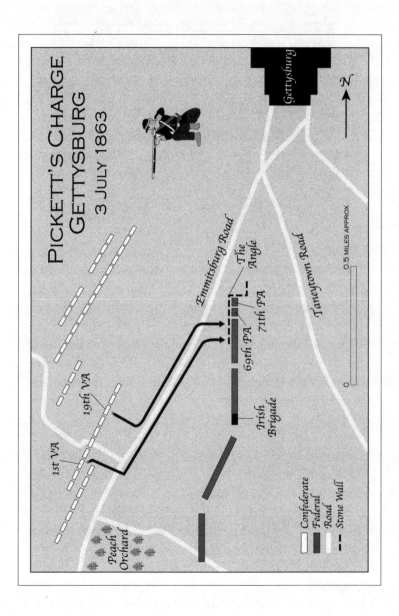

PICKETT'S CHARGE
GETTYSBURG
3 JULY 1863

Gettysburg

N

Emmitsburg Road

Taneytown Road

The Angle

71th PA

69th PA

Irish Brigade

19th VA

1st VA

Peach Orchard

0.5 MILES APPROX

Confederate
Federal
Road
Stone Wall

A view from the Confederate line at Gettysburg towards the Federal line where Pickett's charge met its end.

Guards, the retreat from Cemetery Ridge was a sad one. They had lost one of their regiment's most famous and well-liked members in the shape of seventeen-year-old Willie Mitchel. Willie was the youngest son of the well-known Young Irelander John Mitchel. At Gettysburg, he served as part of the 1st Virginia's colour guard, a highly esteemed role which the youthful Mitchel cherished. His role reflected his popularity among his comrades, who later remembered Mitchel, and the little insect collection the boy had always carried with him, with great fondness. Gettysburg was Mitchel's first and last battle. He fell about 300 yards from the wall, having already been wounded at the halfway point. There were many with Irish nationalist sentiments among the ranks of the blue coats along Cemetery Ridge and it would doubtlessly have saddened them to know they had cut down the son of an Irish nationalist hero.

But they too mourned the loss of a senior Irish nationalist. About 200 yards to the left of the 69th Pennsylvania stood the remainder of the Irish Brigade. They

The 69th Pennsylvania's monument at Gettysburg.

had watched Pickett's charge move across the field and reach its high-water mark to their right. Now they took a few Confederate prisoners, who surrendered themselves rather than retreat under fire, into their line. Although they could not have known it then, Captain James McKay Rorty, who had been detached to serve with an artillery battery on the previous day, lay dead on Cemetery Ridge. Rorty was a soldier of the 69th New York and the second ranking Fenian in the Army of the Potomac.[22] Of course, the 69th Pennsylvania had been at the centre of events and had suffered much more severely. McDermott later wrote about the frightful loss of life:

> The regiment lost all its field officers in repulsing this charge ... There were also four line officers killed and six wounded, and the two lieutenants of Company F taken prisoners. Of the non-commissioned officers and privates there were 39 killed, 80 wounded, and sixteen taken prisoners, making an aggregate loss of 151, while the aggregate strength of the regiment on entering the field the morning of 2 July was 258 . . . It is doubtful

183

that history can show as complete an annihilation of a similar charging force as that of Pickett's Division in that desperate closing scene of the Battle of Gettysburg.[23]

McDermott's reference to an annihilation without historical parallel certainly had a ring of truth at his time of writing. The full frontal assault on an entrenched enemy is reminiscent of what occurred at Fredericksburg, and what occurred frequently during the First World War some fifty years later. In all, over 50 per cent of the 12,500 men who had made the charge lay dead or wounded on the field. Casualties for the Irishmen of the Montgomery Guard are difficult to ascertain, though official reports indicate that casualties for the 1st Virginia Infantry Regiment were extremely high. In all, the 1st Virginia had taken 209 men into battle. Only forty of them waded their way through the dead strewn across the field and back to the Confederate line. Thus, the Irish were centre stage at Gettysburg, where a small Virginia company and a much larger Pennsylvania regiment assured the Irish place at the heart of one of American history's most famous moments.

The Confederacy had suffered a massive defeat. For an army that had always been outnumbered and outgunned, sustaining a defeat of the magnitude of Gettysburg was indeed a hammer blow. Another blow followed the very next day when, in the western theatre, the city of Vicksburg fell to the forces of Ulysses S. Grant.

Chapter 12

Vicksburg and Sabine Pass

In the west, Federal General Ulysses S. Grant had been driving towards the Confederate stronghold of Vicksburg for several months. Vicksburg controlled the middle stretch of the Mississippi River, thus Federal gunboats could not sail past the fortress city without risk of destruction. Downstream from Vicksburg, a second Confederate fortress at Port Hudson, Louisiana prevented Federal gunboats from sailing up the river. Vicksburg was tough to attack from both land and water, as it was located on high bluffs commanding the river below and guarded by the vast Yazoo Delta. By July 1863, Federal forces had already made numerous unsuccessful attacks. In May 1862, Admiral David Farragut moved up the river after he had captured New Orleans and demanded the surrender of Vicksburg, but had insufficient troops to force the issue and returned to New Orleans. He returned with a flotilla in June, but their attempts to bombard Vicksburg into submission also failed. Farragut continued his bombardment throughout July but never attempted a landing and eventually retreated once again.

In the autumn of 1862, General Halleck directed Grant to move against Vicksburg, allowing Grant to develop the campaign on his own initiative. Grant first planned a two-pronged attack that he and Sherman would lead. Sherman would take his half of the command down the river and Grant would advance down the railroad towards Oxford, where he hoped to lure the Confederate army into an attack, thereby enhancing Sherman's chances of taking Vicksburg. However, Grant's advance was impeded by Confederate cavalry raids and Sherman's frontal assault at Vicksburg was repulsed, with many casualties. Now Grant changed tack and initiated a programme of canal digging in the area around Vicksburg. The idea was to transport troops via these newly constructed canals without having to navigate under the Confederate artillery on the bluffs at Vicksburg. A number of canals failed owing to low water levels, Confederate guerrilla operations and the felling of trees across them. Still undeterred, Grant kept up the pressure on the city and his next attempt was the boldest of all.

Grant decided to move his troops along the western bank of the Mississippi and cross the river south of Vicksburg, then attack the city from the south and east. Federal gunboats succeeded in running the bluffs at Vicksburg and moving enough transports to assist Grant in his crossing to the south. A feint attack at Snyder's Bluff and a cavalry raid through central Mississippi by Colonel Benjamin Grierson then drew Confederate troops out of Vicksburg and distracted them while Grant crossed the river.

On 30 April, Grant crossed the Mississippi River at Bruinsburg and moved his forces east until they encountered Confederates at Port Gibson. This small Confederate garrison was easily pushed aside and Grant continued east towards Jackson, which had to be secured in order to cut the Confederate line of communications and supply and ensure that no garrison at Jackson could threaten Grant's flank while he moved on Vicksburg. Meanwhile, Confederate reinforcements already arriving at Jackson were ordered to move west towards Raymond.

As they moved into the town, they were unaware that two Federal divisions were heading in their direction. When Federals were eventually spotted in the area, Brigadier General John Gregg mistakenly concluded that his brigade was confronted by a lone Federal brigade in search of supplies and consequently decided to lay a trap for his foe, using one of his regiments to blockade a bridge on the Utica Road. This regiment was to lure the Federal brigade into a fight before it could cross Fourteen Mile Creek, with his remaining regiments placed in position to spring the trap on the unsuspecting Federals. Two regiments were placed near the lower Gallatin Road, which ran almost parallel to, and just east of, the Utica Road. When the Federals were engaged at the bridge, these two regiments were to swing west and attack the Federal flank. One of those regiments was the 10th Tennessee Infantry, or Sons of Erin.

The Tennessee Irishmen had been imprisoned after the fall of Fort Donelson. We have seen that James Mulligan of the 23rd Illinois reported that a large number of Irishmen from the Tennessee regiment were considering switching sides and fighting for the Union. However, when a list of Confederate prisoners wishing to defect was published at Camp Butler, Illinois on 19 March 1862, only five men from the 10th appeared among the names. The bulk of the regiment was paroled at Vicksburg in September 1862, reorganised on 2 October 1862 and declared exchanged on 10 November 1862. The 10th Tennessee would once again be commanded by Randal McGavock.

As the lead Federal regiment of a column some miles long reached the bridge, Gregg's three artillery pieces opened fire. Soon Federal artillery made its way to the head of the column and began to reply. It was 10.00 a.m. and the Battle of Raymond was under way. While the Irishmen waited on the Confederate left, two further regiments joined in the fight at the centre. The Federals enjoyed a huge numerical advantage, but their lead units were being flanked and they were encountering significant difficulty in deploying the remainder of their force. Now, out on the Gallatin Road, the Irishmen began to swing left, intending to complete Gregg's trap. They moved through the woods between the Gallatin and Utica roads. As the 50th Tennessee emerged from the woods, they were behind the Federals' right flank. From this position, their commander, Lieutenant Colonel Thomas Beaumont, could clearly see the entire Federal division stacked up to his right. Knowing that he was severely outnumbered, he immediately took to his heels and retreated back from whence he had come. This left the Irishmen in a difficult position, as Beaumont's departure left a substantial hole in the Confederate line. As Federals began attacking the Confederate left, it became obvious that Beaumont was gone. Thus, McGavock and the 10th Tennessee were ordered to turn back the Federal assault. As McGavock moved out of the woods, he, like Beaumont, immediately noticed the huge column of Federal forces stacking up against him. Unlike Beaumont, he did not retreat, but attacked. Colonel McGavock now led the charge, and he led his Irishmen straight into the Irishmen of the 7th Missouri Infantry.

The 7th Missouri Infantry was raised primarily in St Louis, Missouri, though the regiment also contained companies from Milton and Clarkesville, Missouri; Belleville, Sumner; and Chicago, Illinois; and even a company from Keokuk, Iowa. The unit was far from exclusively Irish, but the Irish were its principle ethnic component. In all, it is estimated that of some 1,000 men who initially served in the unit, approximately 400 were Irish.[1] These men had seen limited action since mustering into service in June 1861. They had participated in Freemont's Springfield Campaign, three companies of the 7th had fought in several pitched battles against Confederate guerrillas near Kansas City, and most recently the unit had seen some action at Corinth. They had never met another Irish unit in battle, but at Raymond, all that was about to change.

As McGavock rallied the 10th Tennessee and led them towards the onrushing Federal Irish, he suddenly fell dead, most likely the victim of a minie ball. Irish-born Patrick Griffin later claimed to have rushed to his fallen commander's side:

> I was standing about two paces in the rear of the line and Colonel McGavock was standing about four paces in my rear … We had been under fire about twenty minutes when I heard a ball strike something behind me. I have a dim remembrance of calling to God. It was my colonel. He was about to fall. I caught him and eased him down with his head in the shadow of a little bush. I knew he was going and asked him if he had any message for his mother. His answer was: 'Griffin, take care of me! Griffin, take care of me!' I put my canteen to his lips, but he was not conscious. He was shot through the left breast, and did not live more than five minutes.[2]

Griffin was taken prisoner after the battle, but was paroled the following day in order to return to the battlefield and bury his beloved commander. When McGavock fell, Lieutenant Colonel Grace assumed command of the 10th Tennessee as Irishman fought Irishman.

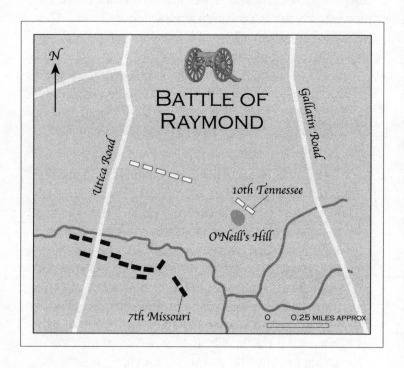

The combat between the two units was intense. In the ranks of the 10th, men like John Ames, John Prendergast and John McElroy continued to fight even after they had been severely wounded. The 7th Missouri was soon reinforced by a few companies of the 32nd Ohio and these two regiments began driving the Tennessee men back. They were rallied and reorganised by the former commander of the 30th Tennessee, Lieutenant Colonel James Turner, who managed to stem the tide. On a hill that would become known as O'Neill's Hill, Captain John G. O'Neill's company were deployed as sharpshooters on the brow of the hill while Turner arranged a line of skirmishers on the slopes below. When the 7th Missouri emerged from the woods below them, Confederate and Federal Irish were once again locked in combat. And the combat was severe. Under a searing May sun, the Irishmen carried only limited supplies of water and much of the moisture in their mouths was used up biting the ends off powder cartridges. The discharge of their weapons would have blackened their faces and added to their overwhelming thirst. These were indeed appalling conditions for the Irishmen.

With O'Neill's men enjoying the advantage of the high ground, they had a clear field of fire across which their fellow countrymen tried to advance. O'Neill's fire was devastating. Soon the men of the 7th Missouri were crawling back towards the shelter of the woods, unable to raise their heads for fear of being picked off by the Irish sharpshooters. Seven of their number were unable to escape, and along with five men from the 81st Illinois, they were taken prisoner by the jubilant Confederate Irishmen. The 10th had avenged the loss of McGavock in brutal fashion. In half an hour of fighting around O'Neill's Hill, they inflicted 150 casualties on their Federal foe without sustaining a single loss themselves. Seventy-three of those casualties were from among the ranks of the 7th Missouri.[3]

The Battle of Raymond ended when Gregg finally concluded that he was greatly outnumbered and withdrew his army from the field, an important action that ensured the Federal capture of Jackson. From an Irish perspective, it was one of those rare occasions where two largely Irish units on opposing sides ran headlong into each other.

Jackson was seized on 14 May, with the Confederate defenders having abandoned the town under the impression that they could not have defended it. Now the railway line to Vicksburg was severed and Grant moved east towards the fortress city, quickly sweeping aside Confederate forces at Champion Hill on 16 May. By 17 May, Grant had almost encircled three Confederate divisions. However, at the Battle of the Big Black River Bridge, they succeeded in escaping towards Vicksburg, burning the bridges behind them. The Irishmen of the 17th Wisconsin arrived at the scene on the evening of 17 May and assisted in constructing the pontoon bridges that kept Grant's army rolling forward. Now all Confederate forces were bottled up in the fortress city and the stage was set for a siege.

The 17th Wisconsin were the first Federal Irishmen to enter the fray. They charged the Confederate works on 19 May and came to within 100 yards of the line. However, owing to poor communications, their brigade failed to advance as one and a withdrawal was quickly ordered.[4] To the south, the Irishmen of the 7th Missouri awaited their call to arms.

Grant's second assault was planned for 22 May. As part of the plan, the 7th Missouri, along with the rest of their brigade, would attack an area known as the Great Redoubt. The Great Redoubt was dug deep into the highest hilltop in

Warren County, Mississippi, just east of Vicksburg. Cannon commanded every possible approach angle from the ground below. In addition, lines of rifle pits surmounted with head logs awaited any attackers who managed to survive the galling cannon fire. One Federal officer described the approach to the position as 'enough to appal the stoutest heart'. Perhaps that was why, when the men of the 7th Missouri heard of their assignment, they wrote letters home to their loved ones and left all of their valuables at the camp. They and the men of the 81st Illinois carried the forty ladders that were to assist them in scaling the bluff of the Redoubt.

With Federal artillery still pounding the fortress, the Irishmen and their comrades reached a little ravine 200 yards short of their imposing target. Here, temporarily sheltered from the fort's artillery fire among the thick cane and bushes lining the ravine's floor, they were ordered to load their weapons and fix bayonets. At precisely 10.00 a.m. they were ordered out of the ravine and advanced towards a bloody date with destiny. Federals were attacking the city all along a seven-mile front before Vicksburg and this small group of Irishmen now led the charge on what was perhaps its strongest point.

As the 7th's green flag moved across the valley, the men who moved with it were under orders to conserve ammunition for close-range fire. They had little option other than continuous forward movement while grape and canister fire from the cannon above ripped through their ranks. Reaching a point about 100 yards from the fort, small arms and cannon fire had actually succeeded in cutting the regiment in two. The commanding officer, Captain Robert Buchanan, had to run from the right wing of his regiment to the detached left wing and order the latter to form up behind the former. Now, as men fell in great numbers around them, the remnants of the regiment moved forward through the bodies of their comrades, often on their hands and knees, until the Confederate ditch was finally reached and they were sheltered from the fire of Confederate cannon. This did not stop the infantry on the heights above from leaning over the embankment and continuing to pour fire into the ranks of the now stationary 7th Missouri.

A new problem occurred when it became apparent that the ladders they carried would be too small to cross the ditch and continue the advance. For one hour, the 7th remained at the base of the embankment, making very little progress in terms of attempting to scale it. Finally, as the dead bodies began piling up, the order was given to retreat. To their credit, there was no panic in the ranks of the 7th Missouri. Buchanan now took it upon himself to allow his men to fire in order to cover their own retreat. They did so admirably and a fighting retreat was made back through the numerous bodies of their fallen comrades. The battle had been fought under the cruel heat of Mississippi's summer sun and a few of the Irish had developed sunstroke, always a serious condition. Six men had planted the green flag on the Vicksburg embankment (one of them was Private Kelley from the 81st Illinois) and all six had been shot down soon afterwards. In all, the 7th suffered its worst day of the war, with six men killed and a staggering ninety-three wounded. They lay on the field beneath the blistering sun for a further two days.[5]

Further north, the 17th Wisconsin had also attacked. Weakened from their efforts of 19 May, they did so at the rear of their brigade. When the attack foundered, the Irishmen were afforded the rather dubious honour of covering their brigade's retreat. All in all, the assaults on Vicksburg cost the 17th fifty-eight casualties.[6] All around Vicksburg, the Federal wounded were dying underneath that cruel sun. As the stench of death rose into the air, one Confederate soldier could only conclude that 'the Yanks are trying to stink us out of Vicksburg'. Eventually, on 25 May, a ceasefire was called and the Federal dead and what remained of the wounded were removed from the field. The assault of 22 May was a failure, but Grant was nothing if not persistent and he would soon try again.

Grant was furious at the casualties that 22 May had cost his army. He needed to come up with a new way of assaulting the town without sustaining heavy losses. North of the Great Redoubt was an area that would become known as the Louisiana Redan. Over the coming weeks, a new plan was put into action. Throughout June and into early July, a series of tunnels was dug and mines exploded under Confederate forces in this area. The 7th Missouri took their turn swinging the pick and shovel throughout the period as mining and blasting moved the Irishmen closer to their Confederate foe. By now, Confederates knew they could not break out and that they could not win this battle. When the end came, the Irishmen were among the first to see it. On 4 July 1863, Confederate forces surrendered at Vicksburg. Captain Buchanan, still in command of the 7th, described the scene as he witnessed it:

> The 7th MO under my command was in the advanced rifle pits one day and while I was at the extreme right of my line close under the 'Pemberton oak.' A flag of truce appeared on the Jackson Road between the 3rd Louisiana Redan and the Black Fort to its left. I immediately commanded cease firing. In a few minutes five officers (mounted) rode towards me led by Gen'l Bowen whom I had known in St Louis and Col. Montgomery who carried the flag. I went forward alone

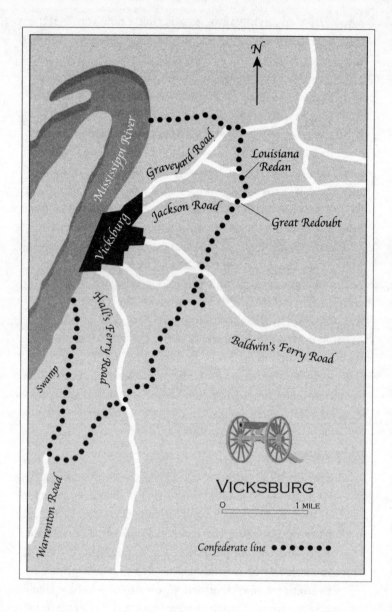

N

Mississippi River

Graveyard Road

Louisiana
Redan

Jackson Road

Great Redoubt

Vicksburg

Hall's Ferry Road

Baldwin's Ferry Road

Swamp

VICKSBURG

0   1 MILE

Warrenton Road

Confederate line ● ● ● ● ● ● ● ●

as they approached and met them about half way between the Oak tree and the fort. After a short interview I sent one of my officers with them to see Gen'l Grant, while I remained with my Regiment.[7]

Meanwhile, Johnson who had been advancing a new Confederate force from Canton fled towards Jackson. One division of the Federal army pursued him, among them the 90th Illinois, which had been mustered into Federal service on 7 September, 1862. It had been raised from among the Irish in various towns and cities throughout Illinois, including Rockford, Galva, Lockport, LaSalle, Joliet, Chicago, Springfield and Belvedere. Company K had the distinction of having been raised across the border in nearby Ottawa. Timothy O'Meara, formally of the 42nd New York, was commissioned as the first colonel of the 90th on the recommendation of none other than Michael Corcoran, commander of the 69th New York at First Manassas. Until November, the regiment had been on guard duty at Camp Douglas, but was then ordered to the front to assist in Grant's first Vicksburg campaign. They first saw action at the Battle of Holly Springs, where Grant had commended the regiment and its commander. In May 1863, they were ordered to join the Federal siege of Vicksburg, but saw little action during the campaign. All that was soon to change, however. Now they pursued Confederate forces in their retreat from Vicksburg.

The march behind Johnson was a dreary and uneventful one for the Irishmen until the evening of 9 July, when the ranks closed to within four miles of Jackson. There, the Irish regiment alone came under fire from a Confederate outpost. The advance was scarcely even slowed as two companies of the 90th Illinois quickly drove the Confederates from the position, allowing the remainder of the division to continue its march on Jackson. In his official report, the Irishmen's brigade commander noted that for this action, 'Colonel O'Meara and the officers and men of his Regiment, the ninetieth Illinois, deserve special mention'. Those officers and men now moved into line under Jackson's guns for the seven-day siege that followed. The 90th Illinois lost only two men, one dead and one wounded, during the siege. On the night of 16 July, the Confederate defenders slipped out of Jackson and across the Pearl River. Federal forces, now growing more ruthless in their attempts to attain victory, burned the town of Jackson to the ground, ensuring that it could never be used by Confederate forces again.[8]

Just days after the disaster at Gettysburg in the east, Vicksburg and Jackson had fallen within a week of one another. The Confederacy was now split in two and it seemed only a matter of time before Federal victory was complete. The Confederacy needed a morale-boosting victory if they were to sustain their war for much longer. Few would have thought that such a victory could be provided by a mere forty-seven Irishmen under the command of a Galway man, Dick Dowling. Against overwhelming odds, the Irish were about to secure one of the most celebrated victories of the American Civil War.

During the summer of 1863, Mexican President Benito Juárez was overthrown and replaced by the Emperor Maximilian. Maximilian's alliance with France meant that a pro-French government now existed south of the Rio Grande. This situation troubled Lincoln because the French had always been supportive of the Confederacy. Now he worried that they might use Mexico as a passage for any material assistance they might wish to offer. Therefore, Lincoln dispatched a Federal force to Texas in order to establish a military presence in the state and to discourage

Maximilian from opening up any form of trade with the Confederacy.

Major General Nathaniel P. Banks led the Federal invasion of Texas in early September. Banks originally planned to lead his forces up the Mississippi and Red rivers into Texas, but low water levels in the Red River forced the expedition to enter the Sabine River from the Gulf of Mexico. At the mouth of that river, in a small, uncompleted fort known as Fort Griffin, stood forty-seven Irishmen of the Davis Guard, 1st Texas Heavy Artillery, commanded by Lieutenant Dick Dowling. These sons of Erin were all that stood between Texas and the Federal army.

Dick Dowling was born in Tuam, County Galway in 1838. He and his parents emigrated to New Orleans in 1846. In 1853, a yellow fever outbreak had taken the lives of the fifteen-year-old Dowling's parents, along with four of his six siblings. Overcoming this tragedy, the orphaned Dowling became a successful businessman in New Orleans. He opened his first saloon at the tender age of nineteen and later owned several others. He also involved himself in high-interest money lending and the cashing of cheques.[9] When war broke out in 1861, Dowling enlisted in the Jefferson Davis Guards, a unit comprised of hand-picked Irish dockworkers from Houston and Galveston.

At 2.00 a.m. on the morning of 7 September 1863, Dowling's sentinel informed him of Federal signals emanating from the blackness at the mouth of the Sabine Pass. Dowling immediately ordered all his guns manned and nervously awaited the dawn. As the sun crept into the sky above Fort Griffin, the Irishmen got their first glimpse of the enemy working feverishly to find a channel up the river. All day, two steamers, assisted by a frigate, sounded the sands for the channel that would permit them access to the river. Dowling's men could only look on, as the Federal ships remained far beyond the reach of their guns. Before the sun went down again, Dowling reported that these three vessels were joined by nineteen other Federal ships of all shapes and sizes. Forces were massing in the gulf and tension was rising in the fort. There was little more to be done but wait for another dawn and the events it might bring.

The Second Battle of Sabine Pass began with the Federal gunboat *Clifton* opening up a barrage on Fort Griffin at 6.30 a.m. on 8 September. The ship was out of range of the Irishmen's cannon, so while cannoneers took cover, the men at the rear of the fort gathered ammunition and made ready their defence. According to Dowling's report, most of the shells were inaccurate and either hissed over the heads of the Irishmen or fell short in the waters at their front. Two struck the fort itself but did little material damage. *Clifton* kept up the bombardment until 7.30 a.m., when it moved further out into the channel. Then, at 11.00 a.m., the Confederate gunboat *Uncle Ben* steamed its way down the channel and anchored close to the fort. The Federal gunboat *Sachem* attempted to engage *Uncle Ben*, but her shells were wide of the mark and overshot the Confederate ship. Once again, the Federal ship broke off the engagement by moving out of range. It was 3.40 p.m. before the Federal ships *Sachem* and *Arizona* attempted to steam up the channel towards the fort. They were accompanied by two other gunboats and eighteen troop transports containing some 5,000 troops.

In the weeks preceding the battle, Dowling's men had been busy placing range markers in the channel. As the ships sailed towards these markers, the Irishmen were able to range their guns precisely. The *Sachem* was the first to experience the Irishmen's devastating accuracy. The entire battery of the fort, consisting of two 32-pounder smoothbores, two 24-

pounder smoothbores and two 32-pounder Howitzers, opened up on the *Sachem*. After only three or four rounds, the ship hoisted the white flag when her boiler was hit. Meanwhile, the *Clifton* was attempting to make her way up the Texas channel and was soon crippled by a shot which broke her tiller and left her drifting helplessly until she ran aground. Beached and unable to manoeuvre, the *Clifton* continued firing on the fort from a mere 500 yards away. She lasted somewhat longer than her compatriot ship and sharpshooters were even able to put some of their minie balls into the fort. Soon, however, the full power of Dowling's six guns were brought to bear on her and the white flag was raised above the decks within twenty-five minutes of her running aground. With two of their four gunboats now surrendered to Dowling's guns, the remaining Federal force abandoned the operation and steamed back towards the gulf. The forty-seven Irishmen captured two gunboats, thirteen heavy-calibre guns and some 200 prisoners without a single casualty from their own ranks. Lieutenant Henry C. Dane of the *Sachem* summed up the astonishing achievement upon being taken prisoner by Dowling. He was quoted as having said: 'And you do realise what you have done sir? You and your forty three men in your miserable mud fort in the rushes have captured two Yankee gunboats carrying fourteen guns, a good number of prisoners, many stands of small arms, and plenty ammunition – and all that you have done with six popguns.'[10]

The Second Battle of Sabine Pass was certainly a major morale boost for the Confederacy. President Jefferson Davis was glowing in his praise for the group of Irishmen who had taken his name. He considered the stunning victory at Sabine Pass as being 'without parallel in ancient or modern warfare'.[11] The amazing victory of this small group became a source of pride for the entire state of Texas. In 1901, a Texas writer brought the incident to fame with a short book, *Brave Dick Dowling; Robert Edward Lee*. He introduced his topic as follows:

> One of the South's greatest victories was won in Texas, and by Texas soldier boys. Sabine Pass, September 8th 1863! Write it in letters of gold. Carve it high on monuments of stone. Grave it on the hearts of the people. A greater deed was never done since the world began.[12]

The legend of the defence of Sabine Pass continued to gain momentum throughout the twentieth century, and on St Patrick's Day 1905, the Dick Dowling monument was unveiled in Houston. The statue of the Irishman was the city's very first public monument.

CHAPTER 13

CHICKAMAUGA AND CHATTANOOGA

After the inconclusive engagement at Stones River, Bragg and Rosecrans had been cautious about moving against one another throughout the early summer of 1863. However, when Rosecrans eventually moved against Bragg, he completely outmanoeuvred the Southern general, so much so that by the end of June he controlled middle Tennessee without having had to commit to a single major battle. He kept up his advance and soon moved into Chattanooga. Confederate forces had been forced to flee the town, as Rosecrans had once again outmanoeuvred Bragg by splitting his army into three and threatening from different directions.

Rosecrans now grew a little overconfident. Thus, when Bragg sent out fake deserters to convince the Federal general of the Confederates' falling morale, he swallowed the bait. He left the three sections of his army isolated and alone while Bragg sought to destroy them one by one. Bragg's plan never came to fruition, as his orders were not obeyed and his chance to destroy Rosecrans' army a wing at a time slipped by. Soon Rosecrans realised the impending danger and began to concentrate his army. The site on which his forces came together was near the Rossville Gap, about seven or eight miles east of Chattanooga on the banks of Chickamauga Creek. The scene was set for one of the war's bloodiest battles. The Irish awaited the carnage.

By now, Bragg was emboldened by the arrival of troops from Virginia under Longstreet and from Mississippi under Johntson, including the 10th Tennessee. On the morning of 18 September 1863, he moved towards Rosecrans' left with the intention of cutting off the Federal forces from their supply base at Chattanooga. As Confederate troops moved north to swing west and cross Chickamauga creek, they skirmished with Federal cavalry and mounted infantry and were joined in this endeavour by the 190 Irishmen of the 10th Tennessee. The Irishmen provided support for the 1st Missouri Artillery Battery as they responded to harassing Federal artillery fire intended to slow their crossing of the creek. The same Irish-born farmers who had made a name for themselves at Raymond's O'Neill's Hill now poured a hail of lead on the Federal artillerists barring their crossing. Curiously, these Federal artillerists were under the command of another Irishman, Colonel Robert H.G. Minty. The artillery duel was eventually won by Confederate forces, who also succeeded in outmanoeuvring Minty using Forrest's cavalry.

As Wood moved his Missouri battery towards the river, the Irish moved with it, all the while keeping up a heavy fire on retreating Federal horsemen. Sustained fire from the Tennessee Irishmen prevented Minty from pulling the planks from the bridge as he went. No Confederate forces could cross the river until Hood's brigade arrived to provide support for the manoeuvre. Hood arrived to the jubilant cheering of Confederate forces. After a brief conference with his officers, the fighting Texan decided on a full frontal assault to force a crossing. Crossing was soon under way, with

Confederate troops, the Irish among them, yelling wildly as they took the bridge. Still in support of the Missouri battery, the Irish now formed part of the lead brigade as Hood stormed south in pursuit of Minty's forces.

Meanwhile, as darkness fell, Federal reinforcements were dispatched to relieve Minty's men. As they pushed up through the ranks of their retreating colleagues, they scanned the blackness for their enemy. At 9.00 p.m., the opposing forces again located one another and a night-time fire fight was under way. In the midst of this confusing episode, the 10th lost their leader, Lieutenant Ted Kelsey. He was replaced by a more prominent Irishman, Robert Paget Seymour, a godson of the Earl of Clanricarde and veteran of the Crimean War. Seymour, an Episcopal native of Northern Ireland, had already gained the admiration of his Irish Catholic comrades, who considered him as Irish as themselves.[1] That night, the Irishmen encamped near Lee and Gordon's Mills, awaiting whatever the morning might bring. They had had a heavy day's fighting, but the Battle of Chickamauga was only beginning.

As the Irishmen slept, one of the war's most confusing battles was taking shape around them. Confederate troops continued to swarm across Chickamauga Creek for the duration of the night. By morning, Major General George Henry Thomas had moved the four Federal divisions of his corps north of Major General Thomas Leonidas Crittenden's corps. The Confederates were unaware of this deployment and believed that Crittenden formed the Federal left. Federal forces were also unaware that large numbers of Confederates had already crossed the creek. Fighting began in the morning when Thomas ordered an attack on what he thought was a small Confederate unit at his front. It turned out that he was actually attacking much larger Confederate numbers than he

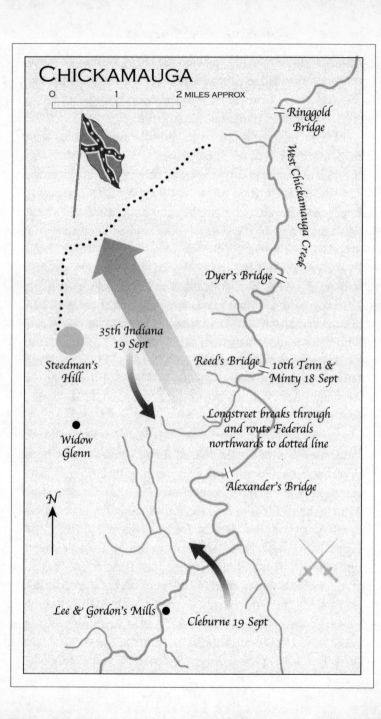

CHICKAMAUGA

0   1   2 MILES APPROX

Ringgold Bridge

West Chickamauga Creek

Dyer's Bridge

35th Indiana 19 Sept

Steedman's Hill

Reed's Bridge — 10th Tenn & Minty 18 Sept

Longstreet breaks through and routs Federals northwards to dotted line

Widow Glenn

Alexander's Bridge

N

Lee & Gordon's Mills

Cleburne 19 Sept

expected and soon a bloody stalemate was reached. Throughout the day, various parts of the Confederate and Federal lines clashed in a see-saw battle as first one side, then the other attacked and retreated. No clear advantage accrued on either side. In the thick of the action were the Federal Irishmen of the 35th Indiana.

The 35th Indiana had arrived near the Chickamauga on the night of 15 September. Looking to the east, the Irishmen could see the Confederate campfires on the far side of the river as they set up camp near Lee and Gordon's Mills. On 16 September, they remained in camp, having captured Privates Donahue, Barrett and O'Donnell, all of whom had been absent without leave. Desertion was now becoming a serious problem and if convicted of the offence, all three would be shot. These three men do not appear to have been convicted of desertion and were readmitted to the ranks. The following day saw mild skirmishing between Irish and Confederate pickets, with no major casualties reported by the Irish. On 18 September, the 35th had another comparatively quiet day. Their pickets clashed with Confederate forces advancing on the river and light artillery fire fell in their camp, but no serious damage was done. On the morning of 19 Septmber, however, the 35th Indiana woke up to heavy firing at their front and remained in the thick of a back-and-forth encounter for the duration of the day. At 3.00 p.m. it looked as though Confederates might finally make the breakthrough to the left of the 35th, so the Irishmen were ordered to the left in support of their heavily pressed comrades.

The desperate battle raged on, but the Confederates made no breakthrough. As darkness crept across the skyline, the Irishmen of the 35th Indiana were ordered back to Crittenden's centre in support of an artillery battery, which involved constructing crude breastworks as quickly as

Major John P. Dufficy.

possible. Major John P. Dufficy, commanding the regiment, later commented that the breastworks 'were of material advantage in providing shelter for the men'. While building them, the men came under a ferocious crossfire from an enemy that now sought to advance on their flank. The fire became so serious that there was no way the Irishmen could hold the position and their brigade commander ordered them to fall back. During the night, they changed their position and were ordered into the reserve behind Wood's division on Missionary Ridge. The 35th Indiana lost twenty-nine men, killed and wounded, on 19 September.

Patrick Cleburne led his division into battle as daylight faded from the evening sky on 19 September. Of the three brigades that Cleburne now commanded, Polk's brigade (Cleburne's old unit) contained the most Irish. The 3rd and 5th Confederate regiments had been consolidated to form a single regiment. The 3rd had contained an Irish company called the Shamrock Guards, and the 5th was itself a consolidation of the old 2nd Tennessee Irish regiment (Walker's) and the 21st Tennessee, which had been one-third Irish. The 5th Confederate has been described as 'one of the Confederacy's great unsung commands', although as was typical of so many Irish units, its commander remembered both their courage and their indiscipline. Polk's brigade also included the 1st Arkansas, with some Irish from Little Rock, Pine Bluff and El Dorado. The 2nd Tennessee (Bates') contained an Irish company, while the consolidated 2nd and 15th Arkansas had quite a few Helena Irishmen in its ranks.

Polk's brigade was not an ethnic unit, yet it was predominantly Irish. At Chickamauga, it went into action with the rest of Cleburne's division.

Cleburne's line started forward at 6.00 p.m., moving through the dense woods and emerging in an open cornfield, where they came under fire from Federal troops behind barricades at their front. Cleburne's dedication to training was telling during this encounter, as his men loaded and fired at an impressive rate. Eventually, with some help from two artillery batteries, Cleburne's command gained the upper hand. The Irish of Polk's brigade were among the first to reach the Federal barricades, although the approach of darkness ended the advance and the Irish and their comrades were stalled once again.[2]

That night, Rosecrans decided to bolster his line by compacting it. Meanwhile, Bragg planned once again to outflank the Federals on their left. However, delayed Confederate attacks met with little success and Bragg changed his tactics again. For the second day in a row, he would attempt to pulverise the Federals in a full frontal assault. Soon, attacks were coming in all along the Federal line. The 35th Indiana met with their first Confederate attackers at 9.00 a.m. Dufficy reported the attacks from that point onwards as 'heavy and unceasing'. At 10.00 a.m. the Irishmen were ordered to move further to their right and make their most significant attack at Chickamauga.

The 35th were to go to the aid of General Baird. Confederate forces had driven through a gap left in the Federal line and were filing into a cornfield to the left of Brigadier General Richard Johnson's division. The Irishmen and their brigade comrades launched a timely attack through the corn and succeeded in driving the Confederate troops from it and through the woods beyond. Having succeeded in addressing this minor weakness in the Federal line, the 35th now formed up on the left of Johnson's second line. From there, they watched Confederates beginning to build up numerical strength at their front, and the inevitability of a full frontal assault must have dawned on them. At 4.00 p.m., the artillery fire began and soon the infantry joined in, raining musket balls into the ranks of Thomas' corps. The 35th Indiana's Irish now stood among them.

The entire southern half of the Federal line had already collapsed. At 11.30 a.m., the newly arrived Longstreet had exploited a weakness created by Rosecrans' plan to leapfrog his units towards Chattanooga. When Brigadier General Thomas Wood's division was withdrawn from the Federal line, Longstreet's men stormed into the gap created and were soon pursuing the entire right wing of the Federal army northwards. Among Longstreet's men were the Irish of the 10th Tennessee. As the Irish regiment steamed westwards, attempting to roll up the Federal right, the first fire they encountered was from the rearguard of Major General Phil Sheridan's cavalry. Sheridan was the son of Cavan immigrants and now, in deploying the rearguard of his cavalry to slow the Confederate advance, he lashed out at an Irish regiment. The Confederate Irish fought back and, continuing their advance, soon had five of Sheridan's cannon in their possession. They assisted their brigade in surrounding a five-gun German battery on Schueler's Hill. In the taking of the battery, several key officers of the 10th's command structure were lost. Captain John Prendergast and Lieutenant Tom O'Connor were both wounded but somehow managed to fight on. Lieutenant Colonel Sam Thompson was not quite as lucky and his wounds left him permanently disabled, while Captain Saint Clair Morgan was the least fortunate, falling dead in the midst of the melee.

Now two-thirds of the entire Federal line were in retreat and Confederates were closing in on Thomas. He was ordered to retreat but could not do so due to the heavy fire he was still encountering. Breaking off and turning his back to the enemy would have resulted in slaughter. Thus, Thomas' command, now including the Irishmen of the 35th Indiana, stood bravely against the full thrust of Confederate forces until sundown, when the arrival of a Federal reserve division prevented Longstreet's capture and the defeat of an entire Federal corps.

Advancing from their fight for the German battery, the men of the 10th Tennessee found some time to parley with 'four very nice looking' Southern ladies who were grateful for the arrival of the Irish at a house which had been occupied by Federal forces. Soon, however, they were back in the deadly business of warfare when the 10th attacked Thomas' command at Steedman's Hill. They were beaten off it in a bloody counterattack by determined Federal troops.[3] Thomas held his line against all the odds. An attack by Cleburne's division, including Polk's brigade and its many Irishmen, also failed to break the Federal line. Eventually, the approach of darkness allowed Thomas' men, including the Irish of the 35th Indiana, to escape the field at Chickamauga.

The 35th Indiana was soon in retreat through the gloomy twilight while still under considerable fire. They retreated towards the town of Chattanooga, where the victorious Confederates would make their next bold move. The Irish had fought well and had taken heavy losses during their stand at Chickamauga. The only blemish on their record was the desertion of Company K's commanding officer, Lieutenant John Duggan, during the battle.[4]

With Federal forces now bottled up in Chattanooga, Confederates laid siege to the town. Bragg positioned troops on Missionary Ridge and Lookout Mountain, from where all supply routes to the Federal army were threatened. With their government desperate to avoid defeat and the capture of Rosecrans' troops, command of all Federal forces in the west was turned over to Grant. Rosecrans was replaced by Major General George H. Thomas, who had made the last stand at Chickamauga. A surprise amphibious landing at Brown's Ferry allowed Hooker to reinforce Thomas' troops with 20,000 of his. Sherman later arrived with 20,000 troops along the same route that Hooker had taken. Among the men arriving with Sherman were the Irishmen of the 90th Illinois.

Meanwhile, Longstreet and Bragg decided that Longstreet should depart with his 15,000-man corps to besiege Burnside's army to the northeast at Knoxville. The departure of Longstreet meant that Bragg's army was severely weakened. When Sherman moved to the northeast, Bragg assumed he was moving to reinforce Burnside at Knoxsville, when in fact he was preparing to cross the Tennessee River northeast of Chattanooga. Meanwhile, on 23 November, Thomas moved his forces out of the town and crashed through the Confederate pickets anchoring his line about halfway between Chattanooga and the Confederates on Missionary Ridge. Bragg did not attack but held his forces in check, not willing to bring on a full-scale engagement over a picket line. As Thomas celebrated a relatively bloodless advance, Sherman prepared to cross the river with the 116 rafts he had secretly constructed. Meanwhile, Hooker was planning his own assault on Lookout Mountain on the extreme left of the Confederate line. This assault saw the first significant action by an Irish regiment at Chattanooga.

In the early morning fog of 24 November 1863, the Irishmen of the 35th Indiana awoke in their camp in Racoon Valley. They knew that a major battle was about to commence

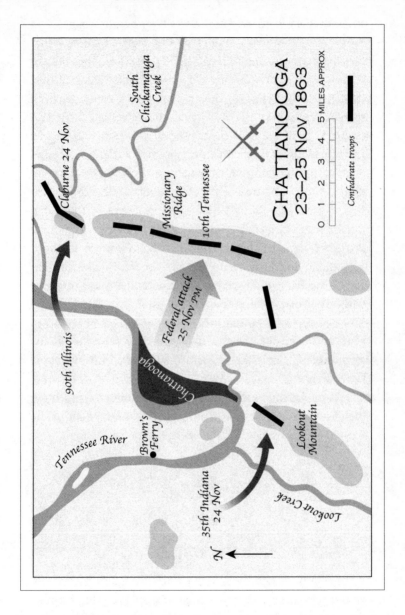

CHATTANOOGA
23–25 NOV 1863

0 1 2 3 4 5 MILES APPROX

Confederate troops

South Chickamauga Creek

Cleburne 24 Nov

Missionary Ridge

10th Tennessee

90th Illinois

Federal attack 25 Nov PM

Chattanooga

Tennessee River

Brown's Ferry

35th Indiana 24 Nov

Lookout Mountain

Lookout Creek

N

when they were ordered to leave all superfluous baggage at camp, a well-known signal to all experienced soldiers that their unit was moving into combat. They moved through the silence of an early morning Georgian countryside, the mist rising from the Tennessee River cloaking their movement in secrecy. Crossing Racoon Creek, the Irishmen were still unaware of where they were headed or where they might encounter a hidden enemy, but soon the orders percolated back along the line that they were to form up into line of battle. Now it became obvious that their mission was to sweep across Lookout Valley, driving ahead of them any Confederate skirmishers they found and ultimately removing the Confederate defenders from the summit of Lookout Mountain. Curiously, Grant had not ordered such an all-out attack; he had merely asked for a demonstration to occur while Sherman crossed the river to the north. But 'Fighting Joe' Hooker saw the advantageous conditions accruing to him and decided that a full-scale assault should be attempted. His decision brought the Indiana Irish into some heavy fighting.

As the Irishmen advanced silently through the morning, their way was peppered with obstacles. Commander of the 35th, Colonel Bernard F. Mullen later reported that:

> The route across the spurs of the mountain was exceedingly rough, deep gorges, rugged ascents and sharp projecting rocks rendering the march toilsome and tedious. Notwithstanding the character of the ground, my regiment, as indeed did the whole brigade, maintained a splendid and unfaltering line.

As they approached the Confederate skirmish lines, tedium would have been a welcome relief. By the time the skirmish line of the Irish regiment emerged from the vale of fog, they were already right on top of their Confederate counterparts and their ranks were hit with what Mullen referred to as 'spattering fire'. As this fire grew more intense all along the line, the Federal advance became somewhat disjointed and the Irishmen found themselves out of line and isolated from their comrades. Undeterred, Mullen did not even stop to fire on the Confederate skirmishers. He knew he had already taken them by surprise, so he simply ordered his men to push on through the skirmish line. They did so and were quickly approaching the outer Confederate line with skirmishers who had not had the chance to reload running before them. As they closed to within 200 yards of the Confederate line, a tremendous volley was unleashed upon them. Mullen simply ordered them to break into a run and charge the enemy line. The Irish now charged headlong at the lightly defended line, unleashing a hearty cheer as they went. They had soon entered the first line of Confederate defences and took them without even firing a shot. Although Mullen noted that the Federal attack had ground to a halt on his left, he continued up the slope and soon the 35th had taken the second line of Confederate defences. In doing so, the regiment succeeded in capturing two Confederate artillery pieces along with several prisoners. At this point, they were ordered to hold what they had and not to advance any further up the hill. The colour bearer of the 35th, Sergeant Jim Somers, then planted the Irishmen's green flag on the second Confederate line.

It had been a most successful morning for the Irish, but as they rested, further Federal regiments galloped up the slope and pursued the retreating Confederates, forming a line in front of them. Sporadic firing continued in front of the resting Irish all day. As the twilight of evening descended, they were once again ordered to the front in order to relieve the 51st Ohio, who had exhausted their ammunition. They succeeded in holding the line until their own ammunition ran out. That night, as the Irishmen slept on the slopes of Lookout Mountain, the defeated Confederates withdrew from the hill. Mullen's report described how they awoke on the morning of 25 November to see the flag of their brigade comrades, the 8th Kentucky, flying from the top of the mountain. What was supposed to have been merely a demonstration had resulted in a stunning Federal success. Federal forces now held the high ground on the left of the Confederate line and a regiment of Irish from the state of Indiana had assisted in taking it.

The 35th had impressed those around them during the action on the slopes of Lookout. Mullen himself was given special mention by Brigadier General Whitaker for 'bravery and the skilful manner' in which he handled his regiment. Major Dufficy's 'gallant conduct' was mentioned in the same list of 'special mentions'. Sergeant Major Powers and Lieutenant Igoe were also mentioned by the brigadier, while Adjutant Gallagher and First Lieutenant Maloney were commended for their 'coolness and intrepidity' and 'daring and courage', respectively.

Meanwhile, out on the right-hand side of the Confederate line, Sherman had successfully crossed the Tennessee and was advancing towards Confederate positions on Missionary Ridge. As he attempted to roll up the right of the Confederate line, Bragg realised the danger he was in. The formidable Patrick Cleburne was dispatched to halt Sherman's advance and his troops were soon holding the line on Tunnel Hill.

The Irishman was with his division boarding trains destined for Knoxville at Chickamauga Station when he received orders from Bragg to return to Chattanooga. As ordered, he took those brigades that had not yet boarded and set out for Chattanooga, where he was ordered to place his command behind Missionary Ridge and act as support for the troops there. He lay in wait until 2.00 p.m. on 24 November, when Bragg finally realised that Sherman had crossed the Tennessee and was attempting to outflank him. Having already detached one of his brigades to Bragg's personal command, Cleburne moved north with three brigades towards where a tunnel of the East Tennessee and Georgia Railroad passed under Missionary Ridge, where he was to form the extreme left of the Confederate line and hold Sherman's advance. Cleburne realised that his under-strength division could not hold such a large gap and immediately informed his corps commander and friend, William J. Hardee. He then attempted to take a small, detached ridge west of the main ridgeline in order to command the flat valley across which Sherman advanced towards Missionary Ridge. Unfortunately for the Irishman, the brigade he dispatched to perform this duty, Smith's Texas brigade, was beaten to the ridge by the Federals and were soon retreating back towards the main ridgeline.

Cleburne was in the process of joining his division to Walker's, south of the tunnel, when he realised the danger unfolding to the north. If Sherman's troops defeated the brigade he had left north of the tunnel and gained a foothold on the main ridge, they would turn the right flank of the entire Confederate army. Now, instead of linking up with Walker's division as instructed, Cleburne decided to leave a gap in the line and send another brigade to the north of the tunnel to check Sherman's flanking manoeuvre. Meanwhile, the bridges over the Chickamauga were destroyed in order to prevent Federals from moving in on his right-hand side.

Cleburne's quick thinking had halted the Federal advance on the Confederate right, but as night fell, the

Irishman worried about a mile-long gap between his and Walker's division. However, Bragg was already ordering his forces to abandon Lookout Mountain on the left and march along the back of Missionary Ridge to reinforce the hard-pressed Cleburne. Cleburne had had an impressive day, but his finest hour was yet to come.

Cleburne did not rest during the night. Instead, he made what he later called a 'moonlight survey' of the land over which his division would fight. The Irishman soon discovered a hill on the northern bank of the Chickamauga that completely commanded his line of retreat. Immediately, he ordered one of his brigade commanders to secure it with two regiments of infantry and a section of artillery. He then inspected and readjusted his defences on Tunnel Hill, ensuring that it could be held against attack from the north and west. He paid particular attention to his artillery placements, which he ensured could command all the low ground across which Sherman might choose to attack. Meanwhile, he had sent for axes, and when they arrived he ordered the construction of breastworks all along his line. Only a brief eclipse of the moon halted Cleburne's night-time diligence. Coming straight towards Cleburne's defences were the Irishmen of the 90th Illinois.

By the morning of 25 November, Sherman had moved 8,000 troops across the river without Bragg being alerted. The 90th Illinois had made the crossing on the morning of 24 November. They had not been involved in the action on that day but were soon called up for the advance on 25 November. They made slow progress through the morning, eventually crossing the railroad in the vicinity of the Tunnel Hill road. All the time they advanced, the Irish were under heavy artillery fire from Cleburne's well-placed guns. They sustained heavy casualties but were grinding out a progress of sorts. Upon encountering the lower slopes of Tunnel Hill, their progress ground to a halt. Cleburne was able to hold the hill against a sustained assault until, at 4.30 p.m., Sherman eventually withdrew. The Irishman had held out against a force that outnumbered his own command by four to one. That night, the Irish of the 90th, along with the rest of their brigade comrades, collected their dead and wounded from the field. Little did they know that their assault had been stalled by the command of a fellow Irishman. Nonetheless, their brigade commander felt compelled to mention by name three Irishmen whom he had found 'in positions too doubtful to admit of explanation' during the battle.[5] Even Cleburne noted stragglers returning to the rear of the Federal line after he had rained artillery fire upon them.[6]

Cleburne's involvement in the battle was far from over. While he and the Irish of the 90th fought it out on the northern end of the field, another group of Irishmen were entering the fray in the centre. At 2.30 p.m., Grant suggested that Thomas move forward into the centre of the Confederate line and take the rifle pits at the base of Missionary Ridge. It was 3.40 p.m. before Grant changed his suggestion to an order and Thomas moved out towards Confederate troops placed on the high ground along the centre of Missionary Ridge. Among those who could see Thomas' forces advancing towards them were the Irishmen of the 10th Tennessee.

The 10th Tennessee had been ordered to man trenches on the slope of Missionary Ridge as soon as Thomas had driven in Confederate pickets in the valley. On the night of 24 November, having spent a quiet day under arms in the trenches, they were moved back to the summit of the ridge. The morning of 25 November saw the Tennessee Irish, along with the rest of their division, come under some sporadic artillery fire while they attempted to work on their defences.

However, the sight of Thomas' forces 'like a huge serpent, uncoiling his massive folds into shapely lines' at their immediate front must have warned them that an afternoon of fighting approached.[7] Work on the defences of Missionary Ridge was at best confused and several difficulties with gaps in the line, disadvantageously placed artillery and a growing disrespect for officers among a group of defenders who could see the problems emerging occurred throughout the morning. Then, at 3.40 p.m., a long line of skirmishers, followed by two battle lines complete with intermittent reserves, began advancing towards the Tennessee Irish and their Confederate comrades. As ordered, skirmishers in the trenches below broke and fled for the main line as soon as they had fired one round into the advancing Federals. Heavy musket fire from the Irish and their divisional comrades on top of the ridge seemed to temporarily check the advance, though in reality the Federals had only been ordered to take the rifle pits below the ridge. They had accomplished that task with unexpected speed and were now considering their next move.

While they pondered, the Irish ran out of ammunition and were instructed to retreat to the downslope of the ridge in order to replenish their supply. The artillery above was supposed to maintain fire on the advancing Federals. Ammunition was replenished, but by the time the Irish made their way back to the ridgeline, the Federals had decided that they would not wait to be decimated from above. Instead, they would take the ridge, and so, without orders from anybody, and much to the annoyance of the watching Grant, Federal troops began charging up towards the crest of Missionary Ridge. They first broke the line to the right of the 10th Tennessee. Soon they were on the left and were now firing into both sides of the Irishmen's division. Disorder reigned and the centre of the Confederate army, including the 10th Tennessee, was soon in rapid retreat. For a time, the Irish regiment helped hold a line about 1,000 yards to the rear of the ridge while Bragg and his disorganised forces retreated across the Chickamauga. The 'bloody 10th' had held out longer than many of the retreating Confederates on Missionary Ridge. Indeed, to their credit, they were the very last Confederate unit to desert the hopeless position and even succeeded in taking a few Federal prisoners with them as they left.[8] Now the attention turned back to the right and Patrick Cleburne.

Cleburne was still successfully holding the Confederate right against overwhelming odds when he heard the news of the centre's collapse. This threatened the rear of his command and plans for a tactical retreat had to be made immediately. He began by dispatching as many vehicles as could be spared over Chickamauga Creek, then placed a line of battle perpendicularly across the ridge to protect the rear. In addition, brigades were dispatched to hold Shallow Ford Bridge and slow the Federal advance on Shallow Ford Road. Nightfall allowed Cleburne to break off the fight at his front and retreat over the Chickamauga after as series of small attacks pushed the Federals hard enough to secure his escape. Cleburne's troops burned the bridges over the Chickamauga as they went. The Cork man had performed admirably at Chattanooga – he had rescued the right wing of the Confederate army. Now he was about to rescue the entire force.

While Bragg attempted to escape over the Chickamauga, somebody had to slow the Federal pursuit. The man chosen for that job was one of the few Confederate commanders who put in an outstanding performance at Chattanooga: Patrick Cleburne. The following day, Cleburne met with Bragg amidst all the confusion of a fleeing army over which the latter had little control. It was during this meeting that Bragg allegedly 'threw his face in his hands and wept like a child and told Gen. Cleburne to guard his rear or the whole army would be lost'. The cooler and more collected Irishman took to the task with relish.

Bragg's shattered army reached Graysville on 26 November. Cleburne still provided the rearguard and he pushed on towards Ringgold. A natural gap formed between the hillsides below Ringgold. Bragg ordered Cleburne to hold that gap and check the advancing Federals there. On the morning of 27 November, Cleburne surveyed the gap. Placing his defences among the tree-lined slope in the darkness of the morning, Cleburne awaited his Federal foe. It was not long before 'Fighting Joe' Hooker's corps trooped into the gap and were most surprised to find Cleburne's division awaiting them. Hooker tried to use his superior numbers to outflank Cleburne on the left and right, but the Confederates held on stubbornly for five hours, until the last of Bragg's wagons and artillery had made their escape further south. Cleburne had rescued the Army of Tennessee and received hearty gratitude from the Southern Congress for his trouble.

Cleburne's military skills were now beyond question, yet the Irishman's popularity was about to dwindle. In early 1864, weary of being outnumbered by Federal foes, he called upon the leaders of the Army of Tennessee to offer slaves their freedom in exchange for military service. His request was met with extreme hostility by the higher echelons of the Confederacy, including Jefferson Davis himself. Cleburne had served the Confederacy admirably, but his suggestion, and the fact that he was Irish and not a West Point graduate, effectively cost him any chance of further promotion.

CHAPTER 14

THE HOME FRONT

Following their comprehensive defeat at Gettysburg, Lee's Army of Northern Virginia retreated back across the Potomac. Lee's ranks were thinned by the battle in Pennsylvania and were further eroded when much of Longstreet's corps were detached in order to assist in the western theatre. Now Lee commanded approximately 50,000 men against the Army of the Potomac's 100,000. Although severely outnumbered, the Southern general still sought to take the offensive. Thus, when he learned that two Federal corps had been detached to assist Grant at Chattanooga, Lee again moved his army northwards. Once again, the Army of Northern Virginia crossed the Rappahannock, with the Army of the Potomac, now under the command of Meade, falling back as Lee continued his pursuit. On 14 October 1863, the first action of the pursuit occurred when General A.P. Hill sent two of his brigades into an action, which he thought would trap a Federal corps. He was wrong, and instead it was three Federal divisions that ambushed and butchered his two brigades at an action generally known as Bristoe Station.

Lee continued to pursue Meade until 17 October, when the approach of colder weather, the length of his supply line and the entrenched Federal position along the Centerville–Chantilly ridge were enough for him to decide that discretion was the better part of valour. Lee turned tail and once again headed south. Federal cavalry attempted to follow him, but were ambushed and destroyed by Jeb Stuart's Southern cavalry. With Lee now on the back foot, the cat-and-mouse game continued as Meade began to pursue him. Lee's army entrenched on the banks of the Rappahannock and awaited the arrival of Meade. However, Meade attacked at night near a place called Kelly's Ford. The surprise night-time attack succeeded in forcing the Army of Northern Virginia to retreat back across the Rapidan River in the direction of the Wilderness. Meade followed them to the edge of the Wilderness. However, his delay in crossing the Rapidan had been long enough for Lee's men to entrench their position near Mine Run. Now, the Army of Northern Virginia lay behind seven miles of earthworks, with cannon placed ideally in order that their arcs of fire intersected.

Meade toyed with the idea of attacking and for a while felt he could break Lee's line. He elected to attempt an attack on 1 December, but when the day dawned he decided that the plan was no longer feasible. Meanwhile, Lee had planned his attack for 2 December, but when the sun rose on that date, the Confederate general found that his foe had already left. With all the manoeuvring of the autumn of 1863 having produced few tenable results, both armies entered their winter camps. The year 1864 would dawn on a country still at war with itself. For the Irish, however, the war was considerably less popular than it had been.

The losses of the Irish Brigade at Antietam, Fredericksburg and now Gettysburg had impacted heavily on the Irish population of Northern cities. While the Irish Brigade may have received a greater proportion of press coverage, other

Irish units were also heavily cut up by the ceaseless fighting. No doubt many Irishmen in non-ethnic units had also lost their lives. Like other immigrant groups, the Irish were among the poorest people in America. Now many homes had lost their primary breadwinners to a war that was not of their making. To add insult to injury, the Federal government introduced a draft scheme that seemed to target the poor, and thus the Irish.

The Draft Act was enacted by Congress on 3 March 1863. However, it was 13 July, in the immediate aftermath of Gettysburg, that the Act began to cause problems. Under its provisions, all men between the ages of twenty and thirty-five, along with all unmarried men between thirty-five and forty-five, were eligible for military duty. The names that would be conscripted were to be decided by a lottery draw in each congressional district. However, those men whose names were drawn had two options available to them if they wished to avoid military service. They could present an 'acceptable substitute' to go in their stead, or hand over $300 to assist in funding the Federal war effort. Quite clearly, these opt-out clauses discriminated against the poorest in society. The Irish immigrant was not likely to have $3 to spare, never mind $300. In addition, it was not likely he could secure a substitute as easily as a wealthier man who could pay for one. The Act was flawed and discriminated against America's poorest people, and recent Irish immigrants fell into that category.

The Irish were not slow to come up with inventive ways of avoiding the draft. Some wore broad hats and declared themselves Quakers, claiming that they could not fight the war as it conflicted with their religious beliefs. Others flocked to British embassies and consulates demanding citizenship of the United Kingdom, which would exempt them from the draft.[1] However, it was the New York Irish who objected most vociferously and violently to the Draft Act.

When names were first drawn on Friday 10 July, all remained quiet. For the duration of the weekend it must have seemed like the draft would go ahead as planned. Then, on the evening of 13 July, a paving slab came crashing through the draft office window in the 9th Congressional District. This was the opening salvo in one of American history's worst riots, the New York Draft Riots of 1863. The draft office was soon on fire and the riot spread along the streets of Upper Manhattan. The police were completely outnumbered and unable to control the mob and soon many police stations were in flames. The offices of the *New York Tribune* also fell to arsonists. The *Tribune* was seen as a pro-Republican newspaper and the streets were wild with rumour that Republican congressional districts did not have the same draft quotas as their democratic counterparts.

Soon African Americans attempting to walk the streets became victims of a mob now completely out of control. Irish and other European immigrants saw freed slaves as serious competition for low-paid jobs and by that time they resented being asked to fight a war that would free a whole new labour force to threaten their jobs. They vented their frustration on the black population of New York and thirteen African Americans lost their lives in the violence. The first African American victims were a fruit vendor and a nine-year-old boy who were attacked on the corner of Broadway and Chambers Street. In addition, the Colored Orphan Asylum on Fifth Avenue was razed to the ground as soon as the mob had looted as much of its content as they could carry. Leslie M. Harris has described the week of appalling violence doled out to the black community:

> Throughout the week of riots, mobs harassed and

sometimes killed blacks and their supporters and destroyed their property. Rioters burned the home of Abby Hopper Gibbons, prison reformer and daughter of abolitionist Isaac Hopper. They also attacked white 'amalgamationists', such as Ann Derrickson and Ann Martin, two women who were married to black men; and Mary Burke, a white prostitute who catered to black men. Near the docks, tensions that had been brewing since the mid-1850s between white longshoremen and black workers boiled over. As recently as March of 1863, white employers had hired blacks as longshoremen, with whom Irish men refused to work. An Irish mob then attacked two hundred blacks who were working on the docks, while other rioters went into the streets in search of 'all the negro porters, cartmen and laborers ... they could find.' They were routed by the police. But in July 1863, white longshoremen took advantage of the chaos of the Draft Riots to attempt to remove all evidence of a black and interracial social life from an area near the docks. White dockworkers attacked and destroyed brothels, dance halls, boarding houses, and tenements that catered to blacks; mobs stripped the clothing off the white owners of these businesses.[2]

It was a peculiar coincidence that one of those charged with implementing the draft in New York was himself of Irish extraction. Robert R. Nugent of the Irish Brigade served as assistant provost marshal of the city, charged with implementing the draft, while he recovered from wounds received at Fredericksburg. When violence broke out, his home was burned to the ground by the mob. Nugent was also centrally involved in meeting the violence of his Irish countrymen with the more savage violence of the Federal government.

Soon, troops were being moved from Pennsylvania towards New York and desperate measures were implemented in order to take back the streets. Being one of the senior military commanders in New York, Nugent was involved in restoring law and order from the beginning. On 13 July, he was placed in command of all regular troops in the city, subject to the orders of Major General Sandford. The following morning, he was placed under the command of General Brown, who volunteered his services in the exceptional circumstances. Troops rolled in from points near and far and the situation was brought under control by 16 July. Troops arriving in the city were well armed and did not hesitate to fire on the rioters. Assisting them were scores of Irish policemen.

The death toll of the New York riots is unknown. The most quoted estimate is Cook's, of 100 civilians killed and 300 injured. Fifty buildings were burned to the ground, including two Protestant churches. The monetary cost of the damage to the city itself was in the vicinity of $1.5 million.[3] The Irish had made their objection to the draft and their lack of support for the war abundantly clear. Future recruitment of Irish and Irish-Americans would be a very difficult task. This led to a loss of Irish ethnicity among many of the units already in the field, who had to replenish their ranks from somewhere, and by mid-1863, Irish units were not very fussy about the nationality of replacements for their fallen comrades. Thus, while they maintained a high proportion of Irishmen among their ranks, they were now far from exclusively Irish.

Support of the war among Irish communities in Northern cities had been dwindling for some time before coming to a head during the draft riots. Susannah Ural Bruce has noted examples of declining Irish support for the war effort as early as the autumn of 1861, after the great romantic rush to war was stalled at Manassas. Concerns regarding the promotion of Irish officers (or lack thereof) within the army and their lack of access to Roman Catholic chaplains were then expressed. Prejudices against, and negative stereotyping of, the Irish may well have given rise to further tensions between the Irish community and the Americans for and with whom they fought. It is even possible that the mysterious disbandment of the all-Irish 14th Massachusetts was owing to concerns in that state at the number of Irish regiments springing up in the army. In these early days, allegations of the underfunding and consequent under-equipping of Irish units also circulated around the campfires.[4] Even so, prominent Irish-Americans like Meagher and Corcoran still supported the war and thus Irish opinion could, at best, be considered mixed.

Praise of the Irish Brigade, the 69th Pennsylvania and the 9th Massachusetts, for their ferocious fighting in the Peninsula Campaign seemed to restore the pride of the Irish-American community in their fighting men. Nonetheless, as news of the appalling losses of Irish regiments engaged on the peninsula began to filter through, the Irish communities of the Northern cities began to question the ways in which Irish regiments were used during combat. Although the Irish were proud of their countrymen's record in battle, they were not overly anxious to commit more of their men to early graves. After a number of newspaper reports failed to mention the parts played by Irish regiments in various actions, many Irish people began to feel that their sacrifices were not appreciated, and as such, in July 1862, Meagher encountered significant difficulty in recruiting more Irishmen for his brigade. However, there was one significant factor that may have contributed to Meagher's difficulty and should not be overlooked: the re-emergence of Michael Corcoran and his recruitment of another Irish brigade.

We have already seen that Corcoran had led the 69th New York Volunteers at the First Battle of Manassas. Taken prisoner in the aftermath of that battle, Corcoran was involved in an event known as the Enchantress Affair, which threatened the execution of captured Confederate privateers by the Federal government. The Confederacy retaliated by threatening to execute Federal prisoners drawn by lot. Corcoran was one of those who faced this sentence. In the end, however, no executions of prisoners on either side occurred and Corcoran was offered parole on condition that he pledged never again to take up arms against the Confederacy. The Irishman would make no such pledge and thus did not secure release until he was exchanged for Confederate prisoners in August 1862. Upon returning to New York, Corcoran's refusal to accept parole as well as his involvement in the Enchantress Affair made him the toast of the town. When addressing the crowd from a hotel balcony in the city, he pledged to recruit another fighting force and return to the front. All the media attention that focused on Corcoran probably assisted in the recruitment of his unit at the expense of Meagher's. Once again, Corcoran targeted the Irish community for recruitment, appealing to them by requesting that they help maintain the US as an asylum for Irish political refugees and in the process receive the military training that might one day help them free their own homeland.[5] Within six weeks, he had four regiments of 2,500 Irishmen ready to join the fight under his command. The Corcoran Legion was born.

Despite the increasing Irish disillusionment with the war, some still felt they could do some service to their homeland as well as their own community. The carnage at Antietam changed all that, however. On the home front, rumours of Meagher's incompetence began to spread. In addition,

One of the recruitment posters for Corcoran's Legion.

Lincoln's Emancipation Proclamation in the aftermath of the Maryland encounter was not greeted enthusiastically by Irish people, who would now have to compete with African Americans in the labour market. The president's subsequent dismissal of George McClellan served only to anger the Irish further. McClellan might have been slow, but at least he demonstrated some regard for the lives of his men. The smashing of their once-proud brigade against the wall at Fredericksburg removed any remnants of support for the war among the Irish population of the Northern states.

Curiously, the story was a little different for their Southern counterparts. Irish immigrants living in the South had had a different experience from their countrymen up north. The persecution of Know Nothing politics simply had not been as severe in the South, where that section had never held any real political power. Indeed, some Southerners had begun to equate Know Nothing politics with abolition. In addition, the Irish found themselves supporting the Democratic Party, something which they had in common with their white neighbours. Even Meagher noted that there were 'no convent-burners, no addlepated ranters, no Know-Nothings' in the South. The Roman Catholic hierarchy's acceptance of their minority status and the adoption of a low-key policy in the South may also have had something to do with native Southerners' tolerance of Irish immigrants.[6] Irish opposition to the emancipation of slaves was also much more at home in the South than the North. In short, the Irish of the South shared many of the political beliefs of their white neighbours. As they had never been persecuted to the same extent as the Irish in the North had been, it was natural that they lent their support to the cause of the South. Those Republicans among them could justify fighting against the Republican government by pointing out that they were freeing a small nation from the aggression of a foreign power. This was something that, in their minds, paralleled the Republican struggle in Ireland. Of course, as time went on, the Irish in the South also suffered because of the war. There is no doubt that many of them would have begun to disagree with the continuance of the struggle, though they never expressed their disagreement publicly. It is fair to say that although the Southern states contained a much smaller Irish population than their Northern counterparts, the Irish population was generally more supportive of their neighbours' war effort than was the case in the North.[7]

Back in Ireland, support for the war was limited to idealistic Fenians who argued that the military training of Irishmen in America would be of benefit to an Irish rebellion against British authority. Other Fenians then argued about the rights and wrongs of either side. Some felt that the American republic should be defended, while others believed Northern aggressors should be driven from the South. Eventually, Fenians bemoaned the mounting Irish casualties, considering it tragic that these men fell while not in the service of Ireland.

In Ireland in general, the rising casualty list is what most influenced people's thinking on the war raging across the Atlantic. Irish newspapers expressed some pride in their countrymen distinguishing themselves on the battlefields of America. After the First Battle of Manassas, the *Waterford News* spoke of Waterford's pride in the glory that Meagher had won for himself. Meanwhile, the *Irishman* praised the Fighting 69th's action at Manassas and contrasted it with the native regiments, who 'ran home to their mother's apronstrings'. However, other publications, like the *Catholic Telegraph* and the *Cork Examiner*, expressed their horror at the loss of Irish life in a foreign war. After Fredericksburg, criticism of the Federal war effort became more commonplace in Ireland. Joseph Hernon Jnr has noted that:

> As the war dragged on, the Irish public became increasingly outspoken advocates of peace. It was the North, in their opinion, that was on the offensive; and it was in Northern armies that most Irishmen were dying and with little respect. Upon the North, then, the Irish placed the onus for continuation of the conflict.[8]

The introduction of the draft was the final straw for many people in Ireland and pro-Southern sympathies began to spill over in the nationalist media. The *Nation* commented:

> Not an Irishman liable to the conscription will be left behind by the military authorities. Irishmen are good fighting material … and so they will be drafted off to die by sickness and the sword, in the vain attempt to subjugate the people of the Southern States.[9]

With such anti-draft sentiments simmering in Ireland, it was little wonder that most newspapers did not unequivocally condemn the New York riots. Instead, the Irish media reacted to the horrific events in New York by generally sympathising with the grievances of the rioters, if not with their methods. Ireland was against the war and against the involvement of Irishmen, so it was not surprising that the island also reacted with some hostility towards the recruitment of any Irishmen on their native shore.

As early as the autumn of 1861, a Dublin newspaper was reporting the presence of Federal recruitment officers in Ireland, most likely targeting the members of recently disbanded Irish militia. However, the general level of poverty in Ireland meant that thousands of potential emigrants were unable to afford their passage to America. American consuls in Galway and Dublin turned away thousands of applicants who promised enlistment in the Federal army in exchange for their passage to America, with American diplomats citing their unwillingness to break the terms of the Foreign Enlistment Act for their refusal. (The Foreign Enlistment Act was a British Act of Parliament which sought to regulate the activities of British and Irish mercenary troops.)

In 1863, the economic climate improved and Irish people began to flock to America, fearing that Britain might bar their way if they did not leave soon. With this increased traffic came increased reportage of Federal recruiting in Ireland. Although many of these reports were little more than rumour, there is some evidence of a low-key American effort to recruit Federal soldiers in Ireland. In October 1863, a former Dublin shop assistant wrote to his one-time employer:

> Sorry I am and that to the heart that I should become the dupe of a Federal recruiting agent, who does not reside far from the old and welcome home of 70 Thomas Street. I am not the only one. You will find young fellows leaving the finest situations in all parts of Ireland foolishly led to believe the falsifying

statements of the Federal agents. They are enlisting young men every day. In fact they are coming out here in thousands and the moment they land they are drafted to the battle field where danger mostly stands. I enlisted in Dublin on the 23rd day of June '63 in the New York Engineers. I received a bounty of 150 dollars which amounts to £30 in English currency.[10]

In 1864, two incidents of alleged Federal recruiting in Ireland brought the issue to a head. In November 1863, a Federal warship, the *Kearsage*, left Cobh (then Queenstown) with sixteen Irishmen on board. While the ship sailed for Brest, Confederate commercial agents in Cork heard of the embarkation and immediately made the British authorities aware of same. Contacts between British and American authorities resulted in the return of the men to Cobh in December. In March 1864, six of the sixteen pleaded guilty to offences against the Foreign Enlistment Act. Now Federal recruitment in Ireland was a proven reality. As if that were not enough, another famous incident occurred around the same time when Patrick Finney was arrested for recruiting in Loughrea, though he was subsequently released owing to lack of evidence. However, it soon became apparent that Finney was recruiting men in Ireland to work for certain companies in America. Upon arriving in America, many of these men found that their jobs did not exist and they were recruited, many of them under some duress, into the Federal army.

Condemnation of Federal recruiting in Ireland came from all sections of Irish society. The only dissenting voice came from the nationalist radical paper, the *United Irishman*, which still encouraged Irish enlistment in an army that was being used to defend a republic that could offer Irishmen freedom from British tyranny. The Fenian paper, the *Irish*

People, disagreed, encouraging all Irishmen to serve their country by remaining at home.[11]

Irish people on both sides of the Atlantic had grown weary of the bloodshed, but the war was far from over. Irishmen on both sides still had some of their bloodiest days ahead of them. A new phase of the war began when Ulysses S. Grant took command of Federal forces and began a policy of all-out, non-stop attack, beginning with his overland campaign of 1864.

CHAPTER 15

THE OVERLAND CAMPAIGN

After the indecisive manoeuvring of the eastern armies during the winter of 1863–64, the Federal government once again changed command of its military forces. This time the man they chose had already forged a reputation for hard fighting in the western theatre: Lieutenant General Ulysses S. Grant.

Small in stature and with a self-destructive alcohol problem, Grant was described by one of his contemporaries as looking like a man who had 'determined to drive his head through a brick wall and was just about to do it'.[1] His temperament, however, suited the war that was coming. Grant was determined and was not frightened by bloodshed, and his ruthless streak drove the Federal army to ultimate victory in a vicious war of attrition. On 12 March 1864, Grant was made General-in-Chief of the Armies of the United States. He would concentrate his own efforts in the eastern theatre, taking command of the Army of the Potomac, while he delegated command in the west to Sherman.

The plan was simple – Federal forces would go on an all-out offensive in both theatres, throwing everything they had at the outnumbered and outgunned Confederates. When success occurred in the east or the west, Sherman or Grant would assist the other in finishing the war. Grant's determination to use his numerical advantage was not good news for the men under his command. The new commander was not afraid of casualties and his campaigns were characterised by much less caution than those of his predecessors. The Corcoran Legion had enjoyed a fairly peaceful war since being mustered into service. But soon these four Irish regiments would move towards the front, just in time for more bloodletting.

On 4 May 1864, Grant began his advance against Lee. He hoped to utilise the same route as Hooker by moving the Army of the Potomac through the Wilderness around Chancellorsville. At the same time, he ordered Major General Ben Butler to move his Army of the James up the Yorktown Peninsula, creating a diversionary threat to Richmond. However, Lee once again moved faster than his Federal counterpart and brought Grant to battle before he had cleared the Wilderness. This encounter lasted three blood-soaked and confusing days. It was known as the Battle of the Wilderness and once again Irishmen played a significant part in the violence.

The Battle of the Wilderness opened on 5 May when Lee sent two corps forward to engage Grant before he could exit the Wilderness and bring his superior artillery to bear on Lee's vastly outnumbered forces. Soon Ewell's corps met with the Federal V Corps, including the Irishmen of the 9th Massachusetts.

The men of the 9th were moved into the line of battle at noon. Skirmishers had already detected the presence of Ewell's corps and were surprised to find Confederates advancing through the Wilderness. The 9th's brigade would support two others of their division as they advanced towards

THE OVERLAND CAMPAIGN

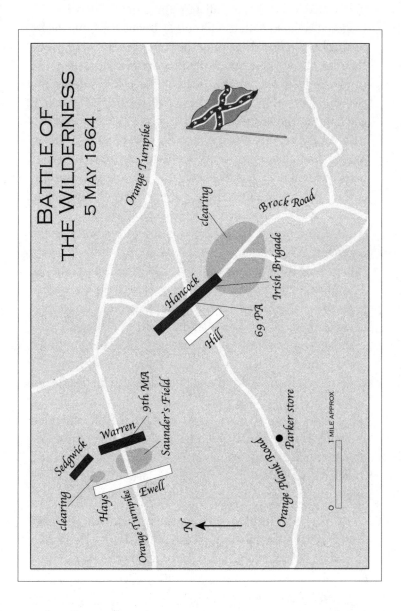

239

the Confederates. About half a mile into the Wilderness, the Irishmen collided with Ewell's corps, driving the Confederate skirmishers before them until they emerged in a 'valley like clearing of several acres'. Now they were under heavy fire from Confederates in the trees at the other side of the clearing. The 9th's commander, Colonel Patrick R. Guiney, was among the wounded at this point. The Boston-born Irish-American later wrote to his wife to express his pride at having had the opportunity to 'shed my blood for our beloved Republic'.[2] His men were now in the maelstrom and it is doubtful that any had time for pride in the Republic. Survival was much more likely the order of the day.

As Lieutenant Colonel Hanley now took command of the regiment, the Irishmen went charging into a trap. Confederate infantry had captured two cannon from the 1st New York Artillery earlier in the day. Now, in an attempt to taunt the enemy, they had placed the cannon in the clearing, decking them out in Confederate bunting and regalia. The Irishmen charged forward, attempting to recapture the guns, but were met with a devastating fire from the woods in front and on their flank. Their rush of blood cost them dearly and as Hanley signalled the retreat back into the woods, twelve officers and 138 men of the 'Irish 9th' lay dead and wounded in the clearing. As Hanley led his shaken regiment towards the rear, their brigade commander galloped up to them and initiated an incident that left a bitter taste in the mouth of one of the 9th's men more than thirty years later:

> When the ninth retired to the brigade line, Colonel Sweitzer, commanding, rushed up shortly afterwards from the rear and demanded of Colonel Hanley in a loud and insolent tone of voice, 'Why don't you take your regiment in?' Colonel Hanley replied, 'We have been in and just come out.' 'Well' said Sweitzer, 'take

'em in again.' Colonel Hanley, without a murmur, gave the order to the men of the regiment, who were then resting on the ground talking about the trap they had been caught in, 'Fall in Ninth.' The regiment promptly formed line of battle and as Colonel Hanley was about to give the order 'Forward!' a staff officer came galloping down towards the regiment, and on nearing it cried out, 'General Griffin's orders are not to take the Ninth in again.' Colonel Sweitzer heard the order and moved off to headquarters, in the rear, without a word. The Ninth resumed its place of rest. It afterwards proved that when the brigade went forward to the attack that its commander, Colonel Sweitzer, remained in the rear and was, therefore, ignorant of what his regiments did, or where they went. General Griffin, however, knew all about them, as that gallant officer did of every regiment in his division.[3]

The incompetence of an immediate superior had nearly returned the Irishmen to a fight that had already ripped large holes in their ranks. It was the intervention of the divisional commander that spared them further casualties. However, while the 9th's Battle of the Wilderness had come to an abrupt and bloody halt, the day's fighting had yet to begin for many of their Irish countrymen.

As the 9th slunk away towards the Federal rear, Hays' brigade was moving into action just a little further north. Hays' brigade still had a number of Irish scattered throughout its ranks, particularly in the 6th Louisiana regiment. They moved into the line at about 2.00 p.m. They were urgently required to fill a gap that had appeared in the Confederate line and thus they made their way through the strangling vegetation as rapidly as they could. Encountering the first of the Federal skirmishers, they drove them easily through the woods until they too emerged in a clearing. Their momentum was their undoing, and as they charged recklessly across the open ground, a line of Federals waited beyond the tree line. As soon as they came within range, the Louisiana men were met with a devastating series of volleys that stopped them in their tracks. Still reeling from the shock of a sudden and high rate of casualties, they tried to reorganise as the Federals advanced from the woods and closed in on two sides. Hays knew he was about to be destroyed and quickly ordered a retreat back through the dead and dying. Hays' brigade took some of the heaviest casualties in its history during this brief and bloody encounter. The already thinned ranks of the ethnically mixed brigade lost 254 men in the Wilderness, approximately one-third of the force it had taken to battle.[4]

The Irish Brigade was part of the Federal army's second corps under the command of Major General Hancock. As such, they clashed with the Confederates of A.P. Hill's corps on the Federal left. After its decimation at Antietam, Fredericksburg and Gettysburg, the regiments had returned to their home in January 1864 for the express purpose of recruiting. They were only partially successful in this task. Although Meagher had arranged a Grand Banquet at City Hall in the New York regiments' honour, complete with marching bands and military regalia, the population of New York, particularly the Irish population, was unimpressed. Enthusiasm for the war had disappeared in the savagery of July's draft riots. The gathering of some 300 survivors and war widows in City Hall was so pathetic that an officer from another brigade proposed a toast to 'the Irish Brigade, what there is left of it'. In Boston, the Irish community had also turned on the Federal war effort. The city's Irish-American newspaper, the *Boston Pilot*, considered that 'the Irish spirit for the war is dead! ... Our fighters are dead.'[5]

With such hostility prevailing among the Irish communities of the North, it was little wonder that the brigade sought recruits wherever it could and not necessarily among the Irish population. In Boston, able-bodied men of unspecified ethnicity were sought out. In Pennsylvania, the recruiters of the 116th emptied the schoolhouses of several upstate towns, regardless of the ethnicity of these soldier boys. In New York, some Irish were gathered for the regiments owing to the cajoling of veterans and the presence of heavyweight Irish-Americans like Meagher and Robert Nugent. Nonetheless, the Irish Brigade that fought at the Wilderness was significantly less Irish than the one which had been cut to ribbons throughout 1862 and 1863. There was still a considerable number of Irish and Irish-Americans within its ranks, though three-quarters of the brigade now consisted of new recruits, and many of them were not of Irish extraction. Although the brigade was slowly changing colour, it maintained a significantly green tinge.

This mixture of Irish, Irish-American and American men formed into line of battle in the Wilderness at 2.00 p.m. on 5 May 1864. Their division marked the left-hand side of their corps. The men stood in one of the few clearings free of trees or shrubbery. The clearing was elevated and commanded a considerable amount of the surrounding landscape, so the site was chosen for placement of almost all the artillery of the second corps. The Irish Brigade operated in support of this artillery. As soon as they had taken their position, they were informed of the presence of the enemy at their front and began constructing breastworks. These works were quickly completed all along Hancock's line, which ran across the Orange Plank Road, with the Irish Brigade to the left of the road. However, all the digging in was in vain – at 4.00 p.m., Hancock was ordered to move his corps forward and drive the advancing Confederates back down the Orange Plank Road until he could link up with the left of Major General Gouverneur K. Warren's corps around the Parker store. The Irish Brigade moved with him. They soon encountered a determined Confederate enemy, but succeeded in driving him back on his right-hand flank. This success on his left was the only advance worthy of report by Hancock, who said:

> During this contest the Irish Brigade ... and Colonel Brooke's (Fourth) Brigade ... attacked the enemy vigorously on his right and drove his line for some distance. The Irish Brigade was heavily engaged, and although four fifths of its numbers were recruits, it behaved with great steadiness and gallantry, losing largely in killed and wounded.[6]

The Irish Brigade had distinguished itself once again, and once again it had paid a high price for that distinction. As darkness fell on the night of 5 May, the brigade was once again in a rather tattered condition. Yet another group of Irish to their right had suffered similar setbacks. Once again, the Irishmen of Pennsylvania's 69th Infantry were on the field.

The 69th had also had a brief period of leave, returning home in March of that year. The regiment had also been recruited up, but remained overwhelmingly Irish. As part of Hancock's corps, they moved towards Hill's Confederates in support of Brigadier General George W. Getty's division of the Federal VI Corps. They fought it out with Confederates in what McDermott described as a 'most stubbornly contested fight'.[7] With darkness falling, neither side was giving ground and the scene was set for another day of fighting.

As soon as daylight crept over the Wilderness, the

desperate struggle recommenced. On the Federal left, Hancock's corps met with some success. The Irish Brigade, still on the left and still licking their wounds from the previous day's engagement, were left with the rest of their division to guard against an expected flanking manoeuvre by Longstreet's corps, which was presumed to have arrived on the field. Meanwhile, the 69th Pennsylvania advanced in parallel with the Orange Plank Road in support of troops from Birney, Motts and Getty's divisions. After another desperate toe-to-toe fire fight in the woods, Hill's Confederates finally gave way and were pushed back almost two miles, where Hancock's weary troops were halted to draw their breath and re-form their line. At about 9.00 p.m. they advanced and engaged the Confederates once again. However, the direction of the battle was about to change, as Longstreet's corps had finally arrived on the field.

Just as the Irishmen of the 69th Pennsylvania were involved in attempting to consolidate the gains on Hancock's right, the Irish Brigade came under intensive fire from Longstreet's corps, who were sweeping in on Hancock's left. Now the whole of Hancock's line staggered and began falling back in confusion. The morning's gains were lost and soon Hancock's corps, including the Irish Brigade and the 69th Pennsylvania, were back where they had started. The Battle of the Wilderness drew to a close as darkness fell. The Federal army had been unable to grind Lee down, but knew they could do better in the open country.

A member of the 69th Pennsylvania later described the ground over which this group of Irishmen had fought in the Wilderness:

> The difficulties under which both sides fought can scarcely be properly described, the ground was covered with a dense growth of pines and cedars whose

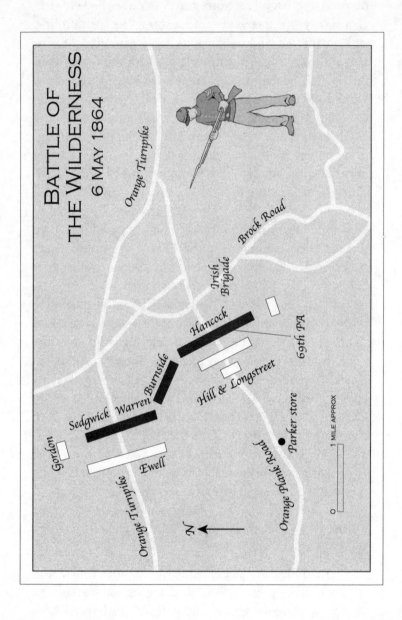

BATTLE OF
THE WILDERNESS
6 MAY 1864

Orange Turnpike

Brock Road

Irish
Brigade

Hancock

69th PA

Sedgwick Warren Burnside

Hill & Longstreet

Gordon

Orange Turnpike

Ewell

Orange Plank Road

Parker store

N

1 MILE APPROX

branches interlaced with each other, and so low as to make the march difficult and trying; in addition to this there was a dense undergrowth of bushes and vines running along the ground over which many were tripped. It was impossible in many places to see more than 20 or 30 yards ahead, and the use of artillery was out of the question … The battle of both days may fairly be said to be battles of musketry, pure and simple.[8]

It was a bloody stalemate. The new Irish Brigade had distinguished itself, but had paid a heavy price in casualties, with more intense fighting still to follow. Grant had gone head to head with Lee in the Wilderness and had suffered enormous casualties. However, the military juggernaut was not stopped, merely slowed down. Unlike the Federal commanders that came before him, Grant seemed unaffected by casualties or setbacks and his vastly superior numbers ensured that his advance could continue. By the night of 7 May, his bloodied and battered forces were again on the move. The Battle of Spotsylvania Courthouse was looming.

Grant decided that he would continue his relentless attritional offensive by slipping around Lee's right flank. Hence he dispatched Warren's V Corps, with the Irishmen of the 9th Massachusetts among them, sixteen miles southeast towards Spotsylvania. However, Lee anticipated this move and sent J.E.B. Stuart's cavalry to meet them. A series of delaying actions were fought by small groups of Confederates in an attempt to prevent the weight of the Federal army from bearing down on Spotsylvania until they had had time to dig themselves in along a fortified line of trenches. The 9th Massachusetts was embroiled in the Battle of Laurel Hill, where eight of its men were killed and eighteen wounded.

Grant's army was slowed down but continued to roll towards Spotsylvania, reaching the town on 9 May. There, they found the Confederates dug in north of the town along a line of trenches some four miles long. Lee had placed his artillery well and would be able to put down heavy enfilading fire on any attacking force. His line had one major weakness – an exposed salient that would become known as the Mule Shoe. The Mule Shoe jutted out from the centre of the Confederate line and extended for about one mile in front of the main trench line. The weakness was first exposed during fighting on 10 May when, after an intensive artillery bombardment, twelve Federal regiments under the command of Colonel Emory Upton slammed into the toe of the Mule Shoe. They succeeded in breaking the Confederate line and it took considerable effort on behalf of the defenders to drive them out. Lee immediately recognised the danger and set about laying a new line at the heel of the Mule Shoe that very night. Unfortunately for his men, however, Grant also recognised Lee's weakness and at dawn on 12 May he sent Hancock's entire 2nd corps right at the Mule Shoe. Among the men that moved with Hancock were the men of the much-depleted (and only partially Irish) Irish Brigade and the Irishmen who still stood among the ranks of the 69th Pennsylvania.

Between 3.00 and 4.00 a.m., the men of the 69th Pennsylvania stepped into line with the rest of Hancock's corps for the massive assault directed at the narrow front of the Mule Shoe. They moved silently and stealthily southwards through the woods until coming upon a clearing created by Confederate troops who had felled the trees to form their defences. They moved onwards toward the resting Confederates until they were within 40 or 50 yards of the pickets. With a rousing cheer, they emerged from the early morning's foggy darkness and charged the surprised pickets, quickly overrunning them and taking the works. The 69th

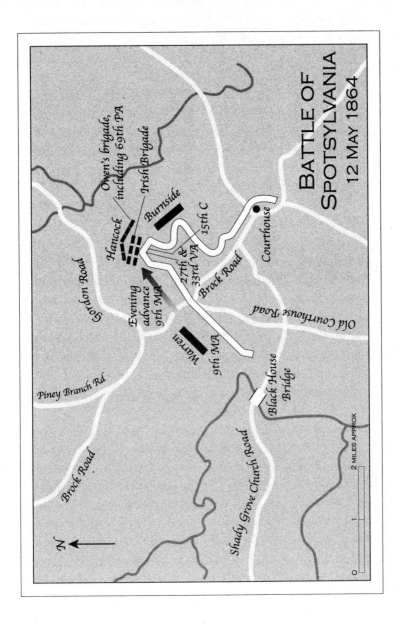

BATTLE OF
SPOTSYLVANIA
12 MAY 1864

Owen's brigade,
including 69th PA

Irish Brigade

Burnside

Hancock

15th C

27th &
33rd VA

Brock Road

Courthouse

Gordon Road

Evening
advance
9th MA

Old Courthouse Road

Warren

9th MA

Piney Branch Rd

Black House
Bridge

Brock Road

Shady Grove Church Road

N

2 MILES APPROX

0   1   2

249

were part of a support division, moving quickly behind the front line troops. Their first engagement was brought on when they collided with Confederates rushing out from the main line attempting to retake the captured works. McDermott later wrote that he knew of no more desperate a struggle for any set of works during the entire war. He also claimed that the 69th had captured the colours of an opposing regiment but had not been given the credit they deserved, as the colours were thrown to the rear and later claimed by another unit.

The Mule Shoe fighting was regarded as being among the most cruel and savage of the war. Casualties on both sides were immense as the same trenches were captured and surrendered again and again. Fr Corby later described the Irish Brigade moving through the morning darkness and towards the Mule Shoe by picking its way through the bodies that already lay thick on the ground from the previous day's skirmishing. They too moved through the early morning fog and quickly fell upon a picket line that was so surprised to see them, they did not even have time to fire a shot. They dashed on over 'open and rolling ground'[9] until they were within 300 yards of the Confederate works. Then, as a withering fire was opened up on them, 'the Irish Brigade gave a wild cheer' that served as the rallying cry for the other troops in their vicinity. They stormed over the works and assisted in taking the first Confederate line, along with much of the famed Stonewall Brigade, still including some Irish from the 33rd Virginia's Emerald Guards and the 27th Virginia's Virginia Hibernians. Lieutenant Thomas Doyle of the former unit later recalled that 'all that human courage and endurance would effect was done by these men on this frightful morning' amid 'fighting that raged with inconceivable violence'.[10] Yet it was all to no avail and the legendary unit was swept aside by Hancock's attack.

At first, the fighting in the Mule Shoe seemed to be going the Federals' way. After he was wounded during the initial melee, Peter Welsh wrote to his wife from his hospital bed:

My dear wife,

I write these few hurried lines to let you know that I got slightly wounded on the 12th it is a flesh wound in my left arm just a nice one to keep me from anymore fighting or marching this campaign we have had a pretty tough time of it we had been 8 days constantly fighting before I got hit that was the greatest battle of the war we licked saucepans out of them my dear wife I think I can get sent to New York to hospital if not I will get a sick furlow to go home … my dear wife do not be uneasy about me I am allright here give my love to all our friends God bless and protect you write to me as soon as you get this and send me five dollars if you can good by for the present

Your loving husband

PETER WELSH[11]

Welsh was wrong on two counts. Firstly, his own wound was more serious than he thought. A victim of the rather primitive medical care that prevailed in the hospitals of the Civil War, Welsh died of blood poisoning on 28 May. Secondly, while the Federals did 'lick saucepans' out of Confederates before he was carried from the field, the fighting soon turned into a vicious stalemate that worked its way back and forth across the Mule Shoe for the remainder of the day. Eventually, the Irish Brigade, along with the rest of the 2nd Corps, were withdrawn late that night.

Among the Confederate defenders of the Mule Shoe were the men of the 1st South Carolina Infantry. This regiment contained one company of Irish known as the Irish Volunteers. They too were caught up in the whirlwind that lasted all day on 12 May and into the early morning of 13 May. As the South Carolinians and Irish advanced into the fight at a portion of the Shoe known as 'the Angle', Confederate General Rodes was reported to have exclaimed, 'There are no better soldiers in the world than these.'[12] The day's fighting in the Mule Shoe cost both sides dearly. Confederates eventually regained the salient as a supporting Federal attack by Burnside was not driven home with the ferocity it should have been and Lee was able to redirect men to shore up the centre of his line.

Burnside's was not the only supporting attack that day: another attacking Federal corps was commanded by Warren and contained the men of Boston's Irish 9th. Daniel Macnamara later described the advance of the 9th as follows:

> General Warren's Fifth Corps, having now but three divisions, made an unsuccessful assault from the right, on Longstreet's left, at about 9 o'clock A.M. The Fifth Corps went forward on the double quick in a drenching rain, through the soft wet mould of ploughed ground, over undulating surface, to within fifty yards of the enemy's earthworks on the hill, when the men commenced to fall under a terrific fire of artillery and infantry. Our wavering lines could not withstand the leaden hail from Longstreet's infantry and deafening batteries. One break in the line brought on another until the disheartened troops fell back in disorder under the withering fire which followed with unerring aim … The Ninth lost 23 killed, 32 wounded and 2 missing or captured.[13]

Later that evening the 9th moved, along with the rest of their division, to support Hancock as the see-saw battle continued at the Mule Shoe. Eventually Confederates regained the Mule Shoe early on the morning of the 13th, then fell back to a more defensible line that had just been constructed to the rear of the salient. Grant had already announced his intention to fight at Spotsylvania even if it took all summer to break the Confederate line, so he was not ready to give up on the idea of breaking Lee in this position. All fell comparatively quiet along the front for a few days while the cigar-chomping firebrand decided his next move. On 18 May, he finally dispatched two more corps to attack the new line in the rear of the Mule Shoe. This brought the Irishmen of the Corcoran Legion into their first major battle in the ranks of the Army of the Potomac.

On 30 January 1863, the Legion had seen their first combat in the Battle of Deserted House. Their performance during that victorious engagement gained them considerable praise from their superiors. In the following months, the legion continued to perform admirably in minor engagements across Virginia. However, in December 1863, they lost their leader when Corcoran fell from his horse while out riding with his old comrade from the 69th and former leader of the Irish Brigade, Thomas Francis Meagher. Allegations that the two friends were engaged in Christmas celebrations heavily dependent on alcohol at the time of Corcoran's death are prominent in some accounts of the incident.[14] His body was taken back to New York, where it was viewed by thousands as it lay in state at St Patrick's Cathedral. The flags in New York Harbor flew at half mast as Corcoran was buried on St Stephen's Day, 1863. Thus, by the time the Corcoran Legion joined Grant for his overland campaign, they were without the leadership of one of

Ireland's most famous soldiers.

Instead, the Legion was now under the command of Colonel Matthew Murphy, and arrived on the Spotsylvania field on the evening of 16 May. They had not arrived without controversy. Murphy brought 1,600 effectives to the fight. The remainder of the legion was reported as straggling in a rather typically Irish manner. On the morning of 17 May, Charles Anderson Dana, Lincoln's eyes and ears at the front, reported to the Secretary of War in Washington, 'Colonel Murphy, with the Irish Legion, reported last evening 1,600 muskets; the remainder, according to Colonel Murphy, being drunk on the road.'

Susannah Ural Bruce has argued that the quality of the Irish soldier had changed considerably between the early days of the war and 1864. The new Irish soldiers were not generally as ideologically driven as their 'older' comrades. Many of them were just off the immigrant ships and had no real ties to America and no entrenched opinions on the political problems of their new home. Instead, they served only to secure the large bounties being offered to them and to earn weekly wages that many immigrants would find difficult to earn during the course of a normal year. The new recruits altered the reputation of the Irish soldier. While excessive drinking and ill discipline had dogged many Irish regiments, by the end of 1864, desertion, poor battle performance and occasional cowardice were traits frequently associated with Federal Irish soldiers.[15]

It is difficult to say how many Irishmen sobered up and arrived at Spotsylvania during the coming days, but at 4.00 a.m. on the morning of 18 May, the legion crossed the entrenchments and prepared to advance on the Confederate line. At this point, two of its regiments, the 164th and 155th New York Volunteers, were ordered to advance by a staff officer of Gibbon's divisional command. This order was given without Colonel Murphy's knowledge and effectively left him in command of only two regiments, the 69th New York National Guard and the 170th New York Volunteers. Murphy took these two regiments across the 'no man's land' between the lines and ploughed straight into the Confederate picket line, driving the pickets from their entrenchments. They then continued onwards through about 500 yards of woods, which had separated the pickets from their main line. Upon reaching the main Confederate line, Murphy halted his two regiments and attempted to ascertain the whereabouts of the separated half of his command. Soon he learned that they were heavily engaged with enemy pickets to his right and rear. Because their ammunition was apparently close to exhaustion, Murphy led his half of the command back to their assistance. By the time he got there, however, Colonel McMahon had already retreated from the position, so Murphy moved his half of the legion into the line in their place. At this point, Murphy was wounded when hit in the left arm.[16] Nonetheless, with the command having devolved to Captain James McIvor, the legion acquitted itself reasonably well. It held the line until ordered to retreat as the full scale of Lee's bloody repulse of Grant's full frontal assault became apparent.[17]

After the appalling losses suffered during Grant's attack of 18 May, the Federal general became convinced that he could not break Lee's line at Spotsylvania. Indeed, he had nearly broken his own army in attempting to do so. However, he had also cost Lee significant casualties, which the Southern general could scarcely afford. Grant broke off the battle and once again slipped south and east towards Richmond. After three minor engagements at Haws Shop, Totopotomoy Creek and Old Church, Lee determined that

Grant's cavalry sought control of the crossroads at Old Cold Harbor. Control of these roads could provide Federal troops with easy access to the rear of the Army of Northern Virginia. He also received reports of Federal reinforcements moving down the James River. If they succeeded in then moving up the York River to White House Landing and moving due west to Old Cold Harbor, they would be dangerously close to linking up with Grant's left flank and moving the Federal line too far south for Lee to deal with.

After serious fighting throughout 31 May and 1 June, Sheridan's Federal Cavalry seized Cold Harbor Crossroads. They were now only 10 miles from Richmond and both armies began to converge on this strategic point. Confederates spent all day on 2 June constructing formidable defences west of the crossroads and between Grant and Richmond. Grant and Meade attempted a breakthrough on 3 June. Among the forces they slung into the bloody and one-sided brawl were the two largest Irish units of the Army of the Potomac, the Irish Brigade and the Corcoran Legion.

The Irish Brigade made their attack as part of Barlow's division of Hancock's corps. As such, they attacked at the extreme southern end of the Confederate line in the early morning at about 4.30 a.m. Part of Barlow's division, including the Irishmen of the 116th Pennsylvania, succeeded in breaching the outer Confederate line and capturing colours, along with some 200 prisoners. However, the ill-fated attack was soon to grind to a bloody halt. Hill's corps was simply too well entrenched and its artillery well placed. The left flank of Barlow's division was severely cut up by artillery fire. Federal artillerists could not even respond, as the ground over which they attacked afforded no suitable gun emplacements. They were soon retreating once again.

Off to their right, the Irishmen of the Corcoran Legion

were not faring much better. As part of Gibbon's division in Hancock's corps, they too had moved out at 4.30 a.m. They moved across the open field only to find that an impassable marsh was dividing Gibbon's troops into two columns as they advanced. As they attempted to navigate this marsh, the Corcoran Legion became one of the many units divided by the terrain. Yet their divisional commander was impressed by the battle performance of one of the legion's regiments. Gibbon later reported:

> On the left, and separated from his brigade, by the swamp, the heroic Colonel McMahon, with a portion of his regiment, One hundred and sixty-fourth New York, gained the breastwork, and, while alongside of his colors cheering on his men, fell covered with wounds and expired in the enemy's hands, they capturing also his colors and the men with it.

But while Gibbon praised the heroics of the 164th New York, he was not nearly as impressed by the performance of another Irish unit, the 69th Pennsylvania. He did not blame the Irishmen for their lack of performance, but rather attached the blame to their brigade commander, Joshua T. Owen of the 69th. It was perhaps a cruel coincidence that in Gibbon's opinion, it was Owen's incompetence that caused the Irishmen of the 69th Pennsylvania to allow the sacrifices made by the 164th New York's Irish to count for nought. Having already castigated Owen for not having his brigade ready to move on time that morning, Gibbon's report continued:

> General Owen, instead of pushing forward in column through Smyth's line, deployed on the left as soon as the latter became fully engaged, and thus lost the opportunity of having his brigade well in hand and

ready to support the lodgement made by Smyth and McMahon.

McDermott, who moved with Owen among the ranks of the 69th, omits any criticism of his brigade commander. He puts the failure of the 69th and their brigade commanders to reach the Confederate works down to the terrific fire they were taking from behind those works. Instead of ordering any further advance, Owen simply ordered his brigade to lie down and start gouging out the sandy soil with their tin cups. The men soon constructed makeshift dug-outs and remained pinned down behind them until darkness set in. That night, entrenching tools were brought forward and the position was hastily made more permanent.[18]

On the Confederate side of the engagement at Cold Harbor, one Irishman stood out above all others – Monaghan-born General Joseph Finegan. Finegan had settled in Florida in the 1830s. He became a lawyer and made some powerful political connections which assured him a prominent position in the military when war broke out. Early in 1862, the Irishman had led some 5,000 Confederates in defence of Florida when a Federal column of similar size landed at Jacksonville. Finegan led his force to strike and defeat the Federals at the Battle of Olustee. A monument dedicated to him stands on the battlefield today. Although Finegan had turned over tactical command for Olustee to Brigadier General Alfred Colquitt, his aggressive confrontation of the Federals brought him to the attention of Robert E. Lee and Finegan was given command of a brigade within the Army of Northern Virginia in the summer of 1864.

At Cold Harbor, Finegan's brigade lay in reserve behind the first Confederate line. They were ordered forward when part of Barlow's division, including Irishmen from the 116th Pennsylvania, made their partial breakthrough. Finegan

Joseph Finegan.

rallied his troops while riding conspicuously up and down the line atop his horse. His Florida brigade charged the Federal troops and drove them from the works they had captured. However, finding that his brigade now occupied a perilous position in full sight of Federal sharpshooters, Finegan ordered two foolhardy charges into the nearby Federal lines that evening. Both charges were cut to ribbons not far from their own trenches. The Irishman had assisted in bolstering Lee's Cold Harbor line, but he had also decimated his own command by ordering tiny portions of it forward in hopeless charges against an enemy that was numerically superior. In short, Finegan's impetuosity led to his confrontation of a Federal division with mere regiments on two separate occasions.[19]

The Battle of Cold Harbor was a spectacular Federal failure. Grant had again failed to break Lee, at a cost of up to 13,000 casualties. The Southern general, by contrast, lost only 2,500 men approximately. For the next three days, the dead and wounded were left to lie under the baking hot summer sun but Grant was reluctant to ask Lee for a truce, thereby conceding that he had lost the battle. By the time he sought such an arrangement on 7 June, it was already too late for many of the unfortunate men who still lay between the lines. On 12 June, Grant finally moved his army south-east across the James River in order to threaten Petersburg, a rail hub for Richmond.

The Overland Campaign was over. Both armies had suffered huge casualties in two months of heavy fighting. However, the losses hit the smaller Confederate army much more severely. Now, the bloodied and bruised armies of the east moved towards the war's inevitable conclusion and the remaining Irish moved with them.

CHAPTER 16

PETERSBURG AND APPOMATTOX

At first, Lee was convinced that the main thrust of Grant's attacks would come against the Confederate capital at Richmond and therefore devoted only a limited number of troops, under Beauregard, to the defence of Petersburg. On 15 June 1864, lead elements of Grant's army attacked the defences at Petersburg and the prolonged siege began.

The Siege of Petersburg represented a shift in Grant's thinking. The Federal general now sought to bottle Lee's forces up and conduct a long, protracted siege, rather than defeat Lee in the open, as he had previously attempted. The ten-month engagement brought the horrors of trench warfare home to the men on both sides. The combat in the trenches during the First World War is reminiscent of the fighting around Petersburg. The Irishmen of three Federal units were significantly engaged in the campaign. Once again, they were the men of the Corcoran Legion, the Irish Brigade and the 69th Pennsylvania Infantry Regiment.

The 69th Pennsylvania fought in the large-scale Federal attack on 16 June and succeeded in driving Confederate defenders from an outer to an inner line of works, but that

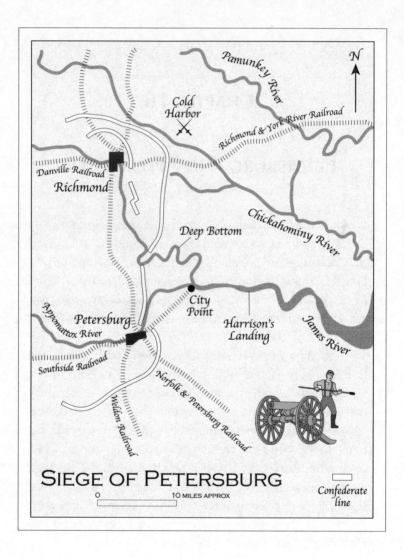

SIEGE OF PETERSBURG

0   10 MILES APPROX

Confederate line

was when the assault ground to a halt. They again fought in continued Federal attempts to break the Confederate line on 17 and 18 June until they were moved, as part of an extended Federal line, to the vicinity of the Jerusalem Plank Road. Here, on 22 June, the regiment encountered the same problems it had had at Cold Harbor in trying to entrench under sustained Confederate fire.

Confederates were not comfortable with the proximity of the Federal line and attacked at noon. At first, their dark uniforms caused the Irishmen to mistake them for Federal comrades. It was only when artillery pieces moved to the front of the dark-clad columns and opened fire on the Federal works that the Irishmen realised they were in a fight. Their surprise cost them dearly and they lost nearly four entire companies before they were able to withdraw from the determined attackers. It was a day of heavy loss for the Irish regiment (107 were killed, wounded or captured) in the midst of a deadly cat-and-mouse game. That night, they reoccupied their original line. The regiment and its brigade comrades were greatly depleted in numbers and on 27 June the Irish regiment was consolidated with the remnants of the 106th Pennsylvania.[1]

The Irish Brigade was also 'discontinued'. Consistently heavy casualties meant that the once-celebrated brigade was unable to avoid its inevitable consolidation with other brigades of its division. On 20 June, the 28th Massachusetts was transferred to the 1st Brigade and in July the 116th Pennsylvania was transferred to the 4th Brigade of the 1st Division, while the three remaining New York regiments were consolidated with the 3rd Brigade. They would form a single battalion within that command.

Sporadic fighting continued in the trenches outside Petersburg until Grant could think of another move to try and break the Confederate line. That move came in the shape of a tactical feint by Grant during the night of 26 July, when Hancock moved his corps, along with two of Sheridan's cavalry divisions, across the James River to threaten Richmond at a place called Deep Bottom. The feint was intended to draw men away from Petersburg, where a huge mine was being laid under the Confederate line, to be detonated in time for a Federal attack there. The Irish Battalion of the 3rd Brigade, the Corcoran Legion and the 69th/106th Pennsylvania moved with Hancock on this long, tiresome, night march.

Hancock succeeded in taking the Confederates by surprise and took their first line of works. The battalion of New York regiments that had once belonged to the Irish Brigade was involved in this attack. However, it was the 28th Massachusetts that gained most praise for its actions that day. Private John Ryan was back with the regiment following a mysterious absence since the Battle of Gettysburg and described the Irish regiment's emergence from a treeline at Deep Bottom as follows:

> The order was given to 'advance' and as we advanced across this opening, we relieved the pickets … they told us when we went through that we would soon stir up a hornets nest. Very soon a Confederate battery opened from the timber on the other side of the opening. Their first shot and shells were directed towards the cavalry. Finally they opened on our skirmish line. They being on a raise of ground, and we being on the level, their shots and shells passed over our heads. We had orders to 'double quick.' In the meantime our batteries were firing on the Confederates and the shots passed over our heads. We advanced as far as the foot of the hill and laid down. At this time, General Miles rode up and sung

out, 'Men let a general lead you.' With that we arose and charged on this battery, capturing the battery complete, consisting of four twenty-pound Parrott rifle guns ... We also took a number of prisoners.[2]

The 28th Massachusetts was a huge part of Hancock's initial success at Deep Bottom and the corps commander praised the regiment for its action.[3] However, when Confederate re-inforcements arrived from Petersburg, Hancock's offensive quickly ground to a halt. He returned to the line in front of Petersburg, leaving some men to guard the bridgehead he had gained at Deep Bottom. The 69th Pennsylvania was involved in some light skirmishing at the First Battle of Deep Bottom, but the Corcoran Legion was not engaged. The Irish were not among the men left north of the James River and returned to Petersburg on 30 July. They were just in time to witness the detonation of the mine and the failure of the Federal attack that followed it.

In the thick of the fight following that detonation were the remaining Irish Confederates of the 8th Alabama's Emerald Guards. When Federal troops attempted to penetrate the gap that the mine had left in the Confederate line, they were pinned down in the deep crater and were unable to get out. Those Confederates who had been lucky enough to escape the blast fired into the hole and swarmed in to win back the salient after some brutal hand-to-hand combat. The Emerald Guards lost men like Moses Chaffin, Patrick Crowley and James Ryan at the crater.[4] The incident was a particularly gory affair, with some 350 Confederates killed in the initial blast, many of their bodies found underneath 10 feet of earth, and over 5,000 Federal casualties sustained.

On 13 August, the Irish Battalion was on the move again. For a time none of the men among its ranks were quite sure where they were going, so closely guarded was the secret. They proceeded to City Point, where they boarded troop transports and steamed down the James River. As they moved along the river, some of the men speculated that they would be returning home to replenish their ranks. They knew they were out of luck when the ships dropped anchor 14 miles downstream of City Point, waited until darkness had enveloped the countryside, and at about midnight, steamed back up the river to Deep Bottom. The 116th Pennsylvania travelled with their old comrades from the Irish Brigade, and their commander later described the disappointment of the men who had begun to hope they were returning to Washington:

> No one thought of sleep. There was no time to even doze while the boys were having such a good time. Were they not on their way to the North! With the tolling of the midnight hour came a sad ending to the Washington dream. The steamer, on which the Regiment was rejoicing and having such a jolly time, slowed up and a tug came alongside with the orders. In five minutes every man knew that it was Deep Bottom and a fight in the morning, instead of Washington and a trip to the North. The singing quickly died away. The river did not seem half so beautiful nor the stars half so bright. Quickly everyone lost interest in the passing shores. The silence of disappointed hope settled over the men.[5]

Arriving at Deep Bottom, they proceeded towards Richmond, engaged in another feint attack. Under a blazing sun, they marched for two hours before coming into range of the guns at Richmond. What followed was to become one of the less celebrated incidents in the history of the Irish Brigade. Their divisional commander, General Francis Barlow, ordered them into the line but later reported, 'I am compelled to say that these troops behaved disgracefully and failed to execute my orders. They crowded off to the right into the shelter of some woods and there became shattered and broken to pieces.' Through the years, allegations of some personal animosity between Barlow and the Irish Brigade have surfaced. Richard Moroney commanded the Irish regiments at that time and he made no mention of this alleged cowardice in his report. However, commanding officers did not usually write critical reports of their own men.

Through 14 and 15 August 1864, Federal troops continued to edge towards Richmond in what was beginning to look like a very successful feint. The Corcoran Legion was involved in some light fighting and sustained a few casualties during this period. By the 16th, temperatures in excess of 100 °F (38 °C) were taking their toll. The Federals were finally turned by Major General Charles W. Field's counterattack. By 20 August the Irish Brigade and the Corcoran Legion were right back where they had started on the southern bank of the James River and saw no further significant action until the Battle of Ream's Station.

This battle occurred when Hancock led his corps along the Weldon Railroad, severing this vital Confederate lifeline as he went. Confederate Major General Henry Heth was dispatched to deal with Hancock's threat and met it at Ream's Station, where he succeeded in overrunning a poorly defended Federal position. The Corcoran Legion was cut to ribbons and after the fight at Ream's Station numbered no more than 200 men. The following is taken from a letter written to Fr Matthew Byrne (whose brother was an officer in the legion) in Buffalo, New York, by Dean Wilson of the legion. It describes the death of the Irish unit.

Then commenced the slaughter. From front and rear they came swarming in with their yells and seizing the artillery turned it immediately on our men ... Captain McConvey was wounded severely and carried about a mile, when the men who were carrying him had to leave him, as the rebels were in our rear and right on top of us ... The Brigade loss was five hundred men. The One Hundred and Seventieth has one officer and about thirty men out of one hundred and fifty ... Many of our troops would not leave the pits at all, preferring capture and imprisonment to running the chances of getting out from under the destructive artillery fire that was concentrated on us from all points, front and rear, right and left ... Their artillery checked their rear from capturing more of us, as they mowed down their own men with the artillery they captured and turned on us. I hope, dear friend, that I will never get in such another 'tight place.' General Gibbon cried; Hancock today and yesterday will let no one approach him.

Gibbon, the divisional commander, was so upset at the losses sustained at Ream's Station that he singled out three regiments which he felt had not performed adequately. These regiments, including the Legion's 164th New York, were temporarily denied the honour of carrying regimental colours. However, after Hancock had pleaded their case to Grant and a more efficient performance was recorded at a skirmish near Hatcher's Run, the three units concerned were once again permitted their flags.[6]

If one Irish unit was butchered at Ream's Station, it seems that another was determined not to be. Once again, the remainder of the Irish Brigade (the consolidated New York regiments) did not distinguish itself during the battle. The 2nd Corps chief of staff, Francis Walker, later bemoaned the behaviour of the entire corps during the action and he singled out the Irish Brigade as symbolic of its decline:

> Concerning the reported ill behaviour of the troops it is enough to say that the two brigades referred to had long been the chief glories of the Second Corps ... Nothing could so clearly show the disorganisation brought about by the terrible losses of this campaign as that such language could truthfully be used about these troops. The Irish brigade left its dead, with their sprigs of green in their caps, close under the stone wall at Fredericksburg; and had shown in every field the most determined bravery ... now according to General Barlow was loath to look at the enemy. It is evident that assaults 'all along the line' had left very little of the old material there.[7]

After the disaster at Ream's Station, the whole of the 2nd Corps returned to the trenches in front of Petersburg. There, they spent the coming months far away from combat, engaged in digging trenches and building roads. The Irishmen were now swinging the pick and shovel for the Federal government. Their character as soldiers and fitness for combat were severely questioned. Widespread desertion dogged the Irish Brigade throughout 1864. Eventually senior officers of the Army of the Potomac took to placing the Irish units in positions where they could be 'easily watched and guarded'.[8] For the surviving members of the original Irish units, the army's treatment of them may well have hurt their pride. Then again, even if they never dared to say it, they may have been glad of an extended break from the firing line.

This break was not to last. As Grant gradually wore Lee down, it was only a matter of time before the last of the Irish soldiers would face the enemy's fire again, and in late October the Irish Brigade was re-formed. It consisted of all the old regiments except the 116th Pennsylvania, which was replaced by the 7th New York Heavy Artillery. The brigade was not nearly as Irish as it once had been, with new recruits and even a new regiment having drastically changed its ethnic character. Nonetheless, they still carried the green flag, were still referred to as the Irish Brigade and still carried with them a few war-weary Irishmen who had survived the horrors of countless battlefields, as well as many newly arrived immigrants recruited almost directly from the quaysides of New York. Those men, and their new comrades, were now commanded by the Irish-born Colonel Robert Nugent and they returned to significant combat early in 1865.

The war had completely stalled in the trenches around Petersburg. The Irish on both sides suffered the appalling hardships of this cruel trench warfare, yet during one brief interlude it appears they may have found one another. After an unsuccessful attack on the Confederate line took the life of the 116th Pennsylvania's Captain Henry Price, the unit's commander later recalled the events that followed:

> After a few days the flag of truce went out, and the body of Captain Price recovered. We learned that on the morning after the assault, an Irishman of a Georgia regiment had seen the body and recognized by the number of the Regiment as a former member of the Irish Brigade. He had tenderly wrapped him in a blanket and carefully buried him.[9]

By March 1865, Lee knew he had only one remaining option: to attempt to break through the Federal lines and threaten their supply depot at City Point. It was a desperate gamble with little hope of success, but if Petersburg and Richmond were to be held, it was the only throw of the dice the

Confederate commander could make. A pre-dawn assault on 25 March was directed at the Federal Fort Stedman. The assault initially broke through, but Federal counterattacks managed to fend off the attackers, cutting off and imprisoning some 1,900 of them. The attack on Fort Stedman weakened other parts of the Confederate line where troops had been withdrawn to participate in the attack. Federal commanders were anxious to exploit those weaknesses and once again the Irish Brigade entered combat.

They moved as part of a Federal counterattack on Lee's weakened left and succeeded in occupying a trench line vacated by its Confederate defenders in the early afternoon. The Irish Brigade was not engaged during the capture of this line, but they were now expected to assist in holding it. They did so admirably, repelling a Confederate charge that, but for Nugent's quick realignment of his units, would have flanked them at about 4.15 p.m. For some time the Irish Brigade withstood the brunt of this attack before it spread out along the line of their division.[10] The brigade had gone some distance towards restoring its former reputation and had ably assisted in dealing the final blow to Lee's hopes of defending Petersburg or Richmond.

On 1 April, Federals managed to take a strategic confluence of roads at a place called Five Forks, sealing off Lee's best escape route from Petersburg and Richmond. On 2 and 3 April they began breaking through the Confederate lines. The Irish Brigade captured approximately 150 prisoners, two artillery pieces and a stand of colours on 2 April. Lee now decided to evacuate the two cities while he still could. He retreated west along the Appomattox River in a desperate attempt to link up with forces under the command of General Joseph E. Johnston in North Carolina.

Grant's forces pursued their defeated foe and the Irish

were centrally involved in the pursuit. The Irish Brigade tangled with retreating Confederates at Sayler's Creek on 6 April, capturing an entire wagon train of supplies. On 7 April they again attacked Confederate troops who had entrenched on high ground near the Cumberland Church in an attempt to buy time for their retreating comrades. The Battle of Cumberland Church was the final action of the famed Irish Brigade. Federal troops twice struck the Confederate line but were unable to break it. It was during this action that the brigade lost one of its greatest heroes. Cork-born Tom Smyth fell after sustaining a fatal head wound. On the occasion of his promotion to brigadier general the previous October, his men in the 63rd New York had expressed the wish that he would one day 'lead us across the ocean to raise to independence and happiness our own dear unforgotten Ireland'.[11] It was not to be and Smyth died two days later on 9 April 1865. After the vicious fight at Cumberland Church on 7 April, the Irish Brigade awoke on the morning of 8 April to find that their enemy was gone, and for them the war was over.

By 9 April, Lee found himself in an impossible position. He could no longer realistically expect to link his forces with those of Johnston. The continuous and relentless pursuit of Grant meant that the Southern general had not been able to stop and resupply his army. He had hoped to do so at Appomattox railway station, but on 8 April a cavalry raid by George Armstrong Custer had captured the railway station and burned the supplies. Now Lee's only hope was to access supplies at Lynchburg. All that stood between Lee and Lynchburg was Phil Sheridan's Federal cavalry. However, when Lee ordered an attack on this cavalry, his subordinate, Major General John B. Gordon, soon discovered that two Federal infantry corps had come up to support it. There was no way Lee could resupply his army and his only option was surrender. On 9 April 1865 Robert E. Lee surrendered the Army of Northern Virginia to Ulysses S. Grant at Appomattox Courthouse, Virginia. The American Civil War was all but over.

Chapter 17

The End of the Matter

Out west, the war had seldom provided much comfort for Confederates. Since Chickamauga and Chattanooga, little had changed. General Joseph E. Johnston had taken command of the Army of Tennessee while Sherman moved his three armies, the Army of the Cumberland, the Army of Tennessee and the Army of the Ohio, against Atlanta. Johnson was outnumbered almost two to one and was almost continuously on the retreat towards Atlanta. His forces generally occupied entrenched positions until Sherman appeared and then usually retreated as soon as Sherman attempted his habitual flanking manoeuvres.

The two generals' first serious clash occurred at the Battle of Rocky Faced Ridge on 7 May 1864. Here Sherman moved two of his columns in a demonstration at Johnston's front, while he slipped a third through Snake Creek Gap towards Resaca, which was chosen as an objective because it was an important rail centre. On 9 May, Federal troops approaching Resaca discovered Confederates entrenched outside the town. This development prompted Sherman to withdraw his troops from the stubborn combat at Rocky Faced Ridge and reunite all his command for an attack on Resaca. By 13 May,

Sherman had concentrated his forces at Resaca and had begun to test the Confederate line.

The Irishmen of the 90th Illinois were engaged in this skirmishing and had one man killed and fifteen wounded. This was their only day fighting at Resaca. They remained in the reserve line until they awoke on the morning of 15 May to find that Johnston had once again withdrawn his forces.[1] During this withdrawal, the Irish of the 10th Tennessee had provided the rearguard at a cost of one man killed and six wounded.[2]

The forces next collided at Adairsville on 17 May, when Howard's advancing Federal corps struck entrenched Confederates two miles north of the town. Sherman began to concentrate his forces in order to give battle, but once again Johnston withdrew, unable to find a suitable line on which to anchor his men.

During a brief pause in fighting around this time, an unusual encounter between two Corkmen occurred. Federal Brigadier General Thomas Sweeny was a committed Fenian. He knew that Patrick Cleburne was in close proximity, and seizing upon what he probably considered to be an opportunity for Ireland, Sweeny sent a courier to find the 'Stonewall of the West'. The courier carried a proposal from Sweeny that he and Cleburne should unite after the war in attempting to recruit veterans to the Fenian banner. Cleburne's reply was to express his wish that both he and Sweeny would have seen enough war by that time and would therefore have no desire to enter into further combat.[3] He was wrong about Sweeny, a man who was known for his hot temper and profanity. He never gave up on the Irish Republican dream and in 1886 he led one of the Fenians' failed Canadian incursions.

The Confederate retreat now continued as Johnston

Tennessee

Chattanooga

state line

✕ Dalton (Rocky Faced Ridge) 13 May

✕ Resaca 13 May

Georgia

✕ Adairsville 17 May

Rome

Allatoona

Pickett's Mill
27 May ✕

Marietta

✕ New Hope Church 25 May

Dallas 28 May ✕

N

Chattahoochee River

Ezra Church ✕

✕ Peach Tree Creek

Utoy Creek

Atlanta

✕ Lovejoy's Station

Jonesborough ✕

ATLANTA CAMPAIGN

0   10   20 MILES APPROX

entered the Altoona Pass. Sherman decided that any attack on that terrain would be too costly and thus he attempted to slip around Johnston's left flank and move on Dallas. However, Johnston anticipated the move and met him at New Hope Church. Sherman concluded that Johnston had but a token force present on the field and on 27 May threw Hooker's corps forward to a dreadful mauling. The man dishing out the punishment was Patrick Cleburne.

Move and counter-move continued throughout the coming days, bringing on engagements in and around Dallas and Marietta. On 20 June, the Federal Irishmen of the 35th Indiana lost their commanding officer and respected Fenian member, Major John P. Dufficy, when he was mortally wounded during hand-to-hand night-time fighting at the Battle of Marietta. On that occasion, Confederates had dented the Federal line where the Irishmen stood and some Federal officers believed that 'the thirty-fifth Indiana behaved badly on account of its officers'.[4] However, the Irish regiment marked the independence day of their newfound home in splendid style when they 'made a brilliant charge on the enemy's skirmish line (which was nearly equal in strength to a line of battle), and, being well supported by the Forty-fifth Ohio, carried the rifle pits and held them, although exposed to a galling flank fire, in consequence of the failure of troops on the left to advance with them.'[5] They sustained casualties of four men killed and six wounded.[6] Soon after that endeavour, what remained of the Irish regiment was detached to guard supply trains until 30 August. Meanwhile, on 27 July, Sherman made a fatal mistake by striking the Confederate left at Kennesaw Mountain. Confederates held high and easily defensible ground in this location and the attack met with a bloody repulse. Once again, Cleburne's division dished out considerable punishment to the attackers. The defeat at Kennesaw convinced Sherman that he would have to break off the engagement and continue towards Atlanta via a series of flanking movements.

Growing weary of Johnston's continuing retreat, Jefferson Davis relieved Johnston of command and replaced him with General John Bell Hood, hoping that the latter commander would attack. Three miles north of Atlanta at a place called Peach Tree Creek, Hood did just that. By now Sherman had divided his command into three sections for the final approach on Atlanta and Hood struck the section led by Thomas. The assault was unsuccessful and, in spite of early Confederate successes, the Federal line held admirably. Hood had proven that his style would be different from Johnston's – he would attack more frequently. Thus, as Federal forces moved on Atlanta, they did not collide with Hood's defenders; rather, it was Hood who collided with them on 22 July at the Battle of Atlanta.

The first part of Hood's plan was to strike the Federal left with Hardee's corps, which brought the Tennessee Irish into action. They marched approximately 15 miles through the night of 21 July and morning of 22 July. First they moved southeast, then swung north towards the left of the Federal line. The 10th Tennessee was part of Bates' division and as such moved on the far right of Hardee's line. Little did they know that they were moving towards the division of the Fenian brigadier general who had recently contacted Cleburne, Thomas Sweeny. The 10th moved through the swampy Terry's Mill Pond and onwards through heavy undergrowth towards Sweeny's line at Sugar Creek, striking it when they burst from the woods in front of him in the early morning. But Sweeny's position was well fortified and the Confederate troops launched themselves forward into a raking canister fire. They were only able to exchange a few

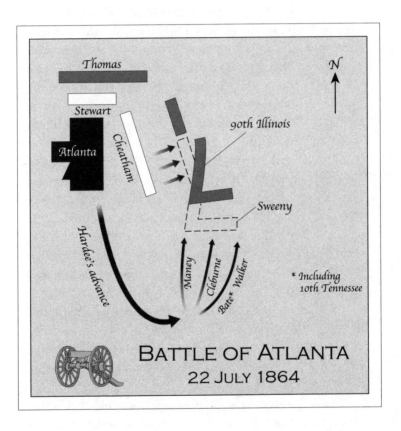

Thomas

Stewart

Atlanta

Cheatham

90th Illinois

Sweeny

Hardee's advance

Maney

Cleburne

Bate* Walker

*Including
10th Tennessee

N

BATTLE OF ATLANTA
22 JULY 1864

volleys with Sweeny's men before they were forced to fall back. The 10th saw no more fighting that day, as they were detached to guard supply trains. Only fifty-three of them were still alive and fit for this duty.[7]

The next Confederate attackers were Walker's division. Among Walker's forces was probably the largest single concentration of Irishmen remaining in the Army of Tennessee. They stood in the ranks of the 1st Georgia Volunteers, a unit that had initially been recruited from the militias of Savannah. As such, the unit contained three distinctly Irish companies: the Jasper Greens, the Republican Blues and the Irish Volunteers. Their membership was comprised of the Irish and Scotch-Irish communities of Georgia. Remarkably, the Atlanta Campaign provided the first taste of major battle that these units had had. Although they were among the first to rally to the flag on the outbreak of the conflict, they had served in several coastal forts, defending them from Federal attack until Sherman's Atlanta Campaign brought major battle to their home state. Some of them had already found the constant marching to and fro under a hot summer sun to be exhausting. At Kennesaw Mountain they found out that exhaustion was the least of a soldier's worries in the midst of a major campaign. By the end of that battle, the Jasper Greens alone had seven wounded and forty-nine missing and possibly deserted.[8]

Walker's attack came just after Bates' had subsided. It was poorly organised and co-ordinated and so ended quickly and in spectacular failure. The Savannah Irish and their 1st Georgia comrades were a part of Mercer's brigade. When Walker was shot down and wounded, Mercer took command of the division. So piecemeal were the attacks of Walker's division that the Irish found themselves as part of the third single brigade flung at three Federal lines of battle cresting a nearby hill, facing 500 yards of open ground between them and the enemy. Only the quick thinking of their brigade commander in withdrawing his unit saved them from appalling slaughter. Bates' and Walker's divisions had both failed spectacularly. The next division to step into the breach that morning was Patrick Cleburne's.

At 1.00 p.m., Cleburne's division attacked to the west of Bates and Walker, expecting to come in on the rear of the exposed Federal left. It was supposed to have been a quick and easy rolling-up operation. Instead it became a bloodbath. Cleburne's men were expected to storm three lines of heavily entrenched Federal soldiers. The first of Cleburne's brigades to hit the Federal line was led by Daniel C. Govan and still contained a small smattering of Irishmen in the ranks of the 1st/15th Arkansas and the 3rd Confederate. They made their way into Federal abatis, but the attack soon spluttered out under canister and musket fire. Then, as further waves of Cleburne's attackers arrived, Smith's Texan brigade succeeded in breaching the Federal line. As Federal troops now abandoned their works in that area, Smith's brigade were now effectively in the rear of the Federal line. In conjunction with another of Cleburne's brigades, they continued to attack the Federals from that position while men from Maney's division moved in at the front. Eventually, their lack of numbers told and the Federals regained the ground they had lost. Cleburne was not finished yet, however. Once more, Govan's men regrouped and hit the Federal line. After three hours of brutal fighting, in conjunction with another of Cleburne's brigades they eventually forced a lodgement in the Federal line to the left of Smith's division.

Meanwhile, out at the Federal front, Cheatham's Confederate division was driving its attack home. This ferocious assault brought the Federal Irishmen of the 90th

Illinois into the action. The 90th had had a peaceful time for much of June, guarding supply trains in the rear. Since then they had been shunted around with the rest of their Federal comrades but had managed to avoid heavy combat. At 2.00 p.m. on 22 July, all that was to change. Lieutenant Colonel Owen Stuart later reported on Cheatham's attack at his front that afternoon:

> At about 2 o clock the enemy attacked the Sixteenth and seventeenth Corps, and my regiment was ordered to deploy to the left and occupy the front of two regiments. In a short time the skirmishers at my front were driven in, and the enemy soon after appeared in heavy columns, advancing to attack. As soon as the skirmishers were all in my command opened fire on the enemy and soon broke their line in my front, and held them in check. They reformed, but were soon broken and forced to fall back in disorder. It was now discovered that they had broken the lines of the Second Division, on our right, and were pouring a heavy fire down our flanks and in the rear. The right wing of the regiment fell back about sixty yards, but were reformed, and went forward to retake the line, when they were ordered to fall back to the lines occupied early in the morning. The regiment was reformed in this line and received orders to advance and reoccupy the line carried by the enemy, which they did, the enemy retiring in great disorder.

The units attacking at the front and to the right of the 90th Illinois were Stevenson's and Brown's Confederate divisions and contained small amounts of scattered Irishmen in the ranks of the 24th Alabama and 9th and 10th Mississippi regiments.

With Cheatham's attack repelled, attention again switched to Cleburne and Walker off to the south. Two of Walker's brigades, including Mercer's brigade and its Savannah Irish, moved in to strike the Federal line from the east, while Cleburne's two brigades, including whatever was left of the Arkansas Irish, continued to fight their way up from the south. Walker's two brigades faced a newly formed Federal line, however, and made very little headway. Their attack soon spluttered out. The Irish Jasper Greens had three men captured and one wounded. Meanwhile, Cleburne's Arkansas brigade, led by Govan, was caught up in vicious hand-to-hand combat at a railway barricade. Their losses were terrible and doubtless some of the remaining Arkansas Irish fell in the fight. Hood's attack had ended in an appallingly gory failure. Yet Atlanta itself was still in Confederate hands.[9]

The Atlanta Campaign rolled on for a further two months, though after Hood's losses at the Battle of Atlanta there was little doubt that the city would eventually fall. Sherman now moved Howard's forces to cut the railway between East Point and Atlanta. Hood moved two of his corps to intercept and destroy this force at the Battle of Ezra Church on 28 July 1864. The battle ended in another defeat for Hood, but the railway was saved. Between 5 and 7 August, another attempt to cut the railway line ended in Federal defeat at Utoy Creek. A Confederate cavalry raid intended to cut Federal supply lines in North Georgia ended in failure at the Battle of Dalton on 14 and 15 August. Federals then conducted a cavalry raid of their own and were partially successful in destroying Confederate railway lines until Cleburne's troops halted their gallop at Lovejoy's Station on 20 August.

Sherman finally decided that a concentrated raid in force

on Confederate supply lines would compel them to surrender the city. On 25 August, six of his seven corps began moving towards the Macon and Western Railroad in the vicinity of Jonesborough. Hood then dispatched two of his corps, under Hardee, to intercept the Federal forces. They met west of Jonesborough on 31 August. By 1 September, Hardee was routed and in retreat. Hood abandoned Atlanta on the night of 1 September, burning all military supplies and installations before he left. (In fact, these great fires are depicted in the 1939 film *Gone with the Wind*.) The fall of Atlanta, coupled with the fall of Petersburg later that year, meant that the Southern dream of independence was over. One celebrated Irish Confederate general was about to meet with his untimely end too.

Sherman followed up his Atlanta Campaign by resting his men in the city for an uncharacteristically long time. This allowed Hood to plan his next move before Sherman could catch up with and defeat him. Hood and Confederate President Jefferson Davis decided that the Army of Tennessee should be moved back towards Chattanooga and threaten Sherman's supply lines, hoping that this would draw the Federals into a decisive battle. This initiated a series of battles known as the Franklin–Nashville Campaign. It was during one of these battles, the Second Battle of Franklin, on 30 November 1864 that Patrick Cleburne fell. It was later alleged that prior to the battle he had spoken of Ireland and its downtrodden state. Comparing Ireland to the South, he asked his men to fight in order that their home would not be subjugated as Ireland was.[10] The 36-year-old general was killed while leading his men in another of Hood's futile assaults at a heavily entrenched and fortified enemy. Just two months before he fell, Cleburne had written:

If this cause that is so dear to my heart is doomed to

fail, I pray heaven may let me fall with it, while my face
is toward the enemy and my arm battling for that which
I know to be right.[11]

His corps commander always remembered the Irishman affectionately and later paid tribute to his deeds:

> …friends and foes soon learned to watch the course of
> the blue flag that marked where Cleburne was in battle.
> Where his division defended, no odds broke its lines;
> where it attacked, no numbers resisted its onslaught,
> save only once – there is the grave of Cleburne and his
> heroic division.[12]

Today the Confederacy's most senior-ranking immigrant
officer is fondly remembered all over the American South.
Counties are named for him in Alabama and Arkansas, while
a Texan lake and city also bear his name. Yet little is known of
him in his native land. (In an interesting aside of the kind to
which historians would not usually resort, I should admit that
while I was born in the very same modern-day Roman
Catholic rural parish as Cleburne, no more than two miles
from his homestead, I had never heard of him before
researching this book.) The 'Stonewall of the West' is much
more a part of American, rather than Irish, historiography.

It seems that Cleburne already had an inkling that his
cause was 'doomed to fail' in October 1864. Very soon, his
words would prove to be prophetic. The decisive battle came
as Hood's depleted army moved in on Nashville. Sherman
had detached part of his command to Thomas, while he
moved towards Savannah with the rest of it. It was during
Sherman's march on Savannah that a horrific scorched-earth
policy emerged, as he attacked the South's ability to wage war
by attacking its civilian infrastructure. On 15 December,
Thomas attacked Hood's forces, initiating the Battle of
Nashville. The Confederate army was routed and in retreat by

the evening of 16 December. With the Franklin–Nashville Campaign now ended in failure, Hood had little option but to move his defeated command back into Mississippi, where he resigned, having forged a reputation as the most reckless of Confederate commanders.

Sherman captured Savannah on 22 December and was ordered to board his men on troop transports so that they could assist Grant at Petersburg. However, he convinced Grant that he should instead march his forces through South Carolina, continuing his scorched-earth policy. Joseph E. Johnston now took back command of the army that Hood had shattered and attempted to operate against Sherman in South Carolina. He simply did not have sufficient forces to do so, however, and after defeat at Bentonville on 21 March 1865, he surrendered the Army of Tennessee to Sherman on 26 April. Although some scattered Confederate forces maintained resistance until the summer, the American Civil War and the Irish participation in it was effectively over.

CHAPTER 18

THE AFTERMATH

Without a doubt, the American Civil War was a defining period for the Irish in America. The image of an Irish Brigade fighting valiantly to preserve the Union was one that conflicted sharply with the prejudiced views so frequently expressed before the war. Of course, anti-Irish prejudice did not disappear, but now the Irish had something with which they could counter it. Whenever their loyalty to their adopted country was questioned, they could, and frequently did, point to their record during America's bloodiest conflict. Over time that record was somewhat embellished in order to ensure that the Irish were depicted as the nation's most fearless and daring defenders. Indeed, Irish-Americans were skilfully able to play on the negative stereotype of the 'fighting Irish' in order to create an image of the Irish super-soldier who often succeeded where lesser men had failed.

In the years immediately after the war, some American newspapers even began to lend tacit support to the Fenian movement when it was mooted that the Irishmen might draw the British army into battle in North America. The British government's support of the Confederacy during the war had annoyed many Northern Americans and the prospect of somebody giving the British a bloody nose was something of which they initially approved. However, by the time the Fenian raids first struck Canada in 1866, that mild support did not extend far enough for Americans to risk another war, this time with the world's super-power, in order to 'liberate' a country of which they knew little, and cared even less. The Fenian raids were interfered with by US troops and ultimately defeated by the British.

Many Irish troops may have given good service to the US, but some still pointed out that the Irish had not given service in proportion with their overall numbers. Frustrations with the Irish voting in blocs were also commonly expressed through the media. Yet it was the Irish tendency to vote in bloc, and the sheer weight of their numbers, which helped them gain immense political power in the late nineteenth and early twentieth centuries. As a result of this power, the Irish gained greater respect. In addition, Irish war heroes were to the forefront in consolidating this power by placing the Irish at the heart of the nation's greatest conflict. Monuments to Irish units were erected on many of the battlefields, ensuring that the nation afforded an equal measure of respect to those Irishmen who had died in its defence.[1]

While the concept of the Federal Irish war hero was helpful for Irish-Americans, Confederate Irish war heroes were considerably less so. However, many of the Irish living in Southern states also flourished after the war. Their assistance to the Confederate war effort gained them some respect and may have assisted a few who advanced themselves in the worlds of business and politics.

***

While researching this book, I journeyed to America in order to survey some of the areas I was writing about and was fortunate enough to walk on the very ground where some of this story unfolded. I experienced the searing heat in which many of these battles were fought and began to appreciate how difficult it was for an Irishman to walk 20 yards, never mind march 20 miles, under such conditions. It was an experience that was both interesting and moving.

Gettysburg is America's greatest monument to the Civil War. All around the vast expanse of the battlefield, monuments to various units and states dominate the modern landscape. In spite of all the monuments, however, it is still more than possible to gain an appreciation of the kind of topography over which these men fought and the close proximity in which many Irish units moved.

For the Irish visitor, one of Gettysburg's monuments will probably stand out more than any of the others. It was the twilight of the evening when I found the Corby statue. It stands behind Cemetery Ridge in the shadow of the colossal Pennsylvania monument. Ural Bruce has advanced the theory that this little bronze statuette of an Irish-American priest 'became one of the most powerful symbols in America of the identity Irish Catholics created for themselves as loyal, active American citizens who also remained true to their ethnic heritage'.[2]

The Corby Monument at Gettysburg.

Thus, as I watched the light fading from the sky behind Fr Corby's enduring image, I was conscious that I was not only looking at a monument to the American Civil War, but also a monument to the hundreds of thousands of Irish people who left Ireland and forged a new life and a new identity thousands of miles from their humble origins. Today, Corby holds out his hand and offers an Irish blessing to all the soldiers who fought on that field, be they Catholic or Protestant, Irish, European, American or otherwise:

Ar a dheis Dé go raibh a n-anamacha.

Appendix I: Organisational Structures

The following is a guide to the organisational structure of forces engaged during the American Civil War.

Army: An army was the largest fighting unit in the war, ranging from 10,000 to 150,000 men. An army usually consisted of several corps comprised of infantry, artillery and cavalry along with various logistical and support units.

Corps: The corps was the largest unit within an army. Armies could consist of anything from two to ten corps. A corps itself included infantry, cavalry and artillery, although some exclusively cavalry corps were organised.

Division: It took two or more divisions to comprise a corps. In theory, a division consisted of about 12,000 men in three or more brigades.

Brigade: A brigade consisted of up to 4,000 men in four to six regiments. As the war wore on and casualties mounted, however, brigades were often drawn from the remnants of up to fifteen regiments.

Regiment: Ideally, an infantry regiment consisted of ten companies of 100 men. Cavalry and artillery regiments had twelve companies. Each company was assigned a letter for its title. However, the letter J was excluded, according to tradition. As the war continued, average regimental sizes fell from the prerequisite 1,000 to as low as 300.

Battalion: Battalions were not a typical part of either army. Occasionally, however, a number of companies formed a battalion, where the sufficient number of ten could not be reached and therefore regimental status could not be achieved.

Company: A company was the smallest unit in service. It was often formed from pre-war militia groups.

APPENDIX II: BASIC WEAPONS AND TACTICS

The following is a guide to the basic weapons and tactics typically used during the battles described in this text.

Artillery: An artillery crew ideally consisted of ten men. A lieutenant and sergeant gave orders, a gunner aimed the cannon and seven men cleaned, loaded and fired the piece. A well-drilled crew could fire three times per minute. Six guns comprised a Federal battery, while four comprised a Confederate battery. There were five batteries to a Federal brigade, or four to a battalion in the case of the Confederacy. Each Federal corps was supported by an artillery brigade, with approximately five such brigades held in reserve by the army. Each Confederate division was supported by an artillery battalion and each corps had a further two battalions in reserve. There was no army artillery reserve.

The three most common types of cannon used during the war were the 12-pound Napoleon, the 10-pound Parrot rifle (each named for the weight of the solid shot they fired) and the 3-inch ordinance rifle (named for the width of its barrel). These cannon fired four types of basic ordinance:

1. Solid shot was a ball or elongated projectile made of solid iron. It was typically used against massed troops at long range or against fortifications.

2. Case shot was a hollow iron shell filled with shrapnel. Gunpowder in the centre of the shell was detonated by a timed fuse, scattering the shrapnel and remnants of the shell among the troops whose ranks it hit.

3. A shell was a round or elongated projectile filled with gunpowder. It could be detonated with an impact or a timed fuse. Timed fuses were frequently used by experienced artillerists wishing to explode the shell over the heads of the troops at which it was aimed.

4. Canister was a tin projectile filled with iron balls that were a little smaller than a golf ball. When loaded with canister, a cannon effectively operated like a large shotgun, spewing innumerable projectiles from its barrel at close-range targets. It was typically employed against infantry advancing on an artillery battery. An earlier form of canister fire (where a lesser number of projectiles were arranged on a threaded bolt in the cannon) was known as grape shot. Grape shot was not widely used during the Civil War, but soldiers frequently referred to canister fire by that name.

Infantry: The standard infantry unit of the Civil War was the regiment. In battle, a regiment was deployed in two long straight lines, or ranks. Frequently a company or two of skirmishers were deployed ahead of these two ranks in order to probe the enemy's line. Regimental flags, or colours, were carried by the regiment's colour company (a duty often performed by Irish companies in Confederate service) at the centre of the regimental line. The colours served as a guide for men who could not hear orders amidst the din of battle.

Infantry men were armed first with smooth-bore muskets, but later with rifled muskets. The rifled grooves on the barrels of these muskets spun the 'minie' balls that they fired. The spinning projectile had an effective range of up to 400 yards and a far greater degree of accuracy.

The most common attacks performed by infantrymen were full frontal assaults and flanking attacks. The full frontal assault was a massed assault directed straight at the enemy's front. The idea was that sheer numbers of men could overwhelm the enemy and drive him from the field. This kind of assault had been popular during the Mexican War fifteen years earlier. By the time of the Civil War, improved firearm and cannon technology allowed the defender an advantage and full frontal assaults were less successful. The other tactic often employed by infantry was a flank attack. This involved moving the attacking force in at the enemy's side, or flank. The attack was difficult to perform but had the advantage of placing 'enfilading' fire into the sides of the enemy's line. (Enfilading fire is commonly known as flanking fire. A line of troops is exposed to enfilading fire when the enemy can direct fire along its longest access; in other words, can fire from the side along the length of their line.)

Cavalry: Cavalry were troops mounted on horseback engaged in operations for which a high degree of mobility was required. The main activities in which cavalry was involved were reconnaissance, delaying actions, pursuit and harassment, and raiding against enemy lines of communications and supply.

The smallest unit of cavalry organisation was a troop. Ten to twelve troops comprised a cavalry regiment. Early in the war, these regiments were attached to larger infantry forces, but as the war advanced and the value of cavalry reconnaissance became more apparent, separate cavalry divisions and corps became an integral part of opposing armies. Cavalrymen were armed with sabres, muskets, carbines (with a shorter barrel than a musket) and pistols. They also carried horse-drawn artillery.

Appendix III: Summary of Irish Units

The following is a list of wholly or substantially Irish units on both sides during the American Civil War. The list is not exhaustive and contains merely those units that are essential to the narrative of this text. Indeed, the information contained here also appears in the main text and is there credited to the various sources from which it was drawn. For the reader's convenience the units appear under Confederate and Federal headings.

Confederate

1st Georgia Volunteer Infantry: This unit was initially recruited from the militias of Savannah. As such, the unit contained three significantly Irish companies. Those companies were the Jasper Greens, the Republican Blues and the Irish Volunteers. Their membership was comprised of the Irish and Scotch-Irish communities of Georgia.

1st Special Battalion Louisiana Volunteers (Wheat's Tigers): Recruited from among the dock workers of New Orleans, this unit was often noted for its substantially Irish composition. Also noted for ill discipline, the unit was disbanded in August 1862, as its soldiers had become unmanageable.

1st Virginia Irish Battalion: This unit, smaller than a regiment, was raised in the railroad and seaport centres of Richmond, Alexandria, Norfolk, Lynchburg and Covington, where clusters of Irish immigrants worked.

2nd/15th Arkansas Infantry: A consolidated regiment with a significant number of Irishmen among its ranks.

3rd Confederate Infantry Regiment: A predominantly Irish unit formed after the consolidation of several Confederate units (2nd Tennessee, 21st Tennessee and 5th Confederate) containing significant numbers of Irishmen and Irish companies.

10th Tennessee Infantry: Raised from among the Irish population of Nashville, this unit was one of only two Confederate regiments that were predominantly Roman Catholic. Companies were also recruited in Pulaski, Clarkesville and McEwen.

15th Arkansas Infantry: Not a specifically Irish unit, however it was Cleburne's first command and had some Irish names scattered among its ranks.

Company K, 15th Alabama Infantry: The 15th Alabama was commanded by Colonel William C. Oates, who described Company K of his Regiment as 'an Irish Company.' Perhaps his own Irish heritage led to Oates' expression of some pride in the fighting prowess of this company, a large part of which were Irish-born labourers, with only a few second generation Irish completing its make-up. When war broke out in April 1861, some ninety Irish immigrants who had settled in towns along the Chattahoochee River enlisted in Company K.

Davis Guards, 1st Texas Heavy Artillery: An entirely Irish company from Houston, Texas, led by Galway-born Dick Dowling. The unit won fame for defending a proposed Federal invasion at Sabine Pass.

Emerald Guard, Company E 33rd Virginia Infantry: Raised in Shenandoah County from among recently arrived Irish labourers on the Manassas Gap Railroad.

Emerald Guards, Company I, 8th Alabama Infantry: The colour company of the 8th Alabama, this unit was solidly Irish. It is estimated that 104 of its initial 109 Irish recruits were born in Ireland.

Emmet Rifles, Company B, 1st Georgia Regular Infantry: An Irish company most likely recruited from among pre-war militia units in Georgia.

Hays' Louisiana brigade: Hays' Louisiana brigade consisted of the 5th, 6th, 7th, 8th, and 14th Louisiana Infantry Regiments. All of these regiments had significant numbers of Irishmen among their personnel. At the beginning of the war the 5th had ninety-four Irish-born men among its ranks. The 6th contained two distinctly Irish companies that were originally intended to form part of a Confederate Irish brigade. Also among the ranks of the 6th was a company known as the Calhoun Guards. The Calhouns took their name from John C. Calhoun, who was the son of an Irish immigrant, and were primarily composed of native Irishmen. The 7th contained four Irish companies among them the 'Irish Volunteers' and

'Sarsfield Rangers'. A Confederate soldier noted that the 7th Louisiana 'was composed mostly of Irishmen.' The 8th included a primarily Irish company known as the Cheneyville Rifles. Company E of the 9th Louisiana was known as the Emerald Guards in acknowledgement of its Irish ethnicity. The 14th Louisiana was of mixed ethnicity. Known as Lee's Foreign Legion, the regiment had initially been intended to form part of a Polish brigade. Yet Irishmen were the most dominant nationality among its ranks and civil war historian Ella Lonn reported that six of its twelve companies were predominantly Irish.

Irish Volunteers, Company K, 1st South Carolina: Colour Company of the 1st South Carolina, this unit formed the nucleus of the regiment. The company was organised in Charleston and was the first to volunteer for service in the war.

Jackson Guards, Company B, 19th Georgia Infantry: Colour Company of the 19th Georgia, this unit was recruited from among the Irish immigrants of Atlanta.

Jasper Grays, Company F, 16th Mississippi: Raised in 1861 from among Irish Catholics in Paulding, Jasper County, Mississippi.

Lochrane Guards, Company F, Phillips Legion Infantry: An Irish company from Macon in Georgia that came to prominence at the sunken road in Fredericksburg.

McMillan Guards, Company K, 24th Georgia Infantry: Raised in Habersham County, Georgia, by Antrim-born Robert McMillan, this unit had a number of Irishmen among its ranks. Its most famous hour came when it defended the sunken road at Fredericksburg.

Montgomery Guards, Company C, 1st Virginia Infantry: A pre-war militia unit raised from among Irish immigrants in Richmond, Virginia.

Montgomery Guards, Company F, 19th Virginia Infantry: Raised in the Charlottesville area, this company was known to have a significantly Irish character.

Montgomery Guards, Company K, 20th Georgia Infantry: A predominantly Irish company recruited in Richmond County, Georgia.

Starke's Louisiana brigade: Among the soldiers of Starke's brigade were two companies of Irishmen known as the Montgomery Guards and the Emmet Guards in the 1st Louisiana under the command of Tipperary-born Lieutenant Colonel Michael Nolan. They were joined by a further two Irish Companies within the 2nd Louisiana known as the Orleans Light Guards and the Moore Guards, the Emerald Guards of the 9th Louisiana, five Irish companies in the 10th Louisiana and a 'significant number' of Irishmen scattered throughout the ranks of the 15th Louisiana. It should be noted that regiments from both Louisiana brigades were transferred from brigade to brigade. It should also be noted that Hays and Starke did not always command these brigades. However, the brigades came to be known by those names. The brigades are described as Hays' and Starke's here, for the sake of simplicity, as the numeration of brigades and regiments could cause confusion.

Virginia Hibernians, Company B, 27th Virginia Infantry: The colour company of the 27th Virginia, this unit was raised in Alleghany County from among the Irish immigrant population.

Federal

7th Missouri Infantry: This unit was raised primarily in St Louis, Missouri. However the regiment also contained companies from Milton and Clarkesville, Missouri, and Belleville, Sumner and Chicago, Illinois, and even a company from Keokuk, Iowa. The unit was far from being exclusively Irish, but the Irish were its principle ethnic component. In all, it is estimated that of some 1,000 men who initially served in the unit, approximately 400 were Irish.

9th Massachusetts Infantry: Recruited from among the immigrant Irish in Boston, this unit was initially funded by Patrick Donahoe, publisher of the Boston Pilot.

10th Ohio Infantry: Recruited from among the Irish immigrant population of Cincinnati, by Major Joseph W. Burke, the unit also contained some German immigrants.

17th Wisconsin Infantry: Recruited from among the Irish immigrant population of Wisconsin, this unit was organised at Madison and mustered into Federal service in March 1862.

23rd Illinois Infantry: Sometimes referred to as the 'Western Irish Brigade' this unit was recruited from among Chicago's Irish immigrant population. *35th Indiana Infantry*: The 35th Indiana consisted primarily of Irish immigrants who had worked on the railroads and canals of Indiana. They came from cities such as Lafayette, Indianapolis, Terre Haute and small river communities like Madison on the Ohio River. Company H was raised in Dayton, Ohio. The regiment was mustered into Federal service in December 1861 and kitted out with dark green coats and green cloth caps.

37th New York Infantry: Known as the 'Irish Rifles' this unit was recruited from among Irish immigrants in New York.

69th Pennsylvania Infantry: Recruited from Irish militia units in Philadelphia this unit was initially designated the 2nd California and credited to the western state. The designation was later changed to the 24th Pennsylvania, then the 68th Pennsylvania, before the unit was finally designated the 69th Pennsylvania in honour of the Irishmen of New York's 'Fighting 69th.'

90th Illinois Infantry: This unit was mustered into Federal service on 7 September 1862. It had been raised from among the Irish in various towns and cities throughout Illinois including Rockford, Galva, Lockport, LaSalle, Joliet, Chicago, Springfield and Belvedere. Company K had the distinction of having been raised across the border in nearby Ottawa.

140th New York Infantry: This unit was raised in upstate New York in the city of Rochester. Rochester's Irish population was significant throughout the nineteenth century and, consequently, large numbers of Irishmen were scattered throughout its ranks. Indeed, the regiment had two specifically Irish companies, C and K. In addition it was led by the Cavan-born Patrick O'Rorke.

Corcoran Legion: The Corcoran Legion consisted of the following four regiments:
- 155th New York Volunteer Infantry
- 182nd New York Infantry (also known as the 69th New York National Guard)
- 170th New York Infantry
- 164th New York Infantry (also known as the Corcoran Guard).

All four regiments were recruited from among the Irish of New York state and city.

Irish Brigade: The most famous Irish unit of the American Civil War, it was at various times composed of six different infantry regiments. They were:

- 63rd New York Infantry
- 69th New York Infantry: Formed out of the old 69th New York State Militia, a pre-war militia unit founded by Irish immigrants in New York in 1851. This was the core unit of the Irish Brigade and was often referred to as the 'Fighting 69th.'
- 88th New York Infantry: Mustered into service in the autumn of 1861, this unit was actually the amalgamation of the old 2nd and 4th New York Infantry regiments. Its men were recruited from among the Irish immigrant populations of New York and New Jersey
- 28th Massachusetts Infantry: This was the second regiment recruited from among the Irish immigrant population of Boston. It did not join the Irish Brigade until November 1862.
- 29th Massachusetts Infantry: A non-Irish unit that served with the Irish Brigade until the arrival of the 28th Massachusetts in November 1862.
- 116th Pennsylvania Infantry: Recruited from among the Irish of Philedelphia in the summer of 1862, this regiment joined the Irish Brigade in October 1862. The 116th Pennsylvania also resorted to recruitment from outside of the Irish community in order to fill up its ranks.

ENDNOTES

Chapter 1
1   Gleeson, David T., *The Irish in the South 1815–1877*, University of North Carolina Press, North Carolina, 2001, p.1.

Chapter 2
1   Tim Pat Coogan, *Wherever Green is Worn: The Story of the Irish Diaspora*, Arrow, London, 2002, p. 254 and p. 255.
2   *Ibid.*, p. 256.
3   University of Virginia, *McCue Family Papers*, Accession #4406.
4   Gleeson, *The Irish in the South*, pp. 24–5.
5   *Ibid.*, pp. 26–36.

Chapter 3
1   Gleeson, *The Irish in the South.*, p. 142.
2   www.confederateflags.org/FOTCflagmakers1.htm.
3   The battles of the American Civil War were often known by two names. Federal forces tended to name the engagements for the nearest river (in this case, Bull Run Creek), while Confederate forces named them for the nearest town (in this case, Manassas).
4   www.historynet.com/wars_conflicts/american_civil_war/ 3035781.html?page=1&c=y.
5   Sean Michael O'Brien, *Irish Americans in the Confederate Army*, McFarland & Company, North Carolina, 2007, p. 43.
6   For a detailed account of the activities of Wheat's Tigers at First Manassas (from which much of my account is drawn) see Gary Schreckengost, '1st Louisiana Special Battalion at The First Battle of Manassas, America's Civil War, May 1999'. This article is currently available at: www.historynet.com/1st-louisiana-special-battalion-at-the-first-battle-of-manassas.htm.
7   Colonel Robert Withers, Official Report, First Battle of Manassas.
8   O'Brien, Irish Americans in the Confederate Army, pp. 45–6.

Chapter 4

1   Ed Gleeson, *Rebel Sons of Erin: A Civil War Unit History of the Tenth Tennessee Infantry Regiment (Irish) Confederate States Volunteers*, Guild Press, Indiana, 1993, p. 21.

2   *Ibid.*, pp. 48–62.

3   *Ibid.*, pp. 69–70.

4   *Ibid.*, p. 82.

5   *Ibid.*, p. 100.

6   *Ibid.*, p. 135–40.

7   *Ibid.*, pp. 142–3.

8   Muriel Phillips Joslyn (ed.), *A Meteor Shining Brightly: Essays on Major General Patrick R. Cleburne*, Mercer University Press, Georgia, 2000, pp. 1–17.

9   O'Brien, *Irish Americans in the Confederate Army*, p. 110.

10 *Ibid.*

11 *Ibid.*, pp. 111–12. See also William Lee White, 'Cleburne's Own: The 15th Arkansas Regiment from Helena to Shiloh' and Carl H. Moneyhon, 'Cleburne's Early War Years: The Emergence of a Leader' in Phillips Joslyn (ed), *A Meteor Shining Brightly*, pp. 34–57.

Chapter 5

1   John F. McCormack, Jnr, in *Civil War Times*, December 1998.

2   Lawrence Frederick Kohl (ed.), William Corby C.S.C., *Memoirs of Chaplain Life: Three Years with the Irish Brigade in the Army of the Potomac*, Fordham University Press, New York, 1992, p. 61.

3   Frank A. Boyle, *A Party of Mad Fellows: The Story of the Irish Regiments in the Army of the Potomac*, Moringside, Ohio, 1996, p. 101.

4   Colonel S.B. Hayman, Battle of Seven Pines, Official Report.

5   A. Milburn Petty, 'A History of the 37th New York Volunteer Infantry' in *The Journal of the American Irish Historical Society*, early 1920s.

6   Daniel M. Callaghan, *Thomas Francis Meagher and the Irish Brigade in the Civil War*, McFarland & Company, North Carolina, 2006, p. 71.

7   Kelly J. O'Grady, *Clear the Confederate Way: The Irish in the Army of Northern Virginia*, Savas Publishing, Iowa, 2000, p. 249 & www.37thtexas.org/html/CoI8thAla.html.

8   O'Brien, *Irish Americans in the Confederate Army*, p. 30.

9   Captain B.W. Leigh, Official Report, Battle of Gaines Mill and Malvern Hill.

10 Michael R. Thomas, 'Confederate Firing Squad at Centreville: First Military Executions in the Army of Northern Virginia', *Northern Virginia Heritage*, Vol. 2, No. 2, June 1980.

11 See www.geocities.com/ddhillman2002/ and O'Grady, *Clear the Confederate Way*, p. 254.

12 O'Brien, *Irish Americans in the Confederate Army*, pp. 57–61.

13 Boyle, *A Party of Mad Fellows*, pp. 119–20.

14 Callaghan, *Thomas Francis Meagher and The Irish Brigade in the Civil War*, p. 76.

15 Christian G. Samito (ed.), *Commanding Boston's Irish Ninth: The Civil War Letters of Colonel Patrick R. Guiney, Ninth Massachusetts Volunteer Infantry*, Fordham University Press, New York, 1998, p. 114.

16 Boyle, *A Party of Mad Fellows*, p. 132.

17 Brigadier General W.M.H. French, Official Report, Seven Days Battles.

18 Major General D.H. Hill, Official Report, Seven Days Battles.

19 Callaghan, *Thomas Francis Meagher and The Irish Brigade in the Civil War*, p.78.

20 Boyle, *A Party of Mad Fellows*, p. 136.

21 William H. Osborne, *The History of the Twenty-ninth Regiment of Massachusetts Volunteer Infantry in the Late War of the Rebellion*, Albert J. Wright, Boston, 1887, p. 152 in Boyle, *A Party of Mad Fellows*, p. 137.

22 Brigadier C.M. Wilcox, Official Report, Battle of Glendale.

23 Brigadier General W.M.W. Burns, Official Report, Seven Days Battles.

24 Anthony W. McDermott, *A Brief History of the 69th Regiment Pennsylvania Veteran Volunteers*, D.J. Gallagher & Co., Philadelphia, 1889, p. 15.

25 Callaghan, *Thomas Francis Meagher and The Irish Brigade in the* Phillip Thomas Tucker, *Irish Confederates: The Civil War's Forgotten Soldiers*, McWhiney Foundation Press, Texas, 2006, p. 43.

27 Callaghan, *Thomas Francis Meagher and the Irish Brigade*, p. 86.

28 *Ibid.*

29 Tucker, *Irish Confederates*, p. 46.

30 Lieutenant Colonel H.S. Campbell, Official Report, Seven Days Battles.

31 Kohl (ed.), Corby, *Memoirs of Chaplain Life*, p. 93.

32 McDermott, A Brief History of the 69th Regiment Pennsylvania Veteran Volunteers, p. 17.

Chapter 6

1 Brigadier General James H. Lane, Official Report, Battle of Cedar Mountain.

2 O'Grady, *Clear the Confederate Way*, p. 92.

3 *Ibid.*, p. 88.

4 *Ibid.*

5 *Ibid.*, pp. 249–59.

6 James P. Gannon, *Irish Rebels Confederate Tigers: A History of the 6th Louisiana Volunteers, 1861–1865*, Savas Publishing, Iowa, 1998, pp. 99–100.

7   *Ibid.*, p. 101.
8   *Ibid.*, p. 103.
9   Brigadier General J.A. Early, Official Report, Second Battle of Manassas.
10 Sandy Barnard (ed.), *Campaigning with the Irish Brigade: Pvt. John Ryan, 28th Massachusetts*, AST Press, Indiana, 2001, p. 54.
11 Travel Brains Inc., *The History Channel: Great Battles of the Civil War*, Manassas II.
12 Colonel Bradley T. Johnson, Official Report, Second Battle of Manassas.
13 Barnard, pp. 55–6.
14 McDermott, *A Brief History of the 69th Regiment Pennsylvania Veteran Volunteers*, p. 17.

Chapter 7

1   Kohl (ed.), Corby, *Memoirs of Chaplain Life*, pp. 111–12.
2   Gannon, *Irish Rebels: Confederate Tigers*, p. 135.
3   For details of Irishmen within the 6th Alabama see O'Brien, *Irish Americans in the Confederate Army*, pp. 74–5.
4   Kohl (ed.), Corby, *Memoirs of Chaplain Life*, p. 112.
5   Joseph Bilby and Stephen O'Neill (eds.), *My Sons were Faithful and They Fought: The Irish Brigade at Antietam: An Anthology*, Longstreet House, New Jersey, 1997, pp. 51–8.
6   Bilby and O'Neill (eds.), *My Sons were Faithful and They Fought*, pp. 51–8.
7   Callaghan, *Thomas Francis Meagher and the Irish Brigade*, p. 104.
8   General George B. McClellan, Official Report, Battle of Antietam.
9   Lieutenant Colonel Patrick Kelly, Official Report, Battle of Antietam.
10 Callaghan, *Thomas Francis Meagher and the Irish Brigade*, p. 103.
11 *Ibid.*, p. 105.
12 Bilby and O'Neill (eds.), *My Sons were Faithful and They Fought*, pp. 51–8.
13 *Irish American*, 18 October 1862.
14 www.thewildgeese.com.
15 Tucker, *Irish Confederates*, pp. 51–2.
16 Barnard (ed.), *Campaigning with the Irish Brigade*, p. 62.
17 O'Brien, *Irish Americans in the Confederate Army*, p. 77.

Chapter 8

1   Carl H. Moneyhon in Joslyn (ed.), *A Meteor Shining Brightly*, p. 55.
2   Lieutenant Colonel Francis Darrs, Official Report.
3   Captain Joseph J. Slocum, Official Report.

4   William L. Burton, *Melting Pot Soldiers: The Union's Ethnic Regiments*, Fordham University Press, New York, 1998, pp. 145–7.

5   Brigadier General B.R. Johnson, Official Report, Battle of Perryville.

6   Colonel L.A. Harris, Official Report, Battle of Perryville.

7   Captain Peter Simonson, Official Report, Battle of Perryville.

8   Wisconsin Legislature, Senate Joint Resolution 7, 2005.

9   Colonel John L. Doran, Official Report, Second Battle of Corinth.

10 Brigadier General Thomas J. McKean and Brigadier General John McArthur, Official Reports, Second Battle of Corinth.

11 For more information on the 35th Indiana see; Brian D Henry, 'The 35th Indiana: Hoosier State's "1st Irish" ' @ www.thewildgeese.com/pages/35thind.html.

12 Colonel Bernard Mullen, Official Report, Battle of Stones River.

Chapter 9

1   Kevin E. O'Brien (ed.), *My Life in the Irish Brigade: The Civil War Memoirs of Private William McCarter, 116th Pennsylvania Infantry*, Savas Publishing, California, 1996, pp. 143–8.

2   Boyle, *A Party of Mad Fellows*, p. 205.

3   McDermott, *A Brief History of the 69th Regiment Pennsylvania Veteran Volunteers*, p. 24.

4   Brigadier General Meagher, Official Report, Battle of Fredericksburg, and O'Brien (ed.) *My Life in the Irish Brigade*.

5   O'Brien (ed.), *My Life in the Irish Brigade*, pp. 156–7.

6   Lawrence Frederick Kohl (ed.), *Irish Green and Union Blue: The Civil War Letters of Peter Welsh: Color Sergeant 28th Regiment Massachusetts Volunteers*, Fordham University Press, New York, 1986, p. 41.

7   Callaghan, *Thomas Francis Meagher and the Irish Brigade*, p. 136.

8   O'Grady, *Clear the Confederate Way*, p. 123.

9   *Ibid.*, p. 250.

10 *Ibid.*, p. 109.

11 *Ibid.*

12 *Ibid.*

13 Kohl, *Irish Green and Union Blue*, p. 42.

14 O'Brien (ed.), *My Life in the Irish Brigade*, p. 165.

15 Callaghan, *Thomas Francis Meagher and the Irish Brigade*, p. 124.

16 Tucker, *Irish Confederates*, p. 59.

17 Brigadier General Meagher, Official Report, Battle of Fredericksburg.

18 O'Grady, *Clear the Confederate Way*, p. 125.

19 Callaghan, *Thomas Francis Meagher and the Irish Brigade*, p127.

20 O'Brien (ed.), *My Life in the Irish Brigade*, p. vii.
21 Colonel Richard Byrnes, Official Report, Battle of Fredericksburg.
22 O'Brien (ed.), *My Life in the Irish Brigade*, p. 181.
23 MacDermott, *A Brief History of the 69th Regiment Pennsylvania Veteran Volunteers*, pp. 23–4.
24 Daniel George Macnamara, *The History of the Ninth Regiment Massachusetts Volunteer Infantry, June 1861–June 1864*, Fordham University Press, New York, 2000, p. 254.
25 O'Brien (ed.), *My Time in the Irish Brigade*, p. 188.
26 Kohl, *Irish Green and Union Blue*, p. 46.
27 O'Grady, *Clear the Confederate Way*, pp. 122–3.
28 Callaghan, *Thomas Francis Meagher and the Irish Brigade*, p. 131.
29 *Boston Pilot*, 7 February 1863.
30 O'Grady, *Clear the Confederate Way*, pp. 120–22.

Chapter 10

1   Myles Dungan, *Distant Drums: Irish Soldiers in Foreign Armies*, Appletree Press, Belfast, 1993, p. 21.
2   O'Brien (ed.), *My Life in the Irish Brigade*, p. 187.
3   O'Brien (ed.), *My Life in the Irish Brigade*, p. 240, note 2.
4   Boyle, *A Party of Mad Fellows*, p. 238.
5   Thomas Francis Galwey, *The Valiant Hours: Narrative of 'Captain Brevet' and Irish-Americans in the Army of the Potomac*, Stackpole, London, 1961, pp. 74–5.
6   O'Brien, *Irish-Americans in the Confederate Army*, p. 90.
7   Callaghan, *Thomas Francis Meagher*, p. 149.
8   Major St Clair Mulholland, Official Report, Battle of Chancellorsville.
9   Gannon, *Irish Rebels: Confederate Tigers*, pp. 157–61.
10 *Ibid.*, p. 156 and Lieutenant Colonel John A. Cress, Official Report, Battle of Chancellorsville.
11 For account of Hays' Brigade at Chancellorsville see: Gannon, *Irish Rebels: Confederate Tigers*, pp. 153–168.

Chapter 11

1   Callaghan, *Thomas Francis Meagher and the Irish Brigade*, p. 152.
2   Jeremiah O'Donovan Rossa, *Rossa's Recollections 1838 to 1898: Memoirs of an Irish Revolutionary*, The Lyons Press, Connecticut, 2004, p. 386.
3   Corby, *Memoirs of Chaplain Life*, pp. 182–3.
4   Stewart, *140th Pennsylvania*, in Boyle, *A Party of Mad Fellows*, p. 267.
5   Murphy, *Kelly's Heroes: The Irish Brigade at Gettysburg*, Farnsworth House, Gettysburg, 1997, pp. 24–6.
6   See Murphy, *The Irish Brigade at Gettysburg*, pp. 26–40.
7   See, Bennett, Brian A, *The Beau Ideal of a Soldier and a Gentleman: The*

Life of Colonel Patrick Henry O'Rorke from Ireland to Gettysburg, Triphammer Publishing, New York, 1996.

8   Tucker, *Irish Confederates*, p. 84.

9   Colonel William C. Oates, Official Report, Battle of Gettysburg.

10 Harry Gilmor, *Four Years in the Saddle*, in Gannon, *Irish Rebels: Confederate Tigers*, p. 196.

11 See Gannon, *Irish Rebels: Confederate Tigers*, pp. 189–99.

12 O'Brien, *Irish Americans in the Confederate Army*, p. 94.

13 *Ibid.*

14 Tucker, *Irish Confederates*, p. 83.

15 McDermott, *A Brief History of the 69th Regiment Pennsylvania Veteran Volunteers*, p. 30.

16 *Ibid.*, p. 31.

17 *Ibid.*

18 O'Brien, *Irish Americans in the Confederate Army*, p. 98.

19 For an account of Irish Confederate participation in Pickett's charge see; O'Brien, *Irish Americans in the Confederate Army*, pp. 94–99.

20 McDermott, *A Brief History of the 69th Regiment Pennsylvania Veteran Volunteers*, pp. 31–2.

21 *Ibid.*

22 Bilby and O'Neill (eds.), *My Sons were Faithful and They Fought*, pp. 91–2.

23 McDermott, *A Brief History of the 69th Regiment Pennsylvania Veteran Volunteers*, pp. 32–3.

Chapter 12

1   Jerry Evan Crouch, *Silencing the Vicksburg Guns: The Story of the 7th Missouri Infantry Regiment, as Experienced by John Davis Evans Union Private and Mormon Pioneer*, Trafford Publishing, British Columbia, 2005, p. 2.

2   Patrick Griffin, 'The Famous Tenth Tennessee', *Confederate Veteran Magazine*, 1905 in Blackwell Drake, Rebecca, *The Exploits of Patrick Griffin: He must have been Irish* at:
    www. battleofraymond.org/history/griffin1.htm.

3   Crouch, *Silencing the Vicksburg Guns*, pp. 69–75 and Gleeson, *Rebel Sons of Erin*, pp. 177–85.

4   Brigadier General T.E.G. Ransom, Official Report, Siege of Vicksburg.

5   Crouch, *Silencing the Vicksburg Guns*, pp. 92–8.

6   Brigadier General T.E.G. Ransom, Official Report, Siege of Vicksburg.

7   Crouch, *Silencing the Vicksburg Guns*, pp. 99–102.

8   Information on 90th Illinois taken from the Report of the Adjutant General of the State of Illinois vol. V, containing reports for the Years 1861–66. Revised by Brigadier General J.N. Reece, Adjutant General.

1900. Springfield, Ill., Phillips Bros., State Printers @ www.illinoiscivilwar.org/cw90-agr.html.

9   Tucker, *Irish Confederates*, p. 97.

10   O'Brien, *Irish Americans in the Confederate Army*, p. 204. The garrison actually consisted of forty-seven men, including Dowling.

11   Tucker, *Irish Confederates*, p. 95.

12   E.G. Littlejohn, *Brave Dick Dowling; Robert Edward Lee*, B.F. Johnson Pub. Co., Richmond, 1901, p. 6.

Chapter 13

1   Gleeson, *Rebel Sons of Erin*, p. 219.

2   O'Brien, *Irish Americans in the Confederate Army*, p. 128–31.

3   Gleeson, *Rebel Sons of Erin*, pp. 231–49.

4   Major John P. Dufficy, Battle of Chickamauga, Official Report.

5   Colonel John Mason Loomis, Battle of Chattanooga, Official Report.

6   General Patrick Cleburne, Battle of Chattanooga, Official Report.

7   Brigadier General William B. Bate, Battle of Chattanooga, Official Report.

8   Gleeson, *Rebel Sons of Erin*, pp. 265–9.

Chapter 14

1   Callaghan, *Thomas Francis Meagher and the Irish Brigade*, p. 166.

2   Leslie M. Harris, *In the Shadow of Slavery: African Americans in New York City 1626–1863*, University of Chicago Press, Chicago, 2003, pp. 279–88.

3   David Herbert Donald, Jean H. Baker and Michael F. Holt, *Civil War and Reconstruction*, W.W. Norton & Company, New York, 2002, p. 229.

4   Susannah Ural Bruce, *The Harp and the Eagle: Irish American Volunteers and the Union Army, 1861–1865*, New York University Press, New York, 2006, pp. 86–98.

5   Ural Bruce, *The Harp and the Eagle*, pp. 111–12.

6   O'Grady, *Clear the Confederate Way*, p. 12.

7   *Ibid.*, pp. 10–46.

8   Joseph M. Hernon, Jr, Celts, *Catholics and Copperheads: Ireland Views the American Civil War*, Ohio State University Press, Ohio, 1968, p. 17.

9   *Nation*, 23 August 1862 in Hernon, *Celts. Catholics and Copperheads*, p. 21.

10   Hernon, *Celts, Catholics and Copperheads*, p. 27.

11   *Ibid.*, pp. 23–37.

Chapter 15

1   Callaghan, *Thomas Francis Meagher and the Irish Brigade*, p. 173.

2   Christian G. Samito (ed.), *Commanding Boston's Irish Ninth*, p. 246.

3   Macnamara, *The History of the Ninth*, pp. 372–3.

4   Gannon, *Irish Rebels: Confederate Tigers*, pp. 226–7.
5   Callaghan, *Thomas Francis Meagher and the Irish Brigade*, pp. 172–3.
6   General Hancock, Official Report, Battle of the Wilderness.
7   McDermott, *A Brief History of the 69th Regiment Pennsylvania Veteran Volunteers*, p. 38.
8   *Ibid.*, p. 39.
9   Major W.G. Mitchell (Aide de Camp to Hancock), Official Report, Spotsylvania and Wilderness battles.
10 O'Brien, *Irish Americans in the Confederate Army*, p. 100.
11 Kohl (ed.), *The Civil War Letters of Peter Welsh*, p. 156.
12 O'Grady, *Clear the Confederate Way*, p. 174.
13 Macnamara, *The History of the Ninth*, p. 387.
14 Callaghan, *Thomas Francis Meagher and the Irish Brigade*, p. 170.
15 Ural Bruce, *The Harp and the Eagle*, pp. 217–18.
16 Colonel Matthew Murphy, Official Report, Battle of Spotsylvania.
17 Colonel James O. McIvor, Official Report, Battle of Spotsylvania.
18 McDermott, *A Brief History of the 69th Regiment Pennsylvania Veteran Volunteers*, p. 43.
19 O'Grady, *Clear the Confederate Way*, pp. 180–85.

Chapter 16

1   McDermott, *A Brief History of the 69th Regiment Pennsylvania Veteran Volunteers*, pp. 45–6.
2   Sandy (ed.), *Campaigning with the Irish Brigade: Pvt. John Ryan, 28th Massachusetts*, pp. 120–21.
3   *Ibid.*, p. 119.
4   O'Brien, *Irish Americans in the Confederate Army*, p. 105.
5   St Clair Mulholland, *The Story of the 116th Regiment Pennsylvania Volunteers in the War of the Rebellion, the Record of a Gallant Campaign*, F. McManus Jnr & Co., Philedelphia, 1903, in Boyle, *A Party of Mad Fellows*, pp. 371–2.
6   Boyle, *A Party of Mad Fellows*, pp. 376–7.
7   Callaghan, *Thomas Francis Meagher and the Irish Brigade*, p. 175.
8   *Ibid.*, p. 176.
9   Mulholland, *The Story of the 116th Regiment Pennsylvania Volunteers*, in Boyle, *A Party of Mad Fellows*, p. 380.
10 Surgeon Charles Smart (Second Corps), Official Report, Siege of Petersburg.
11 Boyle, *A Party of Mad Fellows*, p. 379.

Chapter 17

1   Lieutenant Colonel Owen Stuart, Official Report, Atlanta Campaign.
2   Gleeson, *Rebel Sons of Erin*, p. 284.

3   O'Brien, *Irish Americans in the Confederate Army*, p. 143.
4   Lieutenant Colonel Joseph S. Fullerton, Journal of the Atlanta Campaign kept at HQ.
5   Colonel J.E. Taylor, Official Report, Atlanta Campaign.
6   Colonel August G. Tassin, Official Report, Atlanta Campaign.
7   O'Brien, *Irish Americans in the Confederate Army*, pp. 145–6.
8   *Ibid.*, pp. 146–7.
9   For an account of Irish Confederate participation in the Battle of Atlanta see O'Brien, *Irish Americans in the Confederate Army*, pp. 144–153.
10 Muriel Phillips Joslyn, *A Meteor Shining Brightly*, p. 127.
11 Thomas Y. Cartwright in Phillips Joslyn (ed.), *A Meteor Shining Brightly*, p. 172.
12 *Ibid.*

Chapter 18
1   Susannah Ural Bruce, *The Harp and the Eagle*, pp. 233–262.
2   *Ibid.*, p. 261.

·Select Bibliography

Barnard, Sandy (ed.), *Campaigning with the Irish Brigade: Pvt. John Ryan, 28th Massachusetts*, AST Press, Indiana, 2001.

Bennett, Brian A. *The Beau Ideal of a Soldier and a Gentleman: The Life of Colonel Patrick Henry O'Rorke from Ireland to Gettysburg*, Triphammer Publishing, New York, 1996.

Boyle, Frank A., *A Party of Mad Fellows: The Story of the Irish Regiments in the Army of the Potomac*, Morningside, Ohio, 1996.

Burton, William L., *Melting Pot Soldiers: The Union's Ethnic Regiments*, Fordham University Press, New York, 1998.

Callaghan, Daniel M., *Thomas Francis Meagher and the Irish Brigade in the Civil War*, McFarland & Company, North Carolina, 2006.

Coogan, Tim Pat, *Wherever Green is Worn: The Story of the Irish Diaspora*, Arrow, London, 2002.

Crouch, Jerry Evan, *Silencing the Vicksburg Guns: The Story of the 7th Missouri Infantry Regiment, As Experienced by John Davis Evans Union Private and Mormon Pioneer*, Trafford Publishing, British Columbia, 2005.

Dungan, Myles, *Distant Drums: Irish Soldiers in Foreign Armies*, Appletree Press, Belfast, 1993.

Galwey, Thomas Francis, *The Valiant Hours: Narrative of 'Captain Brevet' and Irish-Americans in the Army of the Potomac*, Stackpole, London, 1961.

Gannon, James P., *Irish Rebels Confederate Tigers: A History of the 6th Louisiana Volunteers, 1861–1865*, Savas Publishing, Iowa, 1998.

Gleeson, David T., *The Irish in the South 1815–1877*, University of North Carolina Press, North Carolina, 2001.

Gleeson, Ed, *Rebel Sons of Erin: A Civil War Unit History of the Tenth Tennessee Infantry Regiment (Irish) Confederate States Volunteers*, Guild Press, Indiana, 1993.

Hernon, Joseph M. Jr, *Celts, Catholics and Copperheads: Ireland Views the American Civil War*, Ohio State University Press, Ohio, 1968.

Kohl, Lawrence Frederick (ed.), *Irish Green and Union Blue: The Civil War Letters of Peter Welsh: Color Sergeant 28th Regiment Massachusetts*

Volunteers, Fordham University Press, New York, 1986.

Kohl, Lawrence Frederick (ed.), William Corby C.S.C., *Memoirs of Chaplain Life: Three Years with the Irish Brigade in the Army of the Potomac*, Fordham University Press, New York, 1992.

Lonn, Ella, *Foreigners in the Confederacy*, University of North Carolina Press, North Carolina, 1940.

Macnamara, Daniel George, *The History of the Ninth Regiment Massachusetts Volunteer Infantry, June 1861–June 1864*, Fordham University Press, New York, 2000.

McDermott, Anthony W., *A Brief History of the 69th Regiment Pennsylvania Veteran Volunteers*, D.J. Gallagher & Co, Philadelphia, 1889.

Mulholland, St Clair, *The Story of the 116th Regiment Pennsylvania Volunteers in the War of the Rebellion, the Record of a Gallant Campaign*, F. McManus Jnr & Co., Philadelphia, 1903.

Murphy, T.L., *Kelly's Heroes: The Irish Brigade at Gettysburg*, Farnsworth House, Gettysburg, 1997.

O'Brien, Kevin E. (ed.), *My Life in the Irish Brigade: The Civil War Memoirs of Private William McCarter, 116th Pennsylvania Infantry*, Savas Publishing, California, 1996.

O'Brien, Sean Michael, *Irish-Americans in the Confederate Army*, McFarland & Company, North Carolina, 2007.

O'Donovan Rossa, Jeremiah, *Rossa's Recollections 1838 to 1898: Memoirs of an Irish Revolutionary*, The Lyons Press, Connecticut, 2004.

Phillips Joslyn, Muriel (ed.), *A Meteor Shining Brightly: Essays on Major General Patrick R. Cleburne*, Mercer University Press, Georgia, 2000.

Samito, Christian G. (ed.), *Commanding Boston's Irish Ninth: The Civil War Letters of Colonel Patrick R. Guiney, Ninth Massachusetts Volunteer Infantry*, Fordham University Press, New York, 1998.

Tucker, Phillip Thomas, *Irish Confederates: The Civil War's Forgotten Soldiers*, McWhiney Foundation Press, Texas, 2006.

Ural Bruce, Susannah, *The Harp and the Eagle: Irish-American Volunteers and the Union Army, 1861–1865*, New York University Press, New York, 2006.

Useful Websites

www.aotw.org (Antietam)

www.civilwarhome.com

www.sonofthesouth.net

www.irishvolunteers.tripod.com (Irish Brigade)

www.28thmass.org (28th Massachusetts)

http://cdl.library.cornell.edu/moa/browse.monographs/waro.html (All the official records digitised and placed on the web by Cornell University)

www.geocities.com/ddhillman2002 (Louisiana Tigers)

www.home.earthlink.net/~japrime/37thnyvi/ (37th New York Irish Rifles)

www.digital.library.villanova.edu/Pennsylvaniana/Pennsylvaniana-00005.xml (Anthony MacDermott's book on the 69th Pennsylvania reproduced in full by Villanova University)

www.thewildgeese.com (A site containing many useful articles on Irish-American history)

www.civilwaranimated.com (Exceptional site containing maps around which the various units move to recreate most of the major battles)

www.battleofraymond.org

INDEX

314

Gaines Creek, 56
Gaines Mill, 55, 56, 58, 59, 60
Gainesville, 71
Gallagher, Adjutant, 216
Galva, 197
Galveston, 199
Gavan, Peter, 145
Georgia, 7, 11, 128
German Fusiliers (Company H, 8th
    Alabama), 52
Getty, George W., 244
Getty's division, 245
Gettysburg, 133, 157, 158, 163, 165,
    166, 169, 170, 174, 182, 184,
    198, 223, 224, 225, 242, 264,
    289
Gibbon, General, 255, 268
Gibbons, Abby Hopper, 227
Gibbon's division, 255, 257
Gibson, Private Drury, 21
Gilbert's Corps, 105, 107
Gleason, Lieutenant, 95
Gleeson, David T., 12
Gleeson, Ed, 35
Glendale, 60, 61, 62, 66
Gordon, John B., 272
Gordonsville, 68, 69, 121
Govan, Daniel C., 281, 283
Grace, Colonel, 189
Grant, Ulysses S., 29, 195, 212, 214,
    219, 220, 223, 236, 237–238,
    247, 253, 259, 261, 263, 264,
    268, 269, 271, 273, 286
  at Corinth, Mississippi, 112
  at Fort Donelson, 32–33
  at Old Cold Harbor, 256
  Shiloh Battle, 38
  and Vicksburg, 156, 184, 185–186,
    192
Grapevine Bridge, 50
Graysville, 222
Great Redoubt, 192, 195
Green, W.C., 49
Gregg, John, 187, 188, 192
Gregg, Maxcy, 57
Grierson, Benjamin, 186
Griffin, General, 241

Griffin, Patrick, 189
Griffin's division, 135
Grover, 77
Grovetown, Battle of, 76
Grovetown woods, 74, 77, 80
Guiney, Patrick R., 135, 240

Habersham County, Georgia, 128
Hagerstown, 86, 89
Hagerstown Pike, 90, 92
Haggerty, Colonel, 23
Halleck, General Henry W., 37, 104,
    185
Hamilton, Joseph, 128
Hamiltons' Crossing, 151
Hancock, General Winfield S., 148,
    158, 242, 243, 244, 245, 248,
    251, 253, 264, 265, 267, 268
Hancock's troops, 130, 144, 248, 256,
    257
Hanley, Colonel, 240–241
Hanlon, Joseph, 151–152
Hardee, William J., 41, 217, 284
Hardee's Corps, 278
Harpers Ferry, Virginia, 6, 86, 89, 103
Harris, Leslie M., 226
Harrison's Landing, 64, 65, 66
Harrodsburg, 112
Hatcher's Run, 268
Haws Shop, 255
Hayman, S.B., 49, 150
Hays, Harry T., 75
Hays' Louisiana Brigade, 76, 77, 78, 85,
    89, 90, 103, 150–151, 154, 158,
    170, 171, 172, 173, 241, 242
Helena, Arkansas, 39, 40, 208
Helena, Montana, 160
Henry Hill, 23, 25, 26, 27, 28
Henry, Isaac, 23
Henry, James, 49
Henry, Mrs, 23
Hernon Jnr, Joseph, 233
Heth, Henry, 267
Heth's division, 157
Hill, A.P., 55, 57, 60, 68, 102, 103,
    157, 223, 242
Hill, D.H., 58, 65, 86, 88